MANY HEARTS, ONE VOICE

ABOUT THE AUTHOR

Melinda Tognini's feature articles, travel writing and personal essays have appeared in magazines and anthologies in Australia and the US. She completed a Master of Arts in writing, which was the basis for this book. Melinda is passionate about telling 'invisible' stories – those stories absent from or sidelined in the dominant narratives of our history – and empowering others to find their voice. After growing up surrounded by the bush, bauxite and beaches of North East Arnhem Land, she now resides in Perth with her husband and two children.

MANY HEARTS, ONE VOICE

The story of the War Widows' Guild in Western Australia

MELINDA TOGNINI

Foreword by the Hon. Dame Quentin Bryce AD CVO

FREMANTLE PRESS

First published 2015 by
FREMANTLE PRESS
25 Quarry Street, Fremantle 6160
(PO Box 158, North Fremantle 6159)
Western Australia
www.fremantlepress.com.au

Consultant editor: Janet Blagg
Design and cover: Carolyn Brown
Cover image: *The two flowering red poppies*, Artant, bigstockphoto.com

A catalogue record for this
book is available from the
National Library of Australia

ISBN: 9781925163179 (paperback)

Fremantle Press is supported by the Western Australian State Government through the Department of Cultural Industries, Tourism and Sport.

Publication of this title was assisted by the Commonwealth Government through Creative Australia, its arts funding and advisory body.

Fremantle Press acknowledges the generous contribution of gtmedia, Perth WA, and DFD Rhodes Pty Ltd, Perth WA, to the publication of this book.

Fremantle Press respectfully acknowledges the Whadjuk people of the Noongar nation as the Traditional Owners and Custodians of the land where we work in Walyalup.

CONTENTS

To war widows everywhere –
because your stories matter.

FOREWORD

As a former national patron of the War Widows' Guild of Australia, it gives me great pleasure to write the foreword to this marvellous history of the Western Australian women who organised themselves and laboured to improve the lives of all war widows and their children. Wars are fought on many fronts and for far longer than the official duration of any particular conflict. In many respects, a war for its widows never ends. The loss of their husband, their beloved, and the father of their children, is only the beginning.

At the conclusion of the Second World War, many war widows faced a life of poverty and uncertainty, with limited avenues of support and inadequate financial assistance. The War Widows' Guild was formed to lobby government for greater financial security, and to provide emotional and social support to widows, with the comfort of fellow feeling.

Established first in Victoria by the formidable Jessie Vasey, the War Widows' Guild quickly expanded to include other states, including Western Australia. Soon, groups of war widows around the country were working to influence policymakers and secure for war widows and their families improved pensions, medical benefits and social services.

The Guild also fought hard for recognition and respect, for a place in the Anzac Day commemorations and parades. Their battles were hard-won in a country that did not always acknowledge their struggles with dignity or respect. We commemorate war veterans and the war dead, but little acknowledgement was given to the women who suffered grief and economic hardship after the loss of their husbands;

the women who fought for the rights and needs and recognition of others like them.

And that battle for recognition is just as relevant today. In the vast literature concerning Australian war and post-war history, references to the sacrifices of the war widows, and the work of the Guild, are seldom found. They are simply left out of many official accounts.

That is why this is such an important book: as a previously unrecorded element of Western Australian post-war history, the story of the War Widows' Guild must not be allowed to be forgotten; it forms an integral part of the history of the women in this state.

And for readers of this book, I can almost guarantee these women will not be forgotten. In these pages we meet ordinary women of extraordinary courage and humour, resourceful and tenacious, young and old, working together in a spirit of mucking in and making do. It is heartwarming and inspiring to see how they gather strength and, at times, give the politicians hell.

Who could fail to be entranced and impressed by this group of women who refused to accept their lot, who began with so little and pushed through barriers of class and gender to create a mighty organisation that continues to flourish today? Over seven decades they have continued to show themselves a force to be reckoned with in the state of Western Australia.

I am honoured to have been patron of the Guild and delighted that this beautifully written account of the magnificent women from Western Australia has been produced.

The Hon. Dame Quentin Bryce AD CVO
National patron of the War Widows' Guild of Australia, 2008–2014
July 2015

PROLOGUE

Anzac Cove, 24 April 2008. Dallas Hickman stands on the narrow, stony beach with other members of the War Widows' Guild tour group. It is a bright spring day and the turquoise sea is so clear she can see pebbles on the ocean floor. This should be the setting for a beachside retreat, not the site of a bloodbath.

Dallas imagines her father as a young man, sitting in a pontoon in the pre-dawn darkness with fellow soldiers from the 11th Battalion. He leaps out of the boat into icy water. The air fills with sniper shots, and strong young men discover they cannot beat a bullet. Her father comes ashore under fire. He belly crawls up the beach, bayonet drawn, unable to see the enemy. Peppered with shrapnel, he manages to reach shelter. Unlike his mates, who were killed around him, Dallas's father makes it out of Gallipoli and is evacuated by ship to Alexandria.

Holding a red poppy, Dallas kneels on the sand. She says a prayer for her father, then casts the poppy into the sea. As she stands, Kazim, our Turkish guide, hugs her. He places in her hand a stone, blue-green and smoothed by the sea. 'Do you know what stone this is?' he asks.

'No,' Dallas replies.

'It is a turquoise,' Kazim explains, 'meaning Turkish. I want you to have it in memory of my uncle who was killed on Gallipoli and where your father was, and now we are all here.'

Dallas nods, unable to speak. Jenny Knight, the executive officer of the War Widows' Guild in Western Australia, approaches. Without a word, she embraces them both.

Dallas, who is in her seventies, grew up with stories of Gallipoli. As a young girl, she accompanied her father on nightly walks, and

Dallas Hickman places a poppy in the sea at
Anzac Cove in remembrance of her father.
(Both photos by Jenny Knight)

occasionally he would tell her about his war experiences. He explained that they had to be fit in order to enlist, and were rejected if they had even one filling in their teeth. He told her of a man in his unit, six foot ten, found dead with no visible mark on him: a splinter of shrapnel had penetrated the corner of his eye. Her father spoke to her of Simpson and his donkey, whom he saw clambering up and down the steep crevice of Shrapnel Gully, carrying wounded men to the beach.

Dallas's father had woken at dawn on Anzac Day for many years, reliving his experiences at Gallipoli. Standing in the spot where he landed, she feels she understands him better now than she ever did in his lifetime. She believes her father would have been proud she had come.

❁

Most of the women on this twelve-day tour to Gallipoli, organised by the War Widows' Guild of Western Australia, had become widows as a result of the Second World War, or the more recent conflicts of Korea and Vietnam. Some, like Dallas Hickman, had a personal connection to Gallipoli: their fathers had landed at Anzac Cove during the eight-month campaign. Some had been war widows for decades; others lost their husbands in more recent years. Some were active members of the War Widows' Guild, holding official positions on the executive committee; for others, the main connection to the Guild was through the quarterly magazine. But all had come to remember those who had died, and those who had been left to grieve without ever seeing their loved one's grave.

On Anzac Day, at Gallipoli and elsewhere, we acknowledge those who fought for our freedom. We recognise the returned men, many of whom were physically injured and emotionally scarred. We remember those who sacrificed their lives. But we hear little about those who were left to mourn and carry on without their sons, brothers, fathers and husbands. What became of them? Who remembers them?

The Great War left countless widows to struggle alone the best they could. Nor did it prove to be the war to end all wars, and it was only after a second global conflict that the War Widows' Guild was founded to offer support to and advocate for women widowed by that war. The organisation quickly expanded to include those bereaved by the First World War and, in the following decades, those of all subsequent conflicts. Members fought for public recognition and the expression of their loss. They fought to have a war widow's pension seen as compensation for their husbands' lives rather than a government handout. They wrote letters, met with politicians and, long before Twitter and Facebook, they used the media to their advantage. They campaigned for subsidised aged-nursing care and they built affordable housing three years before government subsidies were introduced for such ventures. They persevered when faced with hurdles, and fought for their rights at a time when men had the louder voices and determined the rules. While the War Widows' Guild received support from other organisations in its endeavours to secure improved benefits for those widowed as a result of war, it can be argued that many of the benefits war widows enjoy today are a result of the courage of those early Guild members who overcame a life of poverty, social isolation and invisibility.[1]

Since in 2015 we marked the centenary of the Gallipoli landings and the 70th anniversary of the end of the Second World War, where the focus has often been on the men who fought, it is right to pause and reflect on the struggles and achievements of the War Widows' Guild. The stories of this organisation, and of individual women, deserve to be remembered, honoured and celebrated.

CHAPTER 1

WARTIME IN WESTERN AUSTRALIA

'Falling in love,' Marjorie Chapple heard Charles Learmonth say. For a moment, she thought he was referring to 'some blonde' he had seen across the dance floor at the Karrinyup Golf Club. 'No, it's you I'm in love with,' he told her.[1]

It was July 1941 and Marjorie and Charles had known each other just over a year. She had always enjoyed his company, but never expected the friendship to become anything more serious. 'I could never understand why he felt happy to invite me to go out with him,' Marjorie reflected many years later. 'I felt more like a sister than a girlfriend. I had no brother and the relationship we shared filled that gap.'[2]

Marjorie Chapple in 1941. On the right Marjorie wears her VAD uniform.
(Courtesy of Marjorie Le Souef)

Their friendship was complicated by the circumstances of the Second World War. A trained pilot, Charles Learmonth was a member of No. 14 Squadron based at RAAF Pearce north of Perth, and he was impatient for an overseas posting. Marjorie had recently begun training for the Voluntary Aid Detachment (VAD) at the Davies Road Military Hospital in Claremont. The VAD had been established by the Red Cross during the First World War. Its members were given medical training and they worked in hospitals, convalescent homes, hospital ships and blood banks. Initially unpaid, voluntary aides (VAs) were remunerated for their work from January 1940, and from June 1941, were permitted to serve overseas.[3]

'I loved Charles,' said Marjorie, 'but I had not anticipated marrying him. At that stage, I had volunteered to go overseas with the Voluntary Aid Detachment to join the AIF in the Middle East.'[4]

On 13 November 1941, Marjorie Chapple was posted to the Northam Military Hospital, where she and the other VAs were immunised, issued with kitbags and told to be ready for departure. Foreseeing separation due to their postings, and having doubts about a wartime marriage, Charles considered breaking off the relationship, but he was unable to do so. 'I love her,' he wrote in his diary, 'and always will, more than anyone else in the world.'[5]

In the early hours of 24 November, Charles was called to join the search for the HMAS *Sydney*, which had failed to arrive in Fremantle. As he flew his plane along a stretch of the West Australian coast the following day, he saw a number of seamen on a beach north of Carnarvon. Believing they were survivors of the *Sydney*, he dropped them a pipe and tobacco and was mortified when he later discovered they were in fact from the German raider *Kormoran*, believed to have sunk the *Sydney*.[6] After six days the search was called off and, on 30 November, Prime Minister John Curtin informed the nation that HMAS *Sydney* had been lost, along with all 645 of her crew.

With departure for the Middle East imminent, Marjorie was given embarkation leave on 5 December and spent most of the weekend with Charles. Then came the news that was to change the direction of the war. Japan had bombed Pearl Harbor. 'Men and women of Australia, we are at war with Japan,' John Curtin announced in a national broadcast on 8 December. All leave was suspended. Australian troop deployments to Europe and the Middle East were temporarily cancelled. This brought uncertainty about Marjorie's posting, but she and the other VAs were told to keep their bags packed. Marjorie and Charles discussed marriage and became engaged, but decided not to announce it officially until their postings were more definite and a wedding date could be set.[7] Despite there being no specific departure date, Marjorie attended a farewell party for thirty-two VAs at the Adelphi Hotel on 11 December. Two days later, Charles received a posting as a flying instructor to Nhill, only one hundred miles from his parents' property in country Victoria.[8]

Marjorie and Charles spent Christmas apart. On Boxing Day, Charles briefly returned to Western Australia but the closest Marjorie came to seeing him was when he flew his Hudson plane low over the Northam Military Hospital. 'Everyone thought the Japanese had arrived,' Marjorie remembered. 'Except me of course.'[9]

His Majesty King George VI commented on the separation and suffering the war was producing when he broadcast his Christmas message to the Empire. 'Christmas is the festival of home,' he said, 'and it is right that we should remember those who this year must spend it away from home.' He later added:

> All those separations are part of the hard sacrifices that the world demands. It may well be that it will call for even greater sacrifices. If that is to be, let us face them cheerfully together. I think of you, my people, as one great family, for that is how we are learning to live. We belong to each other, we all need each other and it is in sacrificing for the common good that we are finding our true life.[10]

A fortnight later, on Sunday 11 January 1942, Charles wrote to Marjorie's father asking for permission to marry her. Mr Chapple initially replied, 'I'll have to think about it. She's still a bit young.' But, a few days later, he gave his blessing and Charles sent Marjorie an engagement ring. Still in Northam, Marjorie was in sick bay at the time, suffering from sinusitis, but this did not prevent her celebrating with her fellow VAs and a keg of beer.[11] Marjorie applied for a discharge from the army, so she could join her fiancé in Victoria.

❀

While Marjorie waited for her discharge, Edna Ramage awaited news of her husband, Acting Sergeant George Robert Ramage, more commonly known as Bob. He had been sent with the 2/4th Machine Gunners to join the 8th Division in Singapore. 'We intend to hold Singapore,' British general Arthur Percival declared on 9 February 1942. Less than a week later, on 15 February, Singapore fell to the Japanese.

Then, as Edna endured the uncertainty, the war arrived on the Australian mainland. On 19 February, Japanese planes bombed Darwin. John Curtin told the Australian public he had 'been advised by the Department of the Air that a number of bombs were dropped this morning.'[12] The full extent of the damage and the number of casualties were not made public for some time, the *West Australian* reporting that the bombs had a 'limited range in the death and destruction which they wrought.'[13] The Japanese attacked Broome less than a fortnight later on 3 March, leaving about seventy people dead, then Townsville, Katherine, Derby, Wyndham, Onslow and Port Hedland.[14]

The war was too close for Edna Ramage. What if the Japanese moved further down the coast? What then? Edna contacted her sister, who lived in the gold mining town of Kalgoorlie, 550 kilometres east of Perth. The children would be safer there. Her daughter Laurel, aged ten, complied and travelled to Kalgoorlie to stay with her aunt, but twelve year old Ken refused to go; he remained in Perth to finish school and keep an eye on his mother.[15]

Edna eventually received news that Bob was a prisoner of war in Singapore, and later found out that he had been sent to work on the Burma Railway. Her anxieties were relieved only momentarily by occasional, heavily censored prisoner-of-war cards. She occupied herself by working in a tent-making factory;[16] this helped her feel she was contributing to the war effort, and provided camaraderie during her husband's absence.[17]

IMPERIAL JAPANESE ARMY.

I am interned at The War Prisoners Camp at
Moulmein in Burma.

My health is (good, ~~bad, poor~~)
I have not had any illness.
~~I have been in hospital~~.

I am (~~not~~) working (for pay at *1.5 CENTS* per day).
~~My pay is~~ ~~per month~~.

I am with friends *FROM WEST AUSTRALIA. HOPE ALL HOME ARE WELL. LOVE TO YOU ALL. AM ALWAYS THINKING OF YOU AND KIDDIES. KEEP SMILING*

From *Bob Ramage.*

WX 9059 SERGEANT. R. RAMAGE.
DARLING. EDNA AND CHILDREN.
AM SAFE AND WELL UNWOUNDED. DO
NOT WORRY. HOPE ALL AT HOME ARE
WELL. ALL MY LOVE
BOB

Two of the POW cards Edna Ramage received from her husband.
(Courtesy of Laurel Taylor)

✿

Marjorie Chapple finally received a discharge from the army in mid-March, but 'no one at Northam had the authority to sign it.' A Roman Catholic army chaplain solved the problem by organising for her to travel to Perth in the back of an ambulance.

I had leave for one day – on arrival at Perth, I asked the driver to drop me off at the [Army] Barracks in Francis Street. I knocked on every door until I found someone who had the seniority to give me my freedom.[18]

Marjorie returned to Northam by a more conventional mode of transport, the train. She presented her signed discharge papers, underwent a medical examination and, by nine o'clock the following morning, she was officially out of the army and headed back to Perth.

On arrival at the Perth Railway Station, I left my luggage in the cloakroom and proceeded to my father's office to collect the car. Fortunately, I took a devious route through the shops. At Aherns I bought a blue tweed suit, top coat, a blue dress and coat with a hat to match which I thought I would be able to wear for my wedding. Walking down Hay Street with all my boxes of clothes, I spotted an attractive white evening dress in Shirley's window. It fitted and that added to my trousseau wardrobe. With my father, I collected the army luggage still intact waiting to be unpacked in the Middle East.[19]

Her father took her home to Peppermint Grove to join family friends who had evacuated from Singapore and were staying with the Chapple family. At midday the following day, Marjorie's friend June Perry phoned to say she was catching the interstate train to Melbourne at three that afternoon.

It just didn't dawn on me that I might be on it and it was not until 2.25 pm when my father returned to his office and found the message that I also could have a ticket to Melbourne. Fortunately, the car was at home. We loaded it as quickly as possible with all my Army gear, shopping from the previous day and a trunk my mother had filled with my trousseau … I drove to the station as quickly as possible and arrived just before 3 pm. The station staff were wonderful, unpacked the car, raced down the line with it all and put

*it on the train … I leapt on to the train, as it was about to
take off. June and I just looked at one another, neither of us
able to believe what had happened.*[20]

After a four-day train journey, Marjorie arrived in Melbourne with
less than a week to organise a wedding. She married Charles on
Saturday 28 March 1942 at St John's Church of England in Toorak.
Before long, Charles's squadron was transferred to Richmond,
New South Wales, and Marjorie moved with him.[21] Then, in early
September, Charles's squadron received its departure orders. He
left for further preparations and training in Far North Queensland
before finally reaching the war front in New Guinea on 25
November 1942.[22]

❁

Charlotte 'Gloria' Carr had met her husband, Wilfred MacDonald,
at Rottnest Island; she was with a group from the Claremont Tennis
Club, and he was on an army bivouac. They married on 19 April
1938 and bought a house in Bay Road, Claremont; a son, Alexander,
was born two years later on 23 September 1940. An engineer,
Wilfred was stationed outside Darwin with the Royal Australian
Engineers (RAE), to build bridges. The men camped in a valley
near their workplace, with the machinery and other equipment
at the top of the hill. On 30 October 1942, an unattended truck
rolled down the hill and ploughed through a tent. Ten men were
injured in the incident, and Wilfred MacDonald was killed.[23] Soon
after his death, Gloria and two year old Alexander moved to live in
Dwellingup, where her sister ran a greengrocer and drapery store.

Jean Elsie Ferguson saw first-hand the injuries that war could
inflict. In January 1939 she had joined the Australian Army
Nursing Service Reserve while training in midwifery at King
Edward Memorial Hospital. She then served as a nursing sister in
England, Palestine and Egypt before returning to Australia to work
at military hospitals in Queensland. She married Captain John
Ferguson on 25 February 1943 in Tenterfield, New South Wales.
Seven months later, on 7 September, John was stationed in Port

Gloria MacDonald
(Courtesy of Patricia Milne)

Moresby with the 2/33rd Infantry Battalion when an American Liberator bomber, loaded with bombs and fuel, crashed just after take-off from Jackson's aerodrome. John Ferguson was among fifty-nine Australians killed; another ninety-two were wounded.[24] A month later, still raw with grief, Jean Ferguson sailed for New Guinea to work with the 2/11th Australian General Hospital (AGH) at Buna, Madang and Aitape, where malaria was rampant.[25]

Two days after the Liberator disaster, Gwen Forsyth and Rose Heath, whose husbands belonged to the 2/28th Battalion in New Guinea, also became widows. The battalion's orders were to cross the flooded Busu River near Lae. Cables needed to be secured on the other side of the river before the men could cross, and that job fell to Arthur Forsyth. Although an accountant in civilian life, he had been on the professional boxing circuit, and was a strong rower and swimmer. He made the journey once and returned safely to his battalion. But more cables were needed, so again he headed into the river. This time, Arthur was swept away by the strong current, following suspected sniper fire.[26]

Rose Heath's husband, Private George Heath, a stretcher bearer, met a similar fate. It is believed that he was 'hit by enemy fire, and washed down in the river'[27] as he crossed the Busu. Along with at least a dozen more men, Arthur Forsyth and George Heath were

Telegrams Rose Heath received after her husband went
missing while on active service in Papua New Guinea.
(Courtesy of David Heath)

reported 'missing, believed killed in action.' In official records, the crossing of the Busu has been described as 'a remarkable achievement and must rank as the highlight of the Lae Campaign.'[28] But it was a costly achievement.

Gwen Forsyth's youngest son Alan met his father only twice, shortly after Alan's birth when Arthur was on leave from training in Northam, prior to his deployment to New Guinea. Rose's son David has no memory of his father either, although her daughter Maureen recollects standing outside their house at the age of four or five, when a man in uniform walked into view and she was told to run and greet him.[29]

✿

After having almost been killed on his first operation, when his Boston was hit by anti-aircraft fire, Charles Learmonth survived

WX 5421,
Lt. Col. H. Boyd Norman,
2/28 Aust. Inf. Bn. A.I.F.

6 Oct/43.

Dear Mrs. Heath,

It is with sincere regret that I write to you to express the deep sympathy we all feel in the loss of your husband.

The notification you received will be I believe (Missing believed killed in Action". Much though I wish I were able to give you some hope, I fear by now you should not consider your husband's return.

It was early in the advance on Lae that the battalion came to a river crossing that will forever remain an epic in our arms. The river was crossed, and the far bank captured, under the most difficult possible conditions.

It is feared that your husband was hit by enemy fire, and washed down in the river.

From my observations during the crossing and from my military experience I must say that I do not believe your husband is alive today. Thorough search has been made in every place possible, and no sign of several, has been found.

My dear Mrs. Heath I do not know how to adequately express my sorrow for you in this great loss. I know that it is the wives, and mothers, who pay the greater price, and we grieve for you. Your husband was one of that noble band, the stretcher bearers, of whom I can never speak highly enough. We can ill afford to lose any of them. Their devotion to duty, their gallantry in action, is recognised, and is the admiration of all soldiers. I know of no other job in war that calls for greater unselfishness, more courage, and devotion than does that of the stretcher bearer.

In your sorrow I hope that you will think of these things and have pride in the fact that your husband was one of them.

I pray you may be given strength to bear your burden, and comfort in your sorrow.

It is my earnest wish that no more sadness may cloud your further way in life.

Yours sincerely,

HUGH BOYD NORMAN.

Rose Heath received a condolence letter from
her husband's commanding officer.
(Courtesy of David Heath)

almost a year in the tropical jungle of New Guinea, leading his team in numerous bombing and strafing attacks on the enemy.[30] In September 1943 he was promoted to Wing Commander and awarded the Distinguished Flying Cross (DFC). He was then granted leave on 15 October 1943, followed by a new posting as Commanding Officer of No. 14 Squadron at RAAF Pearce, north of Perth.[31] Marjorie and Charles were reunited, albeit in wartime Perth and living on base.

On 5 January 1944, Marjorie uncharacteristically begged Charles not to fly the following day. She'd had a premonition. The next morning she again asked him to remain grounded. As he was leaving their quarters on the RAAF base, she suggested he take the afternoon off, but he wouldn't hear of it. 'Look, Darl,' he said, 'don't worry. I'll call you on the phone when I get back in a couple of hours.'[32]

The phone call never came, and late in the afternoon the Pearce station commander, Group Captain Stan Brearley, appeared with his wife at Marjorie's door. It was a moment Marjorie would remember for the rest of her life. 'There's been an accident,' Captain Brearley informed her.[33]

While flying near Rottnest Island, Charles's Beaufort plane had plummeted into the sea, splitting in two upon impact. The Beaufort planes had been plagued with malfunctions and accidents, involving fatalities, but no cause had ever been found. Charles Learmonth would be remembered as a hero because his quick thinking led to an understanding of the problem. 'Sorry chaps,' Charles radioed as the plane went down, 'can't get her out, trim tabs appear jammed. This looks like it.' There were no survivors, and no bodies were found, despite rescue crews being nearby.[34]

Marjorie returned to her parents' home in Peppermint Grove until March 1944, when she accepted an invitation to visit Charles's parents, Noel and Edith Learmonth, at Carramar, their home in rural Victoria. The 1200-acre property, which had been in the Learmonth family since the 1800s, was twenty miles east of Portland, and two miles north of the small town of Tyrendarra. The smell of baking emanated daily from the weatherboard homestead, and tea and cake were served each afternoon. Marjorie helped where she could. At night, she listened to the radio and read from a collection of old classics by the light of a kerosene lamp.[35]

One day in May 1944 Marjorie answered a phone call from the local postmistress; a telegram had arrived from the Minister for the Army, Frank Forde, to say that Charles's brother John had died in a German prisoner-of-war camp on 10 May. Noel and Edith Learmonth had now lost not one but two sons since the beginning of the year. Marjorie remained with her parents-in-law until accepting a position as a hospital visitor for the Red Cross at Heidelberg Military Hospital in Melbourne.[36]

Like the Learmonths, thousands of families received news of the loss of a loved one via telegram. The telegram that Phyllis Thomas opened informed her that her husband Albert's plane had been shot down over Germany. There was uncertainty as to whether he was dead, or had survived and become a prisoner of war. Only after months of living in limbo came the terrible confirmation that he had indeed been killed in action.[37] Compounding her grief was the fact that many of the items returned with her husband's kitbag did not belong to him. The night he died had been chaotic, both in the sky and at the base. Personal belongings of those missing and presumed killed were scooped into the nearest bag to clear the way for new arrivals. Albert's watch was returned, but the face and glass were missing. There was a signet ring but it was plain gold, whereas his bore an onyx stone. Phyllis was also distressed over a pair of small wooden clogs she had given him for good luck. She discovered too late she was only supposed to give away one; the other was to be kept so that he would return to reunite them.[38]

Many years later, Phyllis wondered how her husband would have adjusted to the mundane job of newspaper proof reader if he had ever returned. Some ex-servicemen had suffered horrific injuries, yet when they arrived home, they were expected simply to adapt to civilian life.[39] She thought about how war must change a man, but her thoughts could never be more than speculation.

❀

Jessie Mary Vasey waited apprehensively at her country property, Wantirna, at the foot of the Dandenong Ranges in Victoria. Her husband, Major General George Alan Vasey, was en route to take command of the 6th Division in New Guinea, and had been due in Cairns around 4 pm on Monday 5 March 1945. It was now 7 pm; she should have received word by now. Perhaps Beryl Riggall, whose husband Bill was with George, had heard something. Jessie dialled Beryl's number.

'Beryl, have you heard anything – that they've arrived?'

'No.'

'I've got this feeling … I don't like it, something's wrong.' Jessie hung up, unable to shake her uneasiness.[40]

TELEGRAM

443 MELBOURNE 71 6-28 P

LETTERGRAM // MRS A E THOMAS
35 GOODE ST SOUTH PERTH PERTH WA

INFORMATION RECEIVED THROUGH INTERNATIONAL RED CROSS FROM GERMAN
AUTHORITIES THAT ONE OTHER MEMBER OF YOUR HUSBANDS CREW
FLIGHT SGT D J CHASE ROYAL AIR FORCE LOST HIS LIFE STOP CREW

TELEGRAM

COMMONWEALTH OF AUSTRALIA—POSTMASTER-GENERAL'S DEPARTMENT.

CONSISTED OF SEVEN MEMBERS STOP REGRET NO FURTHER NEWS OF YOUR HUSBAND
WARRANT OFFICER ALBERT EDWARD THOMAS SINCE LETTER DATED
26 TH AUGUST 1944

The telegram sent to Phyllis Thomas after her husband's plane was shot down.
(Courtesy of Patricia Milne)

COMMONWEALTH OF AUSTRALIA

Casualty Section,
DEPARTMENT OF AIR
391 Lit. Collins Street,

AIR MAIL

MELBOURNE, S.C.1

IN REPLY QUOTE RAAF. 166/39/266(21A)

Dear Madam,

It is with deep regret that I have to inform
you that the death of your husband, Warrant Officer Albert
Edward Thomas, has now been presumed, for official purposes,
to have occurred on the 23rd April, 1944.

The operation in respect of which your late
husband was reported missing took place on the night of
22nd/23rd April, 1944, and Air Ministry has presumed that
the Casualty occurred on the 23rd April, 1944.

The Minister for Air and members of the Air
Board desire me to extend to you their profound sympathy.
It is hoped that the accompanying enclosures will contain
information of assistance to you.

Yours faithfully,

(M.C. Langslow)
SECRETARY.

Mrs. P. Thomas,
35 Goode Street,
SOUTH PERTH.   W.A.

Phyllis Thomas had to wait several months for the letter
confirming her husband's death.
(Courtesy of Patricia Milne)

Phyllis Thomas (left) with her daughter and a friend.
(Courtesy of Patricia Milne)

THOMAS (W/O Albert Edward, RAAF, attached to RAF), previously reported missing in air operations over Germany, now reported lost his life, April 23, 1944. Buried Nth Military Cemetery, Dusseldorf; beloved husband of Phyllis, dear father of Patricia.

THOMAS, A. E. (W/O.)—In loving memory of Bert, killed in air operations over Germany, April 23, 1944; son-in-law of Mr and Mrs J. M. Jolly (South Perth), brother-in-law of Gladys (Mrs Watson), Marjory (Mrs Meadly) and Maurice (AIF).

THOMAS, A. E. (W/O).—In fond memory of Bert, killed in air operations over Germany, April 23, 1944; brother-in-law of Marj and George Meadly.

Notices in the *West Australian* for Bert Thomas,
including one from his wife, Phyllis.
(Courtesy of Patricia Milne)

25

The evening before Jessie farewelled her husband they had dined with friends. She would miss him terribly, but understood his desire to be with his men again and did not begrudge him that. Conversation turned to the other men who had enlisted. Major General George Alan Vasey, known in some military circles as 'Bloody George' for his robust language, had been concerned about his men and their families at home from the time he spent fighting in the First World War. '[The men] come to me … time and again, Jess … especially before a show,' he said, 'and say … "Sir, if anything happens to me you'll see that my wife and kids are all right?" And I tell them …"Yes, you know bloody well I will."'[41]

After a battle, he paid attention to the families of the men who had died. 'The first thing I do is call for the casualty list,' he once explained to nurse Ruth McLennan while recovering from polyneuritis. 'It weighs heavily … to realise … you have no option but to be responsible for creating all these widows, fatherless children, these mothers robbed of sons.'[42]

For her part, Jessie had helped establish the AIF Women's Association in Melbourne in 1940, becoming its secretary at the inaugural meeting. She met a number of widows through her work there, and did what she could to support them. As early as 1941, Jessie petitioned Prime Minister John Curtin, proposing that a furniture grant be given to war widows. Although a £75 grant was provided the following year,[43] overall, Jessie felt 'very despondent' about the 'desperate position' of these women, how little assistance she was able to offer them and the lack of interest shown by the rest of the community.[44]

'Stick to it,' George encouraged. 'After this is over, you will have all the help I can give you.'[45] On the morning of his departure, he said, 'Now don't forget, look after the war widows because the bloody government won't.'[46]

Now, with both her sons away, one working for Ships Water Transport and the other boarding at Geelong Grammar School, Jessie waited alone for confirmation of George's arrival in Cairns. At 10 pm, a car appeared in the driveway. This could only mean bad news. Jessie opened the door to Major General Charles Lloyd and Bishop John McKie, who confirmed her fears. The RAAF Hudson in which General Vasey was travelling had crashed just outside Cairns Airport. There were no survivors.[47]

Jessie maintained an air of calm, but later she broke down.[48] She and George had been married for twenty-three years. Despite his active service overseas, they had shared so much: their sons George and Robert, their travels to India, the Depression, their home Wantirna, and a concern for the women widowed by war. How could she continue without his encouragement and practical support? And their sons? How was she to break the news to them?

A search of the crash site had failed to find the men before nightfall,[49] but salvage operations continued for several days. The search team eventually recovered Major General Vasey's body, along with those of Major General Downes and Lieutenant Colonel Bertram, but the bodies of three others were never found. In the days and weeks after her husband's death, Jessie received hundreds of condolence letters. Those offering their sympathies included Prime Minister John Curtin, Major General Akin of the US Army, General Vasey's fellow soldiers, Ruth McLennan, who had once nursed him back from near death, and the army drivers who had transported him wherever he needed to go. The letters expressed admiration for both his leadership capabilities and his approachability. As was typical of condolence letters of the day, many suggested that Jessie should find 'comfort and satisfaction' that her husband was a 'fine man' who had done a 'splendid job'.[50] The fact that he had 'rendered such wonderful service to the Empire' ought to provide consolation in her time of 'great sorrow'.[51] Archbishop Booth wrote of Jessie's 'innate courage' that General Vasey 'would have loved to see taking foremost expression at a time like this.'[52] Jessie replied, 'For myself, I find it almost easy to be brave, but nowhere can I find peace or comfort.'[53]

Unable to cope with returning to her work at the AIF Women's Association, she wrote:

> *After so many long years of anxiety my husband's death finds me very weary. I hope you will not feel that I am deserting the Association ... but I am very sad that I never did accomplish the thing I hoped most to do, establish some form of special help for war widows.*[54]

Major General Vasey had promised support and assistance upon his return. His wife, who had worked so hard during the war to help war widows, had now become one of them.

⚜

In June 1945, a different group of service wives and children, married not to Australians but to visiting American servicemen, began the long journey to their new homes in the United States. At the time, Marjorie Learmonth was still working for the Red Cross at Heidelberg Hospital, and the organisation asked her and two other women to chaperone 108 war brides and 38 babies from Melbourne to Sydney. There the number swelled to 279 women and 85 children before the group travelled on to Brisbane. Marjorie thought the war brides were wonderful girls, and a great loss for Australia:[55]

> *We didn't hear one complaint although the conditions in which they were travelling must have been from out of the ark because most of the railway carriages had been in museums … I had two workers with me and we literally didn't sit down between Melbourne and Brisbane. We were on the job the whole time.*[56]

In Brisbane, Marjorie and the other Red Cross workers transferred the women and children over to the care of the American Red Cross, who embarked with them for San Francisco aboard the SS *Lurline* after an introduction to the American tradition of coffee and doughnuts.[57] Marjorie returned to Heidelberg Military Hospital for a time before moving back to her parents' house in Perth.[58] It was here in her childhood home that Marjorie heard the news that hostilities had ceased.

With John Curtin's untimely death in July 1945, the duty fell to newly appointed Prime Minister Ben Chifley to address the nation on 15 August: 'Fellow citizens, the war is over.' Finally, after almost six years of war and four days of speculation and premature celebrations, peace was official. In Western Australia, the local newspapers captured images that have become part of popular memory: a throng of people descending on the centre of Perth; men in suits, and women and children, crowding into St Georges Terrace, William Street and Hay Street; a man raising his hand, his fingers forming the V for victory; a group of young people walking arm in arm, holding souvenir flags declaring 'VP Day'; the Union Jack hanging from the second storey of a city building. Seven thousand servicemen and women marched along the Terrace and down to the Esplanade to participate in a thanksgiving service.[59]

But not everyone joined in the city's festivities. Marjorie Learmonth woke on VP (Victory in the Pacific) Day to the whistles of steam trains sounding continuously. Instead of joining the crowds in the city, she spent the day at home, thinking about Charles and all that she had lost.[60] It is unlikely that Gwen Forsyth felt like rejoicing either. Left with two young boys to bring up alone, she probably wondered what the future held.

For Edna Ramage and her children, VP Day was filled with sadness after hearing that her husband and their father would not be returning home. Whenever Edna's brother had heard of a train or ship arriving, he went to meet it, asking for any news of Bob Ramage. Eventually, he had come across a man who had been in the same prisoner-of-war camp and recalled a September night in 1944 when fellow prisoners brought Bob into the camp after a long day on the Burma Railway. Suffering from dysentery, he died soon afterwards. Edna had received a card from Bob that same month.[61]

Similarly, after three-and-a-half years of uncertainty, Madge Anketell finally received official notification that her husband had died from his wounds. Madge's husband, Lieutenant Colonel Michael Anketell, commanding officer of the 2/4th Machine Gunners, was wounded just days before the fall of Singapore, and although she had been informed of his injuries, she had heard nothing further since then.[62] Even now she received conflicting information. The *West Australian* reported that he was killed when the Japanese bombed the hospital in which he was being treated.[63] In fact, he had been shot in the thigh and seriously wounded on 12 February 1942. He had been evacuated to hospital and underwent surgery, but never recovered.[64]

Kathleen Marguerite Kuring, Rita to those who knew her, would never have certainty as to her husband's fate. On a windy day in

September 1941, Lieutenant Colonel Herman August Kuring had disappeared off rocks at Rottnest Island. Stationed there as the commanding officer of the 10th Garrison Battalion, he had left his driver and car to walk the last half mile to Wilson's Bay. A search of the area failed to find him, but his hat was discovered floating in the ocean. Rita found herself alone with two children to raise, amid rumours that her husband was a German spy. The speculation was fuelled further by the sinking of the *Sydney*, despite a thorough investigation concluding that he had fallen from the cliff and drowned.[65]

Sheila Barron too was grieving. In 1927, she had married Robert Marriott, but was widowed two years and two children later. Nine years on, she met and married Norman Barron. They ran an orchard in Forrestfield and Sheila gave birth to two daughters before the outbreak of the Second World War. Like Gwen Forsyth's husband, Norman Barron joined the 2/28th Battalion. This was earlier in the war; while Arthur Forsyth served in New Guinea, Norman went to Tobruk, where he survived for six months before being killed in action. Just before her thirty-eighth birthday, Sheila was widowed for a second time.[66]

Marjorie Learmonth, Edna Ramage, Madge Anketell, Rita Kuring, Gloria MacDonald, Gwen Forsyth, Jean Ferguson, Rose Heath, Phyllis Thomas, Sheila Barron and Jessie Vasey were just a small number of some ten thousand war widows[67] across Australia for whom VP Day was tainted by grief, the hopes and dreams for their post-war futures dashed.

CHAPTER 2
THE WAR WIDOWS' GUILD BEGINS

After VP Day came repatriation, and the men adjusting, with varying degrees of difficulty, to being husbands, breadwinners and fathers. The federal government aimed for full employment for the male population, with priority given to ex-servicemen. It offered assistance in the form of retraining or study through the Commonwealth Reconstruction Training Scheme and incentives to take up land or build houses through the War Services Home Scheme. Married women, many of whom had joined the workforce during the war, were expected to return to full-time domestic duties.[1] But the traditional role of wife and mother was not possible for everyone; war widows faced an uncertain future.

A widow's grief was exacerbated by the fact that the allotment given to her from her husband's pay was cancelled upon his death. The basic pension of £2.10 per week paid to the wives of men killed on active duty[2] was less than half the basic wage, although even this was more than twice the pittance offered to widows of civilians. Furthermore, there existed in the Repatriation Act a morality clause which could see a war widow's pension cancelled altogether if authorities deemed her 'immoral'.

A war widow with children needed to be both breadwinner and nurturer. Some managed to juggle the two roles. In Perth, Gwen Forsyth returned to nursing to support herself and her boys. Rather than undertaking hospital shift work, she made home visits on behalf of several GPs, fitting them in around her sons' routines.[3] For many war widows, though, this flexibility was not available; they faced a choice of living in poverty or finding work and being an 'absent' mother. On top of this was a sense of isolation and loneliness, as others welcomed home

Booklets detailing the assistance available to war widows
and their children as part of post-war reconstruction.
(Courtesy of Patricia Milne)

loved ones and resumed 'normal' family life.[4] Edna Ramage perceived
that while her neighbours were friendly, the women could not fully
appreciate her situation because their husbands had returned to them.

Jessie Vasey had graduated with a Bachelor of Arts with first class
honours from Melbourne University in 1921, unusual for a woman at
that time, and could have chosen to use her social connections and
educational qualifications to earn a comfortable living. Instead, she
remained concerned about the future of other war widows and their
children,[5] and in spite of her own weariness and grief, her husband's
final words to 'look after the war widows' propelled her forward.

Jessie had been making the most of any opportunity to raise
awareness and fight for the rights and livelihoods of war widows, even
before VP Day. When General Vasey was killed, John Curtin had sent
a condolence letter to Jessie, writing 'Australia owes to him a very great
debt of gratitude.'[6] Jessie replied immediately, using the back of the
Prime Minister's letter to draft her response:

*He believed that with men of good will, all things are possible
... I do wish that for his sake and the sake of all the men who
have endured so much for Aust[ralia] your government could
find it in their hearts to deal more gently with their widows.*[7]

The condolence letter Jessie Vasey received from Prime
Minister John Curtin (top) and her draft reply.
(VFP, MS3782, NLA)

On 4 July 1945, Jessie had also written to Frank Forde, Minister for the Army and Acting Prime Minister at the time. Jessie told him that war widows were despairing, and raised the issue of accrued leave pay (payment given to servicemen in lieu of leave) that had been withheld from many war widows due to a technicality. She also mentioned the lack of affordable housing opportunities for war widows. In theory, the war service loans offered to ex-servicemen were available to war widows, but in practice, a war widow's pension alone was insufficient income to meet the criteria for such loans. She wrote:

> *The Minister of Repatriation explained in the House that widows were not eligible for War Service Homes because their pension was too low. What other homes can they afford? All the widows I contact who live in reasonable homes tell me that relatives are paying the rent, a precarious position for fathers die and charity grows cold.*[8]

And believing that a person should not protest without being prepared to find an answer, she offered a solution:

> *Is it beyond the resources of the country for which these men died to [lease] their widows houses at a nominal rental and, while these houses are being built[,] to pay them a rental allowance or, if they already own homes, a small upkeep allowance?*[9]

But Jessie Vasey was just one woman speaking out in a world where men had the louder voices. Citing 'the dismal lot of the average war widow' and 'bureaucratic indifference' she concluded that war widows across the country would have to 'pull together' if the fight for better pensions and conditions was to be won.[10] One group, the War Widows and Widowed Mothers Association (WWWMA), had been established in Victoria in 1922 to lobby the federal government to provide First World War widows and their dependants with medical benefits. In 1927, the WWWMA had convinced the government to remove the means test on war widows' pensions, allowing the women to augment their pension with paid employment should they wish.[11] But whereas the WWWMA only existed in Victoria, Jessie envisioned a national organisation.

The families of deceased servicemen were also offered assistance by other organisations such as the Ugly Men's Association in Western Australia, and Legacy nationally, but Jessie was not content with what she perceived as charity; her aim was to facilitate self help.[12] When she discovered that the Commonwealth Reconstruction Training Scheme (CRTS) included a provision for war widows to undertake training, with the CRTS providing funding for qualified instructors for approved courses,[13] she conceived the idea of teaching widows to weave. Now, she pointed out, 'weaving and such, the world over, have done a great deal to bring healing to broken lives.'[14] (Jessie had observed beautiful weavings created by poor women in India when she accompanied George there in the inter-war years.[15]) Weaving skills could enable widows to earn an income to supplement the pension. Most important, weaving could be done at home, at a time convenient to the women, so that children who had already lost one parent would not lose another to paid employment outside the home.

In October 1945, barely six months after the death of her husband, and two months after VP Day, Jessie placed an advertisement in the newspaper and sent letters to 2400 war widows in Victoria, outlining her vision for a craft guild for war widows. 'During my long connection with soldiers' families, I have felt, always, that the sacrifice demanded of the war widow and her family by the community was a very terrible one,' the letter began. Jessie went on to describe the final conversations she had with George, and his promise of help.

My husband never came back to give me that help, but his words remain for me the goal at which I aim and at which I hope the War Widows' Guild will aim – "their loss itself is more than enough to suffer." [16]

In a society that was grief weary and considered loss to be a private matter,[17] Jessie publicly acknowledged hers, and expressed her belief that the best qualified to help war widows were those who had suffered similarly.

For a long time I felt that real help for widows could only come from among themselves, now, as one of them, I am sure of it. It is only the women who have faced the problems and the terrors of that long walk in the shadows who can understand what the other widow must face and know how to give a helping hand. In grief and bewilderment we must all grope for some meaning to life; for me the one anchor to which I cling is the thought that I must go on, that I must not be a drag on the victory for which my husband laid down his life.[18]

She alluded to the problems war widows faced when it came to housing, the difficulties of maintaining existing friendships and the need to find 'new interests and a new circle.' She believed that in a group such as the one she proposed, 'it will always be found that someone else has had to face your problems, and it is half the battle to be able to talk matters over with someone who understands and wants to help.' She held that weaving had social as well as financial benefits:

For us, on our meagre pensions, these hobbies have the great advantage of bringing pleasure and profits and friends.[19]

Jessie concluded her letter with a call to action: 'It rests with us, the war widows, to make our Guild a power in the land.'[20]

Kitty Gahan was one of approximately two hundred widows who responded to Jessie's letter and gathered at Melbourne's Assembly Hall on Saturday 22 November 1945. When Kitty's husband had enlisted at the start of the war, she moved away from her family in Mildura to Melbourne. Among all her friends, she was the only one to have lost her husband, and she found it difficult to cope when the husbands of her friends returned. Out of a job, and unsure of what to do next, Kitty listened intently to Jessie Vasey.[21]

Jessie, referred to by most of the women as Mrs Vasey, was older than the majority of them, with a commanding, compelling presence. Articulate and smartly attired, she seemed so capable, confident and knowledgeable that she gave Kitty and the other widows hope. In hearing other widows' stories, Kitty discovered others who understood her experience.[22]

MOUNTAIN HIGHWAY,
WANTIRNA, VIC.
October, 1945.

Dear

During my long connection with soldiers' families I have felt, always, that the sacrifice demanded of the war widow and her family by the community was a very terrible one. In spite of my hopes and efforts very little has been done for them, especially for that group of women for whom living on a beggarly pittance will mean a complete alteration in their way of life. It hurt my husband very much that the families of the men he had loved so greatly, the men who had died so uncomplainingly for Australia, should suffer privation and want because of that sacrifice. Our last evening together was spent in discussing ways of improving their conditions with some of our friends, and then General Vasey said : "Stick to the war widows now and when I come back you shall have every atom of help I can give you. To me their position is incredible, surely their loss is itself more than enough to suffer." My husband never came back to give me that help, but his words remain for me the goal at which I aim and at which I hope the War Widows' Guild will aim—"their loss itself is more than enough to suffer."

For a long time I felt that real help for widows could only come from among themselves, now, as one of them, I am sure of it. It is only the women who have faced the problems and the terrors of that long walk in the shadows who can understand what the other widow must face and know how to give her a helping hand. In grief and bewilderment we must all grope for some meaning to life ; for me the one anchor to which I cling is the thought that I must go on, that I must not be a drag on the victory for which my husband laid down his life.

Widowhood for most of us, will mean the loss of the circle and the interests which we shared with our husbands. If we are to go on we must find new interests and a new circle ; it rests with us alone to build happy homes for our children. All this seems quite hopeless of accomplishment when most widows have to face the fact that only the barest necessities can be paid for out of the present pension. This is surely where we can help ourselves. If we grouped ourselves together, as in the proposed Craft Guild, and shared our hobbies, if we found new interests and told our friends about them, ways and means would soon be found to foster and encourage those interests. In a group, too, it will always be found that someone else has had to face your problem, and it is half the battle to be able to talk matters over with someone who understands and wants to help.

There is a wealth of human kindness only awaiting direction. Since I started to make inquiries about weaving as a craft for our widows so many who love this work have offered their help and their services ; even from far away Canada has come details of a big scheme there and textbooks and pamphlets as well to help us. Many people would gladly send in books and magazines for a reading group, and hundreds of garden lovers would share seeds and plants if they knew where to get into touch with our widows. For those who want to own books there are the very excellent English book clubs whose small subscriptions could probably be shared with several others. All these are things which could be done through the Guild.

Since it is possible to learn such crafts as weaving, pottery, cooking, dressmaking and a host of others through the training schemes free of all charge, it seems very foolish not to take advantage of this opportunity. Weaving and such, the world over, have done a great deal to bring healing to broken lives, and for us, on our meagre pensions, these hobbies have the great advantage of bringing pleasure and profits and friends.

Then there are other matters about which widows should concern themselves. The community, as a whole, is a very busy one. Not many of them even noticed when the Minister said that widows on pensions were being refused War Service Homes as their finances were not good enough. As the Act stands he may have been quite right, but what a cruel state of affairs that reply uncovered. If a widow is not to get a War Service Home, at a total cost of about 22/- weekly, how is she to live and where ? The chances of renting a Housing Commission house at a lower rental are about one in a thousand. Surely the price of a man's life should be a shelter for his family. There is a very strange regulation by which recreational leave pay and war service leave pay although credited to the soldier and in his pay book is not paid over to his family when he is killed—surely a very cruel injustice. All wages awards are subject to cost of living adjustments— why not pensions ? Why is the first child of a living soldier allowed 21/- living allowance and the same child only allowed 17/6 when his father is dead ? He eats just as much. These and other anomalies could be corrected if enough women grouped themselves together to do it. Governments listen to numbers.

During the long and difficult years of the war women have shouldered heavy burdens ; the war widow may never lay hers down. Yet it is no mean destiny to be called upon to go on for a man who has laid down his life, as Christ did, to save mankind from the power of the Beast. Our husbands fought against hopeless odds and overcame them ; we can do the same for from their sacrifice will come our strength. It rests with us, the war widows, to make our Guild a power in the land.

Yours sincerely,

J. M. VASEY.

Jessie Vasey's letter sent out to all war widows describing her vision.
(Guild archives, WA Branch)

37

Accompanying Jessie Vasey on stage was Rachel Grieve, an experienced weaver who had spent twenty years overseas before returning to Australia in 1937. While abroad, she had worked and studied in a variety of fields including teaching, illustrating and psychology before developing an interest in weaving. She would spend the rest of her life devoted to weaving, and became a highly sought after instructor of the craft,[23] with samples of her work still held by the Australian National Gallery in Canberra and the National Gallery of Victoria.

Following a talk and demonstration by Rachel Grieve, Jessie Vasey addressed the audience, encouraging them that 'things would be different if they banded together, sought companionship in their shared experiences, became a sisterhood.'[24] When she finished speaking, a motion was carried 'that those present form themselves into the War Widows' Craft Guild with power to add to their number.'[25]

'Mrs Vasey should be president,' a woman called out.

'If you want me to be president, someone will have to nominate me,'[26] Jessie responded.

Muriel Cula, whose husband had been killed in New Guinea, nominated her, Mrs Sewell seconded the motion and Jessie Vasey duly accepted the position. An interim committee was elected until a constitution could be written, with Beryl Riggall taking on the role of honorary secretary.[27] Subjects discussed at the meeting included the fact that payment for servicemen's accrued recreational leave, which could be as much as a hundred pounds, was not available to the widows of men who died between 1 July 1942 and 1 April 1945. The meeting protested 'emphatically against the withholding from dependants of the pay due to the deceased servicemen in lieu of recreational leave.'[28]

Helen Seager, a journalist for Melbourne newspaper the *Argus*, wrote supportively about Jessie Vasey and her 'new venture'. While Jessie was reluctant to ask for money, Helen Seager knew the Guild needed financial assistance to buy looms and other equipment, and for establishing a crèche for the children of trainees. She encouraged readers to send donations, writing, 'Let us help them make the War Widows' Guild weaving as famous a name as we can. The start is all they need.'[29] The appeal reached the £1000 mark by the first week of January.[30] Letters also arrived, some from women who had only

Why a Guild

Community quite ignorant   -   Mrs. Dowell -   high old time   maid

Saving from extinction etc. - community's finest asset - down into
sub standard group ...

Raising pension   -   doubled -   not for luxuries, but for decencies
clean sheets, baths - home with a verandah.

½d. a day
No compensation for sorrow   -   'To me their position is incredible

Country cannot afford it

Cost of the war in vain - go under

Immigration - millions paid - healthy Australians

Other bodies do things for widows - League - Legacy &c.

Special spheres - oo overlapping at all

Saving from extinction - last war's widows, bitterness, neglect,

frustration. Loss of interests and circle "Welcome Home" P.O.W.

War neurosis - anxiety state   (Mrs. Dick)

Comfort - widows all being together have interests in common

Living on the pension means loss of interests - Hurtful remarks

Idea of the Guild took shape

Reconstruction   -   full use   -   not for mothers' encouragement

After training - what?.   Tools - raw materials - markets.

Link up - country dressmaking - C.W.A. etc.

Weaving - why?   Creative and curative - Done in the home

Selling: assured market

Position abroad
          Rodier - Mrs. Mairet - leads the trade and sets an
          example to the world of what good weaving is

          Times expert - Marriott

          Influence Australia - wool - flax

      Proud woman - uncharted seas
          Highland Home Industries Ltd.
          Searle Scheme in Canada.

Not weaving alone -   first only.

Loom

Books and magazines in circulation

"Own business" -

Accrued leave pay 17/6 - 21/-

Furniture grant

Tribute to the Dept. of Repatriation -

Fear and trepidation   "never defeated" unless you say you are"

Exactly 1 year ago - now 4 Guilds

Jessie Vasey's notes for 'Why a Guild'.
(VFP, MS3782, NLA)

recently received official notification of their husbands' deaths. One letter indicated the support Jessie's initiative provided:

> *If it wasn't for the Guild I would have no hope to cling to just now. I have just heard officially that I have been a widow for three and a half years. Despite all my anxiety for so long the shock is still terrible and still bewildering. It is the mere thought of the guild and all it will mean to us lonely ones that saves me from despair.*[31]

Lessons in weaving and other crafts began in Victoria in January 1946 under the instruction of Rachel Grieve. By the end of the year, the Victorian Guild was training seventy-seven war widows, thirty of them full time.[32] With financial assistance from the Red Cross, Jessie Vasey also established a day nursery for children aged between two-and-a-half and five years.[33]

For Jessie, the formation of the War Widows' Craft Guild in Victoria was just the beginning. She was determined to develop the organisation into a force to be reckoned with or, as she described it, 'a power in the land.'[34] She would not waver from her mission to improve the lives of thousands of women whom she felt had not only lost their men, but had been forgotten by the rest of the nation.[35] Believing that a larger membership base would mean greater political influence, Jessie Vasey set out to develop the Guild interstate. Over the next twelve months, she initiated branches in New South Wales,[36] South Australia[37] and Western Australia.

On Wednesday 27 November 1946, two hundred widows attended a meeting at Anzac House, the Returned Services League (RSL) headquarters in St Georges Terrace, Perth. At the request of Esther Whitelaw, wife of General John Stewart Whitelaw, the Friendly Union of Soldiers' Wives assisted with the arrangements, and provided the widows with afternoon tea. Marjorie Learmonth attended, being encouraged to do so by General Whitelaw.[38] Gwen Forsyth, Jean Ferguson, Edna Ramage, Madge Anketell, Rita Kuring and Phyllis Thomas were also present.

'Few people realise how hard it is for a war widow to make do on her inadequate pension,' Jessie Vasey told the gathering. She stressed the

Dear Sir,

We are anxious to bring to your notice our War Widows' Craft Guild and its needs as we think it would appeal to you as worthy of consideration when you are disbursing such charitable trusts as may apply to us.

Before going into the question of what the Guild does, I would like to assure you that in no way does the work we do overlap that done by Legacy. The salary of the Organising Secretary of the Sydney Guild is being paid by the President of Sydney Legacy, who is himself quite satisfied of the need of the Guild and the fact that there is no overlapping. May I draw your attention to the fact that Legacy's splendid work is done for children in a certain age group and, where necessary to the well-being of the children, for their mothers; but that all widows whose children are not members of Legacy or who have no children are of course outside its orbit. There will also be as well those women who are very seriously in need of help of various kinds, not necessarily financial, who do not and would prefer not to come within the usual charitable group. For this particular class of woman the practice of a good handicraft is of inestimable value.

All war widows can obtain training through the Department of Post War Reconstruction, but the conditions are such as to make it impossible for the war widow with children or other family obligations to afford to take part in the classes. This Guild has set itself to pay fares and expenses for part-time trainees so that no woman will have to take full-time training and neglect her children in order to get Government allowances, or refuse her training for the sake of her family. As is usual with all Government schemes, there are a great many gaps in Reconstruction set-up. Once the individual widow has received her training, she is no longer their responsibility and she has to buy her tools of trade as well as find her markets and raw materials. These are the things we propose to do for her. As far as possible trainees, such as the weaving trainees, will be guided and advised in their work by specially talented people. Our procedure in this matter has been modelled on the extremely successful work undertaken by Highland Home Industries Limited and by the Swedish Crafts Associations, all of which are prosperous bodies.

At the present moment there does not exist any body whose work it is to see that Government regulations, where they apply to war widows, take any cognisance of her particular needs. Up to date she and her family have been, as it were, "also-rans" in the Service Acts; for example, because (as we have been told) there was "no one to put the war widow's case" Repatriation Act was not amended to increase the allowances for children when the Service Mens' Childrens' Allowances was raised, which has resulted in the anomaly that a dead service man's first child receives 17/6 per week and the living service man's child receives 21/- per week. I would remind you that by some fantastic reasoning a widow is still considered a dependent and is paid as such. She is expected to provide her own living needs, rent for her family and

all the extras that children need on the absurd sum of £2/10/- weekly.

May we ask that you give our Guild your sympathetic consideration?

Yours faithfully,

One of the many letters Jessie Vasey wrote requesting support for the newly formed War Widows' Craft Guild.
(VFP, MS3782, NLA)

importance of speaking up, reporting that the previous repatriation minister had once said in parliament that war widows' pensions must be adequate because he had never had any complaints.

> *I do not want you to go about labouring the question, making out that we are ill-treated. That only leads to frustration. But do everything you can to help – write to your Federal member, talk the problem over with sympathetic members of the public, enlist the sympathy of your local RSL branch. It is only when requests are supported by strong public opinion that they carry weight.*[39]

Jessie identified the mixed messages given to war widows about their place in post-war Australia:

> *When a married woman wanted to work the men's cry was 'Woman's place is in the home,' yet when a war widow asked for an adequate pension so that they might stay at home, they said, 'Oh, she can work to augment it.' Widows seemed to be regarded as a cross between a criminal and an imbecile; some man had always got to decide exactly what they should do and how they should do it.*[40]

As she had done in Victoria, Jessie promoted the benefits of undertaking training under the Post-War Reconstruction Scheme. Doing so as a group under the auspices of a craft guild would not only give the women extra income, but it would bring them 'a fresh interest, new friends and a break away from the domestic ties of their homes.'[41]

Two days after the meeting at Anzac House, the provisional committee of the War Widows' Craft Guild WA met there, with Jessie Vasey taking the chair. Those present voted to apply for registration as the War Widows' Craft Guild.[42] Temporary committee members were elected unopposed, with Marjorie Learmonth to be chair. Jean Ferguson and Madge Anketell agreed to share the vice-presidency, Lucille Rickards was elected secretary, Muriel Jones became assistant secretary and Mrs G. Smith the treasurer. Although she did not take an official role, Gwen Forsyth was part of the inaugural committee, as were Edna Ramage, Phyllis Thomas and Peggy Walker, all of whom would take advantage of the weaving training.[43] The committee discussed ways to have their voices heard, and to encourage others to participate, and decided to arrange regular monthly social gatherings for friendship and mutual support. They agreed to send a circular to all war widows in Western Australia, informing them of matters connected with the Guild, such as craft classes and repatriation benefits, and encouraging them to write to their federal members regarding accrued leave pay. It was also resolved to 'request the appointment of a war widow on any board dealing with the allocation of Canteen Funds on behalf of war widows or their children', and to seek the Red Cross's assistance in establishing a day nursery for pre-school age children whose mothers were widows and training or working full time.[44]

While in Perth, Mrs Vasey took the opportunity to address Legacy, the Red Cross Society, and the state executive of the RSL at separate engagements. She encouraged cooperation between the RSL and war widows, suggesting that the RSL could help war widows 'by performing men's jobs around their homes, such as mending gutters and cutting lawns.'[45] Speaking to Legacy, an organisation of ex-servicemen established after the First World War to look out for the dependants of deceased servicemen, she referred to the ambiguous marital status of war widows:

The widow is a rather odd animal. Under certain conditions she is a single girl; under others she is a married woman. Under reconstruction training she is not allowed to keep her pension if she trains. It is deducted from a single girl's training allowance.[46]

Jessie made no secret that she thought the war widows' pension was pitiful, with or without the training allowance. While conditions were better for war widows than for widows of civilians, Jessie Vasey never considered the war widows' pension to be satisfactory. And with Guild branches now set up in four states, and branches in Tasmania and Queensland to be established in 1947,[47] the fight for improved compensation was about to heat up.

R.S.L. AND WAR WIDOWS.

Mrs Vasey Seeks Co-operation

An appeal for greater co-operation between the Returned Servicemen's League and war widows was made by Mrs. J. Vasey, widow of the late Major-General G. Vasey, former G.O.C. of the Seventh Division, A.I.F., when she was entertained at Anzac House yesterday afternoon by the State executive of the R.S.L. Mrs. Vasey arrived in Perth from the Eastern States recently in connection with the organisation of a West Australian branch of the War Widows' Guild.

She said that the organisation of the guild was practically the last request of her late husband. War widows felt that they were almost social outcasts, and there was need for greater co-operation between them and the R.S.L. She would like members of the R.S.L. to help war widows by performing men's jobs around their homes, such as mending gutters and cutting lawns. War widows should be given an opportunity to participate in the disbursement of profits of the Australian Army Canteen Services. She was hopeful that the deciding board would include a war widow who would possess the power to emphasise the needs of war widows.

"It rests with the R.S.L. to make certain that the dead soldier has his canteen profits passed on to his family," she said. Mrs. Vasey expressed the opinion that war widows' pensions were inadequate.

The president of the State executive of the R.S.L. (Mr. J. M. W. Anderson) was chairman. Among those present were Mrs. J. S. Whitelaw, wife of the G.O.C., Western Command, and representatives of the State executive of the R.S.L. Women's Auxiliary, the Friendly Union of Soldiers' Wives and the War Widows' Guild.

WAR WIDOWS' GUILD

MRS. J. VASEY'S VISIT.

Australia-Wide Movement.

In the course of an Australian-wide tour to establish a War Widows' Guild in every State, Mrs. J. Vasey, widow of the late Major-General G. Vasey, former G.O.C., of the 7th Division, A.I.F., is visiting Perth.

Mrs. Vasey said yesterday that the aim of the guild would be to obtain better conditions for war widows. For many years she had been worried by the problems which these women faced, and had decided to establish a movement, on a Commonwealth-wide basis, which would work to overcome their disabilities. It had, she added, been one of her husband's ambitions.

The guild was already well established in Victoria and N.S.W., and had got off to a good start in South Australia and Tasmania. Early next year she planned to visit Queensland to launch a branch of the guild there.

Mrs. Vasey, who will spend about two weeks in this State, will outline the objects of the Guild at a meeting to be held in Anzac House today at 2.30 p.m., to which all war widows are invited.

Jessie Vasey's visit to establish the Guild in Western Australia attracted the attention of the local press. These are just a few of the articles that appeared in the *West Australian* between 27 November and 5 December 1946.

WAR WIDOWS' GUILD

IMPROVED STATUS SOUGHT

Scope for Craftsmanship.

The securing of a reasonable pension for war widows as its long-term objective, and meanwhile to see that they obtained all benefits to which they were entitled, were the aims of the War Widows' Guild, as outlined by Mrs. J. Vasey, widow of the late Major-General G. Vasey, former G.O.C., of the 7th Division, A.I.F., to a crowded meeting of war widows at Anzac House yesterday. At the request of Mrs. J. S. Whitelaw, wife of the G.O.C., Western Command, the meeting was arranged by the Friendly Union of Soldiers' Wives, whose president (Mrs. H. Dean) presided.

Few people realised how hard it was for a war widow to make-do on her inadequate pension, said Mrs. Vasey, and she urged everyone present to make up her mind that, quietly but firmly, she would set out to do something to remedy the position.

Women, she pointed out, would always get the terms they deserved. If the war widows did not say they were dissatisfied, they could not blame the Government for not taking action to better their conditions. The former Minister for Repatriation (Mr. Frost) had said in the House on one occasion that he thought war widows' pensions must be considered adequate, because he had never had any complaints! Her own husband had always held that nobody had the right to criticise without being prepared to do something to remedy the wrong.

"I do not want you to go about labouring the question, making out that we are ill-treated," continued Mrs. Vasey. "That only leads to frustration. But do everything you can to help—write to your Federal member, talk the problem over with sympathetic members of the public, enlist the sympathy of your local R.S.L. branch. It is only when requests are supported by strong public opinion that they carry weight."

THE WEST AUSTR.

WAR WIDOWS.

LIGHTENING THE SHADOWS

Guild's Work Outlined.

"No war widow is quite a normal person," said Mrs. J. Vasey, widow of the late Major-General G. Vasey, in an address to the Perth Legacy Club on Tuesday. "You cannot possibly count out the fact that she has suffered bereavement after years of terrible anxiety and faces the future without any hope because there is no hope in it. All she sees is prices rising and her pension staying where it is.".

Mrs. Vasey said that with the formation of a branch of the War Widows' Guild in Western Australia the guild was now established in every State except Queensland.

"All through the war," she said, "I had tried to help war widows. When they first came to me in 1939 as the mothers of the men who were going away to the war I suddenly realised to my horror that I could recognise the widow of the 1914-18 war when she came into a room with other women. It had put, I felt, a terrible mark on her, and I wondered why we as a community had never been able to do more to relieve them of their burdens. The first trouble is the inadequacy of the pension. I think that, unless we realise what it means to a woman to live always with the fear at her shoulder that her children are underfed and will miss the privileges and not have the place in life that would have been approximately theirs had their father lived, and unless we do something to relieve that woman of that fear we are going to force down into a sub-standard in our community the families of some of the finest men we have ever had."

Many of the children of war widows, she said, had been found

WOMAN'S REALM.

SOCIAL NOTES.

(By "Avon.")

Mrs. G. A. Vasey, who is visiting Perth in the course of an Australia-wide tour to establish War Widows' Guilds in every State, was the guest of honour at a late afternoon party on Sunday given by Dr. and Mrs. Douglas Gawler in the garden of their Claremont home. Among those present were Mr. and Mrs. J. Dimmitt, Mr. and Mrs. A. G. Symington, Mr. and Mrs. John Morrison, Mr. and Mrs. J. L. Paton, Mr. and Mrs. Roger Goode, Mesdames J. S. Whitelaw, J. E. Hendry and F. Farmaner and Miss Norma Rolland.

*   *   *   *   *

WOMAN'S REALM.

SOCIAL NOTES.

(By "Avon.")

Lady Mitchell, the president of the West Australian Division of the Red Cross Society, attended the luncheon given by Mrs. A. W. Jacoby at the Karrakatta Club on Monday to enable members of the executive of the Red Cross Society to meet Mrs. G. A. Vasey, who came to Perth to establish a War Widows' Guild in this State. Among those present were Mesdames R. A. Cameron, R. A. Forsaith, P. G. Hulbert, W. Hedges, C. Learmonth, F. Lefroy, A. G. Symington, N. Temperley and Miss E. Mower.

*   *   *   *   *

The social aspect of Jessie Vasey's visit featured in the 'women's pages' of the *West Australian*.

❀

Nationally, the problems were the same all over the country. War widow pensions, introduced during the First World War, were covered by the *Australian Soldiers' Repatriation Act*. Replacing the state-based War Councils in 1918, the Repatriation Department's main function was to assist in the re-establishment of veterans in civilian life, especially in terms of employment, training and medical assistance.[48] Where a man lost his life during active service overseas, the Repatriation Department assisted his widow and children in the form of a weekly pension. In 1916, a war widow's pension (which also covered de facto widows[49]) was £2 10s per week, approximately 90 per cent of the basic wage of £2 15s 16d.[50] Initially, a war widow lost her pension if she remarried, but, from 1916, she could retain her pension for two years after the wedding; however, this provision was abolished in 1931, a measure attributed to cost cutting necessitated by the Depression.[51]

In 1947, a war widow's basic pension remained at £2 10s, with some additional payments depending on the number of children and the rank of her husband. By contrast, the basic wage had increased to £5 9s 1d.[52] In Jessie Vasey's view, the pension was not only insufficient to live on, but also an inadequate recompense for the loss of one's husband. Furthermore, she believed that the war widow's pension ought to be viewed as compensation, not charity.[53]

On 4 March 1947, the eve of the second anniversary of General Vasey's death, the government announced that war widows would receive a pension rise of five shillings, effective from 1 July 1947.[54] Jessie Vasey wasted no time in protesting against such a pathetically small increase. She fired off letters to several politicians, including Harold Holt, then the Member for the Victorian seat of Fawkner.

Dear Mr Holt

FREEDOM FROM WANT
FREEDOM FROM FEAR

*These were the things our men died to give us, yet their
families must exist in privation and penury on a level
far below the basic wage while others enjoy the benefits
purchased by their deaths. To us it seems that the pensions
are only a mockery in a land which prides itself on its
standard of living. Must our men sacrifice not only their
own lives but that of their families also?*

*In Victoria it costs on an average thirty shillings to feed
and clothe a child in a decently run orphanage, we must
keep two children on 37/– (including endowment). Surely
the dead serviceman's child needs as much as the orphan?
Up to date few members of Parliament have shown any
interest in this matter, are you one of them? Guilds are now
Australia wide, and, in each state, we want to know who will
work for decent conditions for war widows and war orphans.*

Yours sincerely

*J.M. Vasey
President.*[55]

Jessie was further outraged by an announcement in early June that federal members and senators had voted to increase their own pay by 50 per cent, from £1000 to £1500 per annum.[56] Not afraid of a fight, Jessie Vasey decided a forthright approach was needed if war widows were to achieve a substantial increase in benefits.[57] On 2 July 1947, approximately two thousand war widows and supporters crammed into the Melbourne Town Hall for a mass rally.[58] Numerous politicians were invited; only a handful attended, one of them Harold Holt. Robert Menzies, who knew General Vasey from their school days together, sent his apologies and a donation.[59] The War Widows' Craft Guild banner hung across the entrance of the hall. Inside, more banners hung from the balcony, including one which said, 'The Cheapest Thing Used in the War was the Serviceman's Life' and 'War Widows want Compensation not a Dole.' Under discussion were accrued leave pay, which was still not forthcoming for widows of men who died between 1 July 1942 and 1 April 1945, increased education and medical benefits, and a call for war widow pensions to equal the basic wage.[60] Jessie Vasey asked the women to protest with their vote at the next election.

> There isn't a wife or mother in this hall who hasn't managed men in short pants or long pants. Politicians are only men, with loud voices. If Australian women make up their minds that war widows should have decent conditions, Heaven help the politician who resists them![61]

Jessie continued with a discussion about the sacrifice of their men.

> Australia's wealth and future were paid for in blood, sweat and tears. The cruellest price of all was paid in blood. The war widow paid that price.[62]

The rally made news headlines. Articles quoted Jessie's speech extensively, portraying the war widows' demands as reasonable and justified.[63] On the wave of this attention, Jessie led a deputation to the federal Minister for Repatriation, Herbert Claude Barnard. Although he was prepared to investigate the issue of widows with children, as well as anomalies in educational and medical benefits, he was not prepared to consider a pension rise for childless widows. 'Many of these flappers married these men in a hurry, and a lot of them hoped they would never come back,' he commented unwisely to his secretary.[64]

Jessie overheard the remark and contacted the media. Splashed across the papers was the minister's use of the word 'flappers' to describe childless widows. Mr Barnard was furious. 'Mrs Vasey's statement is a wilful distortion of the facts,' he told the media.[65] Mr Barnard argued that he had meant the term in a complimentary way, and accused Jessie of giving a distorted view of the meeting to the press. He added that he had some understanding of the war widows' plight because he had a war widow in his own family.[66] Jessie retorted that he had used the word 'wretched' to precede the 'flappers' comment, and so there was no way it could be construed as complimentary.[67]

In Western Australia, Guild secretary Muriel Jones sent a letter to the editor of the *West Australian*[68] and state president Marjorie Learmonth wrote to Prime Minister Chifley to protest against Barnard's 'flapper' comment. After a lengthy discussion, the WA executive committee agreed to organise a public meeting similar to the one held in Melbourne.[69] However, they accepted advice from Senator Collett, who had commanded the 28th Battalion at Gallipoli, Egypt, Sinai and France, and was the state president of the RSL for eight years prior to entering politics.[70] Senator Collet suggested that instead of staging a meeting, the Guild should seek representation with Mr Barnard when he arrived in Perth in August.[71]

Jean Ferguson, now matron at the Repatriation General Hospital, Hollywood (previously the 110th Military Hospital), also raised the issue of pensions at a meeting of Ex-Service Organisations. She said that Marjorie Learmonth would 'appreciate it very much if the organisations could support the appeal for a bigger pension for War Widows with children, who really need more help.'[72] Mr Growcott, Deputy Director of Reconstruction, asked whether the Guild could supply details about the number of widows involved, the total amount of income required, the number of children and the degree of hardship experienced. To address these questions, Marjorie Learmonth asked members to keep a budget indicating their expenditure, to provide evidence that the pension was inadequate.[73]

Marjorie Learmonth, inaugural state president in Western Australia.
(Courtesy of Marjorie Le Souef)

Marjorie Learmonth, Jean Ferguson and Gwen Forsyth met with Minister Barnard on Monday 4 August 1947.[74] Senator Dorothy Tangney, Australia's first woman senator, introduced the deputation and then Marjorie Learmonth spoke, reinforcing the inadequacy of the war widows' pension. As requested, members had kept records of their budgets and expenditure from which Marjorie concluded the women could not manage without greater assistance. 'Either they must work or appeal to a welfare fund,' she said. 'This proved that war widows found it impossible to manage on their present pension.' Marjorie requested that the children of war widows be eligible for their allowance and medical benefits until the age of eighteen, instead of sixteen, as few children were able to live independently at sixteen. She also asked that war widows 'be granted access to the facilities at the Repatriation Hospital, Hollywood, for any specialised treatment deemed necessary, and to the department's panel of specialists.'[75]

Minister Barnard stated that he was still 'not prepared to recommend an increase in the pensions of childless war widows, who were able to earn an economic wage' but he was 'fully prepared' to assist those who were 'aged or infirm or mothers of large families or young and physically incapable of earning their living.' He added, 'Frankly I regard war widows and their dependants as a primary responsibility of the government, but just how far we can go on helping them has to be decided.'[76]

The *West Australian* reported that the war widows received an 'attentive' and 'sympathetic' hearing from Minister Barnard.[77] Marjorie Learmonth, on the other hand, was no more impressed with Mr Barnard than Jessie Vasey had been. 'He had the reputation for letting people speak to his back,' she recalled years later. 'That was easy for him as he sat on a swivel chair. For us it was the height of rudeness.'[78]

Despite the animosity between Mr Barnard and the War Widows' Guild, another five-shilling pension increase was announced in September, along with a domestic allowance of 7s 6d per week for widows with one or two children, and accrued leave pay of servicemen who died while on active service prior to 20 March 1945.[79] The amount of leave pay depended on the time a woman's husband had spent in the armed forces, ranging from 14 days' pay for a man who saw less than a year's service, and up to 42 days' pay if he served his country for three years. The widow of a deceased prisoner of war would receive the equivalent of 14 days' pay regardless of when he died.[80] This would have directly benefited women such as Gwen Forsyth, Jean Ferguson and Marjorie Learmonth, all of whom had lost their husbands during that period.

Marjorie spoke about the role of the Guild in securing these added benefits in a radio interview on 2 September:

> *I do not think there is any doubt that the 5/– pension rise although ridiculously inadequate in comparison with the cost of living was due to the fact that the Guild existed.*[81]

She added that the War Widows' Craft Guild would become a force that refused to be ignored:

> *In the past war widows have been overlooked on many occasions. It is taking time to bring us up to date with our*

entitlements, but in the future the politicians will know he or she will have to answer to a representative of thousands of women who are members of the War Widows' Craft Guild, if we are forgotten.[82]

There was no question that there was a great deal more work and campaigning to do, but the war widows' persistence and political pressure was beginning to pay dividends.

CHAPTER 3
A PLACE TO CALL HOME

The initial problems confronting the war widows in Western Australia included finding somewhere to meet and assessing the viability and practicalities of establishing a weaving course. For the first few months, members met in each other's homes, with committee meetings conducted at Anzac House.[1]

On 11 March 1947, Jean Ferguson, vice-president of the Guild and assistant matron at the Repatriation General Hospital, Hollywood, attended a Post-War Reconstruction meeting with representatives from other ex-service organisations, including the Totally and Permanently Disabled Soldiers Association and the Australian Legion of Ex-Servicemen and Women, seeking information regarding the training scheme available to war widows. Mr Wood, deputy director of the Ministry of Post-War Reconstruction, confirmed what Jessie Vasey had told Legacy about the training allowance. While undertaking training, a war widow received a living allowance of £3 5s, plus a further £1 for the care of her children. The catch was that her war widow's pension of £2 10s would be deducted from this amount. There was general agreement at the meeting that the allowance should be *in addition* to the pension, otherwise the benefit of participating in the training was substantially reduced.[2]

Mr Phillips, deputy director of industrial training, expressed concern that not many war widows had yet enrolled in training. Jean Ferguson explained that this was primarily due to the lack of suitable rooms in which to conduct classes. From Mr Phillips' perspective, however, the establishment of a weaving centre was being delayed because of insufficient enrolment numbers. 'All widows who intend to train should immediately submit an application,' he said.[3] And if there were war widows unable to commence immediately, 'they should still apply and then defer,' added Mr Wood. 'As soon as there are enough applicants, I will assist in the search for accommodation,' Mr Phillips promised.[4]

Following the meeting, the Guild approached its members, and a number enrolled in training. That same month the Guild moved into rooms at Army Records, situated in the 28th Battalion Drill Hall in Lord Street, East Perth.[5] The Guild now started the process of setting up its own weaving school by submitting a formal application to the Ministry of Post-War Reconstruction.[6] The classes would operate under the auspices of the Perth Technical College, but it was the Guild's responsibility to find staff and equipment,[7] and materials such as linen and cotton threads.

Anticipating a positive response, the Guild ordered six large looms and approached Kitty Gahan to teach. Kitty had been among Rachel Grieve's first trainees in Melbourne, and had initially known little about weaving:

> Apart from liking all sorts of hand work, I hadn't done anything remotely connected with weaving, and I didn't imagine that I would be capable of doing such work. When I first visited our Guild in Victoria, and saw the work being done, I was fascinated but rather doubtful of my ability to follow suit. However, I decided to take the chance ...[8]

Kitty had displayed flair for the craft, and just over a year later, had become an instructor. Weaving classes commenced unofficially at the Guild rooms in Lord Street, although applicants did not receive their training allowance until the school was formally approved and opened.[9] The Guild also employed one of its members, Mrs McEvoy, as a clerk to deal with administrative work.[10]

The women had the option of keeping finished articles for the cost of materials, or selling them through the Guild. While the war widows learned to make rugs on large looms, many of them produced fine linen, which was in high demand in the post-war period. Products included tablemats, tapestries, furnishings, travel rugs, and material for winter skirts.[11] 'There is such a variety of both useful and beautiful things to be made, that one is spared the boredom of too much repetition of the same thing,' commented Kitty Gahan in a radio interview. 'In weaving, one's own creative ability has the opportunity for expression, and it is really quite a thrill to see the actual fabric growing under your own hands.'[12]

Some doubts over the viability and suitability of a weaving school in Perth were cast at a Post-War Reconstruction meeting on 29 July, even though the group had supported the venture in March, and the

Weaving School students. Back (L–R): Ruth Engwell, Beatrice (Trixie) Davey, Gwen Forsyth, Edna Ramage, Mrs Hill, Ethel May Jones. Front (L–R): Mrs J. Kelly, Eleanor Burnside, Wyn Spence. (Courtesy of Helen Treloar)

Weaving School students. Back (L–R): Ruth Engwell, Wyn Spence, Mrs Hill, Ethel May Jones, Gwen Forsyth, Edna Ramage, Fanny May Collins, Beatrice (Trixie) Davey. Front (L–R): Kitty Gahan, Peggy Walker, Mrs Butler, Mrs Smith, Marjorie (Madge) Davidson, Eleanor Burnside, Mrs J. Kelly. (Courtesy of Helen Treloar)

weaving school had now been officially approved. 'Is it wise to train for weaving in uncertain conditions?' a representative of one organisation asked, presumably in reference to the rations and shortages that were still occurring.[13]

Mr Growcott, the meeting chair, replied that 'the market would remain pretty buoyant for a considerable time', while currently there was 'a fairly well defined demand for woven articles and on that basis training had been approved.' Mr Leslie, MLA, believed that 'there would always be a market for weaving' and Miss Pearce concluded the discussion by stating:

> *in nearly every case a woman chooses to do weaving because it is something that she can do in her own home – she visualises learning this craft and doing it in her spare time. Therefore, there would not be the volume of work turned out which would flood the market.*[14]

By September, there were ten students enrolled in the six-month full-time weaving course and seventeen enrolled in its part-time equivalent. Edna Ramage was one of the full-time students. Many found that part-time studies were more compatible with their commitment to homes and children. Even so, over time, several pulled out of the course. Some realised that weaving was not for them, or left due to work commitments or remarriage. Others took to it naturally and thoroughly enjoyed it.

Some women discovered that although they did not want to weave, belonging to the Guild was still beneficial.[15] But not all war widows joined the organisation, imagining it to be a 'gloomy affair'. Kitty Gahan was quick to allay this perception:

> *The interest the women have found in the work is apparent in their faces. A number of them were in a very nervy state when they started, having only heard definite news a few months previously after varying periods of uncertainty. The companionship of others who understand how they were feeling was of great value, and contrary to what one expected in such a gathering, there was no suggestion of any gloom.*[16]

Edna Ramage was one of those who found great comfort and companionship at the Guild. Full-time work eventually drew her away from Guild activities, but the friendships she formed helped her enormously in the early post-war years, and lasted many years. She was particularly friendly with Betty Thompson and Marjorie (Madge) Davidson, whose husbands had both served with the 2/4th Machine Gunners alongside Edna's.[17] Captain George Alan Jack Thompson had been executed by the Japanese shortly after the fall of Singapore, and Thomas Davidson died in September 1943 while a POW in Thailand.[18] Edna, Madge and Betty met socially outside of Guild activities, and attended dances together.[19]

Ethel May Jones enjoyed the weaving too. Originally from the goldfields, Ethel had worked in a Kalgoorlie munitions factory during the war. Her youngest child was just a baby when she received the news that her husband had been killed on 3 January 1944. After the war, she moved to Perth. She joined the Guild, but had little spare time after caring for five children and working at Boans, and she was unable to continue with the weaving. She was initially granted a six-month suspension from studies in a letter dated 20 July 1948, but a letter dated 5 July 1949 indicated that she had not returned.

Mindful of its aim to help widows, many of whom had young children, the Guild investigated the possibility of setting up a nursery or kindergarten in the city. The kindergarten was to be of service to the women who were working or training full time, and to those who wanted to leave their children for a short time while shopping.[20] The project never eventuated, and during school holidays, weavers were encouraged to bring their children to the Guild rooms, where Muriel Jones minded them during weaving classes.[21]

One of the women to undertake the course, Peggy Walker, showed a particular aptitude for weaving. Although she had no previous experience, she had always enjoyed using her hands. As a teenager in the Depression, Peggy taught herself to cut down clothing to create new items. At seventeen, she taught herself to knit and later she started doing needlework. During the war, Peggy had worked for the Red Cross at the Repatriation Hospital, teaching a variety of handcrafts to bed-ridden returned servicemen. These included using small looms to make scarves and ties, but that had been the extent of her weaving skills until she joined the Guild, where she discovered she was in her element: 'I loved it. Absolutely enjoyed it.'[22]

After Peggy completed the basic course, the Guild proposed sending her to Melbourne to attend an advanced weaving class.[23] The plan was that upon completion she would replace Kitty Gahan, who could then return to Victoria. Approval was not immediately forthcoming from the Department of Reconstruction, so the Guild invited Peggy to be a student teacher in the interim.[24] Authorisation for further training finally came through in September 1947, and Peggy immediately left for Melbourne, while the other women continued under Kitty's instruction.[25]

※

Community groups commonly invite a person of note to become their patron, as a way of raising the profile of their organisation within the wider community. In May 1947, Mrs Dyson had proposed, and vice-president Madge Anketell seconded, that the Guild invite Lady Clara Mitchell, wife of Lieutenant Governor Sir James Mitchell, to be the War Widows' Craft Guild patron in Western Australia. A woman with a long-term interest in community affairs, Lady Mitchell was already involved in a number of organisations, including the Red Cross, the Country Women's Association (CWA), the Girl Guides and Silver Chain. Moreover, she understood the pain of losing loved ones. Her son Gerald had been killed in the First World War, and her only daughter, Jean Anketell, who was also Madge Anketell's sister-in-law, had died in 1946.[26]

When Lady Mitchell replied to the invitation, she was convalescing following a heart attack. It is unknown whether her family connection to Madge Anketell influenced Lady Mitchell's response, but she agreed to take on the role in spite of her illness. She promised to visit as soon as her health improved. Guild members were delighted,[27] and her acceptance established a precedent of asking wives of successive state governors to be the Guild patron.

Just as Lady Mitchell's association with the Guild began, Marjorie Learmonth's ended, for she married Lieutenant Colonel Leslie Le Souef, with whom she had been friends since before the Second World War. During the war, Le Souef had trained and commanded the 2/7th

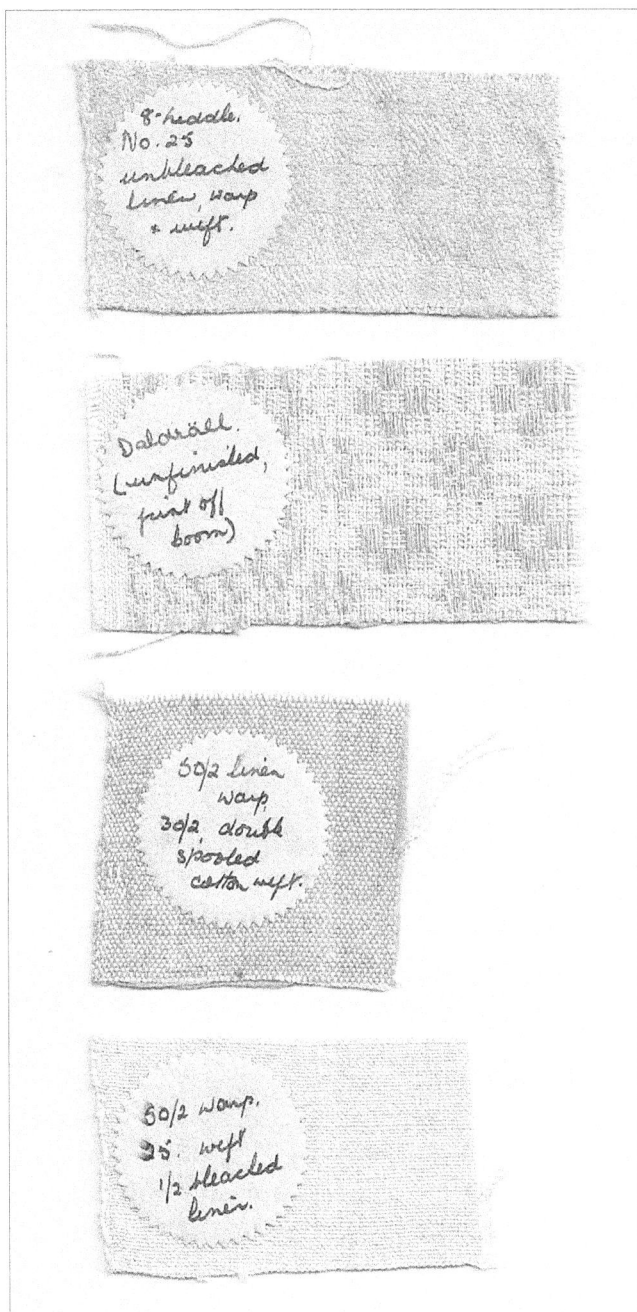

8-heddle.
No. 25
unbleached
linen, warp
+ weft.

Dalaväl.
(unfinished,
just off
loom)

50/2 linen
warp,
30/2 double
spooled
cotton weft.

50/2 warp,
25. weft
1/2 bleached
linen.

Weaving samples.
(Courtesy of Peggy Litchfield)

Australian Field Ambulance. After the Australians were forced to surrender on Crete in May 1941, he survived four years in German prisoner-of-war camps where he used his knowledge of the Geneva Convention to challenge guards and save the lives of many. He finally returned to Australia in February 1946, renewed his friendship with Marjorie and began courting her.[28]

When Marjorie and Leslie married on Saturday 25 October 1947 at St Georges Chapel in Crawley, the Guild presented them with a gift of weaving that included a finely woven tablemat by Peggy Walker. Marjorie's remarriage meant that the Department of Repatriation no longer considered her to be a war widow.[29] As the War Widows' Guild constitution stated that only war widows could be members, she was required to resign from her role as state president and her membership of the organisation she had helped to establish. Nevertheless, Marjorie remained interested and concerned about the Guild and its members, as did her husband Leslie, now a surgeon at Royal Perth Hospital. On one occasion, he assisted a war widow whose child needed an operation she could not afford, by arranging a payment plan and conducting the surgery. The operation was a success, and the widow repaid the debt as agreed. Upon receiving the final payment, Leslie handed the woman an envelope. Inside was the amount she had repaid him, which he now returned to her in full.[30]

With Marjorie's departure from the Guild came the task of electing a new president. This fell to the Guild council, which met every three months and consisted of the executive committee plus additional members interested in the broader decision-making processes of the organisation. At the council meeting on Friday 7 November 1947, Mrs Rosenberg moved, and Gwen Forsyth seconded, that Winifred Fowler be elected state president.[31]

Winifred Fowler's husband had returned from two wars. Promoted to the position of Captain during the First World War, Hugh Lionel Fowler was wounded twice and eventually returned to Western Australia. While lecturing at Claremont Teachers College he met Winifred (née Finch), who was undertaking her teacher training, and they married in 1922. After studying in London for both a Diploma in Education and a PhD in Psychology, Fowler established the Psychology Department at the University of Western Australia

19th June

My dear Mrs Vasey,

We have only just discovered that I thought Lewie had sent you a wire and he thought I had — we were both so very thrilled to read of your much deserved recognition for all you have done for so many women in Australia. Like myself so many war widows have got so much out of the Guild, far more than they could ever give back. Apart from material gains having an association with anyone

Marjorie Le Souef (formerly Learmonth) maintained contact with the Guild after her marriage. Here she congratulates Jessie Vasey on her OBE in 1950. (VFP, MS3782, NLA)

(UWA).[32] He enlisted in the Second World War in 1941, but was soon discharged due to bronchitis and asthma attributed to his First World War service.[33] Undeterred, he re-enlisted in May 1942 to start the Australian Army Psychology Service in Melbourne. He was promoted to the position of major, but in November he again retired due to ill health.[34] He returned to his wife and three children, and his academic work at UWA until his premature death on 27 May 1946.[35]

Not long after her husband's death, Winifred was forced to examine her own mortality when she was diagnosed with a possibly cancerous growth in her breast. She underwent a mastectomy, although the lump was subsequently discovered to be benign. During the operation a lymph node was cut, causing long-term swelling in her arm, and later she suffered further ill-health resulting in several hospital stays. Although not physically robust, Winifred Fowler was a gregarious

Winifred Fowler
(Courtesy of Beryl Haneman)

person who enjoyed the company of others and welcomed many into her home. She took in boarders to supplement her pension, mostly university students or high school students from the country. Well educated and widely read, she was often called on to assist her friends' children with their homework. Evenings were often punctuated by the phone ringing and the caller asking, 'Winnie, can you help me with this?'[36]

In accepting the position of state president, Winifred now broadened her sphere of influence and assistance. One of her first tasks was to attend a national conference in Melbourne in November 1947 with representatives from other state guilds. Peggy Walker, still in Melbourne for her advanced weaving course, accompanied her.

At the conference, members shared a 'growing belief' that there was strength in unity and were hopeful that by 'combining the Guild and fighting as one body' they would 'eventually get somewhere in raising the low standard of living which the government offer[ed] as compensation' for their husbands' lives.[37] Delegates examined and made amendments to a draft national constitution, which stated in part that:

Winifred Fowler (right) with her daughters, Beryl and Margaret.
(Courtesy of Beryl Haneman)

The objects of this Federal body are to discuss and
determine the general policy of the Guilds; to deal with
such matters as may be referred to it by any State Guild or
Guilds; and to control the activities listed hereunder, subject
to the fact that the Federal Executive shall have power
to delegate authority to each State Guild to deal with the
appropriate Commonwealth authority on State matters.
And to follow the original purpose: 'To watch over and
protect the interests of war widows.'[38]

Membership was discussed, in particular whether First World War
widows should be accepted as members. One of the concerns was
that financial assistance provided to the War Widows' Guild from the
Department of Reconstruction was only available to Second World
War widows. Yet any work undertaken by the Guild, such as opening
a hospital, would mainly serve those from the First World War, many
of whom were older and experiencing ill health. The widows from that
earlier war had also suffered greatly, but were without such a leader as
Jessie Vasey to fight for their interests. Furthermore, some state guilds
already welcomed First World War widows; it would be difficult to

exclude them. Conference delegates eventually agreed to accept First World War widows as associate members, with all entitlements apart from the ability to hold office or vote, with an exception made for those who were already full members prior to the conference.[39]

When it came to governance, a national council would comprise a federal president, honorary treasurer, honorary secretary, state presidents, and one other representative from each state. In selecting a federal president, Jessie Vasey was the obvious candidate; it is difficult to imagine anyone standing against her. The possibility of a national patron was discussed, and it was agreed to write to Her Royal Highness Princess Marina, Duchess of Kent, after seeking permission from the federal government. She too was a war widow; her husband, the Duke of Kent, was killed in an air crash in 1942, while on active service. Princess Marina accepted the invitation to be patron, a special privilege as it was unusual for a member of the royal family to become patron of a new organisation.[40]

Other issues pertinent to forming a federal body and developing a national identity were raised. The word 'craft' was dropped from the name, and there was discussion as to whether 'association' should replace 'guild', but it was felt that the word 'guild' had greater meaning.[41]

Visiting the conference on the second day, Senator Dorothy Tangney participated in a discussion about medical benefits and the availability of facilities for war widows in repatriation hospitals, formerly only for returned soldiers. Dorothy Tangney said that she thought Minister Barnard and the repatriation authorities were willing for war widows to use repatriation hospitals provided they used existing medical staff; it would be seen as a slight on hospital staff if widows chose their own doctor. She agreed to discuss the issue of tuberculosis and other chronic cases with Minister Barnard, and, shortly after the conference, she wrote confirming that she was personally taking up the case with him.[42] In mid-February 1948, Senator Tangney fulfilled her promise,[43] and that same month, three war widows with tuberculosis were admitted to Hollywood Hospital.[44] Senator Tangney then visited the Guild on 27 February to address the weaving students and executive committee, who thanked her for her kindness in approaching the minister.[45]

Soon after that, Winifred Fowler took three months' leave due to her own hospital admission.[46] In her absence, Gwen Forsyth took on the role of chairing meetings, and attended the federal conference in June, where issues affecting war widows nationally were discussed, including the Canteens Trust Fund and a proposed Widows and Orphans Panel.[47]

During the war, the army, navy and air force each ran service canteens which sold goods to members at just below retail value. Collectively, the canteens raised almost five million pounds by the end of hostilities. In 1947, the government passed legislation that required surplus patriotic and canteen funds to be given to the Repatriation Commission. Sixty thousand pounds was allocated to relief funds for each of the three services. The remainder was consolidated into a single fund, the Canteens Trust Fund, with the aim of providing relief and assistance to ex-servicemen and their children, including a provision for their education.[48] The Canteens Trust Fund began operating on 1 January 1948, with an education committee and a welfare committee formed in each state to oversee the distribution of funds. In Western Australia, Patricia Connor was selected to represent war widows on the education committee. Gwen Forsyth became the war widows' representative on the welfare committee and at the same time agreed to take on the role of welfare officer within the Guild.[49]

The Widows and Orphans Panel was formed to handle war widows' cases, previously dealt with by the Regional Welfare Committee.[50] The panel was made up of three representatives from Legacy and three from the Guild, giving war widows increased authority in decisions regarding their own members. Gwen Forsyth, Winifred Fowler and May Hiatt agreed to represent the Guild on the new panel, and Mollie Hayes took up Gwen's previous position on the welfare committee. Patricia Connor remained on the Canteen's educational committee until November, when Rita Kuring replaced her.[51]

Peggy Walker had returned from her advanced weaving course in time to spend Christmas 1947 with her children on her parents' farm in Serpentine[52] before starting as weaving instructor on Tuesday 3 February 1948. Classes started at approximately 9 am, with the women working through until 3 pm, finishing in time for their children's return from school. Peggy boarded in the city with Marjorie and Leslie Le Souef for several months, and then with another war widow for a year. But she always caught the train home for the weekends, where her youngest son lived with her elderly parents. She would return to the city on the 6.30 am milk train on Monday morning, or on Sunday afternoon in the winter months. At that time, her older son Graham boarded at Christchurch Grammar School, an expense her job at the Guild made possible.

Beatrice Davey, Wyn Spence and Phyllis Thomas were among those who displayed a talent for the craft. Peggy reflects:

> *Some of them took to it, absorbed it, and were really*
> *interested. Others thought, oh this is easy, like you might*
> *pick up a pair of knitting needles … they suddenly found,*
> *no it isn't easy … I got a reputation, I'm afraid. I don't*
> *tolerate mistakes.*[53]

Peggy believed it was important to set a high standard for the work, something that was crucial when it came to selling the goods. She remembers a conversation she had with one weaving student when she inspected the woman's work and pointed out a mistake.

'Oh, no one will see that,' the woman said.

'You must take it out and do it again,' Peggy told her. 'Then you'll be happy. It will be right.'

'I'm not taking it out.'

'But it's wrong. You can't leave something blatant like that.'

'But I only weave for my friends. They won't look at it.'

'Don't you worry because you've done the work?' Peggy asked.

'No, it's all right.'

Nothing Peggy said could persuade the woman to correct her work, and Peggy refused to help her again.[54]

While many of the weavers, including Peggy Walker, Gwen Forsyth, Beatrice Davey and Phyllis Thomas, learned to weave to supplement their pensions, not all war widows needed the extra income. Eleanor Burnside joined the Guild because of her interest in the weaving, but she was a woman of independent means, having helped run her family's private taxi service for many years. Her husband, Lance Corporal James Wallace, had been killed in the Middle East on 30 January 1941, without ever having the chance to meet his daughter. One of Eleanor's final pieces on the large loom was a rug for a double bed, which she wove in two pieces in a pattern of navy, red, grey and white tartan. She enjoyed anticipating how long the rug was going to be and measuring out the wool accordingly. Eleanor found weaving to be a stimulating and creative task, with no two pieces the same. She did, however, wonder how it could ever truly be a livelihood, because although pleasurable, it was time consuming, and the materials were expensive.[55]

In an attempt to reduce costs, the Guild sought out materials at wholesale prices. Finished articles, including delicately designed fine linens, were displayed for sale in a small room off the main hall. Unfortunately, the Lord Street rooms were not centrally located and so failed to attract sufficient interest from the public. While Peggy Walker was in Melbourne, the Perth Guild had held a display in the window of Foy and Gibsons in St Georges Terrace, as part of the 1947 Show Week. Following the exhibition, the executive committee agreed that the Guild needed to 'secure a shop in a prominent position as soon as possible' to display goods and take orders.[56]

In May 1948, following an article in the *Western Mail*, the Department of Reconstruction and Training offered the Guild an army hut at their premises in Bazaar Terrace (later the Esplanade). No rent would be charged, but the Guild would be required to vacate the premises with a month's notice should the hut be needed for other Reconstruction Training purposes.[57] The Guild accepted the conditions and moved from their rooms in Lord Street to their new home on Monday 24 May 1948. But while the army huts in Bazaar Terrace were closer to the city centre than those in Lord Street, they were not particularly suitable as a shop where goods could be ordered, displayed and sold.

To promote their goods, the Guild held an exhibition at Newspaper House in early September 1948, resulting in a large number of orders being taken, especially for travelling rugs. Particularly popular were those made with school crests or initials in the design. These rugs could be made more efficiently on a large loom, so one was purchased, and in the months that followed it was in constant use.[58] Winifred Fowler ordered a rug in Perth College colours, as she had once taught there; it became a family heirloom, and now belongs to her great-granddaughter, who was a student at Perth College. During the final week of September, the Guild participated in the popular Country

Women's Exhibition, an initiative of the CWA. The Guild entered the weaving section with a scarf, an afternoon tea cloth, a set of cotton mats and a set of linen mats. Members also exhibited in the Reconstruction Training Section of the Royal Show. [59]

By October, all full-time weaving students had completed their course, and the school was now open only two days per week for the remaining twenty-two part-time students. Peggy Walker was allocated space in the Guild rooms to weave for herself on days she was not teaching; however, she found herself constantly attending to Guild business. Believing this to be an unfair arrangement, Winifred Fowler suggested that Peggy be paid as a full-time clerk, a proposal Peggy accepted. [60]

Still searching for a shop, Madge Anketell approached Eric Sandover, a member of the prominent Perth family that owned Harris, Scarfe and Sandovers. He invited the Guild to display its weaving in the Hay Street store's front window. Marjorie Davidson's mother, Mrs Rushforth, also offered them a window in her Barrack Street shop, along with a small counter inside for the sale of goods. Those who had displayed work at the Guild's exhibition at Newspaper House were asked to bring in items to be sold. [61] Then, in March 1949, the *Daily News* ran a story about the Guild, resulting in the use, rent free, of a room as a gift shop in Durham House, opposite His Majesty's Theatre in Hay Street. While the Guild was grateful for somewhere to sell their goods, the shop struggled to make a profit. Tucked away on the first floor, its position was still not prominent enough to attract shoppers. [62] In the meantime, weaving classes were due to finish in June, requiring the Guild to vacate the army huts in Bazaar Terrace, and leaving the war widows without a meeting room or space to socialise. [63] The RSL allowed the Guild to use the Supper Room at Anzac House to hold its AGM, but it was not the same as a space of its own. [64]

In an attempt to draw war widows together socially, Winifred Fowler invited the weavers, together with anyone who had ever served on council, to her home in Stanley Street, Nedlands on the evening of Wednesday 9 March 1949. She hoped that small social gatherings would rouse greater interest in the Guild, but there was also a need for a place to hold larger meetings. Winifred suggested the Guild take over the lease of the Esplanade Kiosk, situated on the Esplanade

Reserve and overlooking the Swan River.[65] Originally established in 1880, and known as the Esplanade Recreation Ground from 1885, the large grassy area between the Esplanade and the river was the site of many activities: religious meetings, concerts, and Sunday afternoon soapboxes, hecklers included. It was also a venue for football, rugby, soccer, lawn bowls, tennis and hockey. Significantly, it had been the location of Anzac Day services since 1916, and the VP Day Service in 1945.[66]

The Esplanade Kiosk had been built in 1928 to replace an old grandstand, and its initial purpose was as a tearoom.[67] Unfortunately it had been neglected during the Second World War and was rather rundown, but it was centrally located, with the potential to be a viable business, and would provide the war widows with a suitable meeting space. Winifred Fowler and the Guild's solicitor, Brian Simpson, had already been to see the lessee of the Esplanade Kiosk in August 1948, hopeful of taking over the lease. They returned to the Guild disappointed; there appeared to be no possibility of acquiring the premises, although the Guild minutes provide no reasons for this.[68]

But once Winifred made up her mind, there was no changing it,[69] and she and Madge Anketell continued to pursue the possibility of leasing the Esplanade Kiosk. Eventually, their perseverance paid off. In August 1949, a year after their initial inquiries, the Esplanade Kiosk became available for lease from the Perth City Council. There was a

The Esplanade Kiosk (foreground) and surrounding city buildings.
(Courtesy of Florence Gordon)

catch: the Guild needed to pay a once-off fee, known as 'key money', of £1100, in addition to its weekly rent.

The Guild had already launched a state-wide appeal for monetary help in June but it was 'apathetically received and the results were very disappointing.' Instead of the £2000 they had hoped for, they collected only £335.[70] Not to be defeated, members gave interest-free loans of amounts from £1 to £50, with the understanding that the Guild would gradually repay the money. In this way, the Guild raised the £1100, and the Esplanade Kiosk lease was theirs.[71] Securing the lease was only the first step, however. There were still weeks of cleaning and renovating ahead of them. 'It was filthy, not just dirty,' Gwen Forsyth reminisced years later:

> Talk about 'Seven maids with seven mops' – we used more than mops. We scrubbed and scraped, we scoured, we cleaned, we oiled and polished, we washed windows and made curtains, we painted all the tea room tables and chairs, we cooked and sewed.[72]

Gwen Forsyth's son Alan remembers those days well:

> If you can imagine Mrs Heath and my mother and Mrs Hiatt, who was very delicate and always looked as though if you sneezed she'd blow away; there they were with shovels, scraping the floor. It was awful. The change rooms were worse still.[73]

Although the women raised the 'key money', refurbishment required extra funds. Money from the Lotteries Commission enabled the Guild to furnish the clubroom. The Soldiers Dependants helped equip the kitchen and tearooms, and the Red Cross donated chairs, tables, cupboards and towels. Members of Legacy offered practical assistance, as did members of the 2/28th Battalion. The men, some of whom most likely fought alongside the husbands of Sheila Barron, Rose Heath and Gwen Forsyth, donated their Sunday mornings to do carpentry work.[74]

The Guild officially took over the Esplanade Kiosk as their headquarters on Monday 26 September 1949. They now had a place to store the rug loom, a handcraft shop, a meeting room upstairs, and tearooms, which they hoped would generate an income. The kiosk's first week of business took place in the midst of renovations. It generated £30 profit, while treasurer Rita Kuring requested that 'all expenses be kept as low as possible.'[75]

Everybody needed to pitch in if the business was to prosper. While the Guild was required to employ some paid staff, such as Rose Heath as manager, many more volunteered, especially on weekends and public holidays. Peggy Walker offered to work in the gift shop for half her salary for two weeks from 10 October, at which time she announced her engagement.[76] She continued on until her wedding in January 1950, when Mollie Hayes agreed to take on the role of saleswoman, and to organise what had become an annual exhibition.

Gwen Forsyth willingly scraped the floor with a shovel, and was even prepared to clean toilets, but she was reluctant to wait on tables. 'I will do anything except waiting,' she said.

'Come on,' another woman cajoled, 'we need everybody who is able to help.'

'I'll never make a good waitress,' Gwen insisted.

The other women prevailed upon her until she relented. Her first customer ordered a meat pie and sauce. Returning with her customer's meal, Gwen tripped and the pie flew into his lap.

'You will never do this again,' the other women informed her.[77]

Rose Heath (second from right) with her mother, Louisa May Pollard, son David and daughter Maureen outside the Post Office Building on the corner of Wellington Street and Forrest Place, circa 1947.
(Courtesy of David Heath)

Gwen had many other gifts and used them to serve the Guild well. She had been an active member of the executive committee since the Guild's inception, shared the position of vice-president, and her 'unlimited energy' found an outlet in other duties. She represented the Guild on the Canteens Trust Fund and Widows and Orphans Panel. She sat on the Guild's business committee and was the liaison officer between the Guild and Legacy. Additionally, she served as the Guild's welfare officer, a role in which she 'begrudge[d] neither time, nor patience … Her sympathetic understanding … helped many a member.'[78]

The early months at the kiosk were difficult for the kitchen staff, with workers 'under their feet laying lino, overhead fixing fluorescent lighting and around them adjusting electrical fixtures for pie-warmers [and] toasters.'[79] But having finally achieved what they'd set out to do, nothing was going to dampen their enthusiasm. Wyn Spence, the Guild's secretary, commented:

> It speaks well for our staff that all these upheavals are taken with a spirit of pride and sportsmanship and that the good work in the kitchen goes on in spite of noise and partial disorganisation.[80]

The renovations did prevent the handcraft shop, now relocated from Durham House, from adequately displaying their goods, although there were many enquiries from interested clientele and numerous orders were taken. The rug loom was in constant use in the lead up to Christmas, with about fifty rugs and half a dozen baby shawls made by April 1950.[81]

The Esplanade Kiosk took up a great deal of the Guild's energies, but it was not the only new endeavour. In September 1949, May Hiatt formed a hospital visiting sub-committee to call on war widows who were patients in Hollywood Hospital.[82] War widows could now be admitted to Hollywood Hospital, as long as beds were available and their condition was not infectious or incurable. Additionally, x-rays and pathological and biochemical testing were available, if they were conducted for the purpose of hospital admission.[83] War widows who were patients in Hollywood praised the accommodation and treatment, especially the attention given by Matron Jean Ferguson. A foundation Guild member and inaugural vice-president, she displayed a personal interest in the war widows, and concern for the welfare of their families.

Another venture, initiated by Guild secretary Wyn Spence, was the formation of a sub-branch in Kalgoorlie. Officially formed on 30 August 1949, the group was small, with an average of eight members at each meeting, but it fulfilled its purpose of providing 'companionship for each other and pleasure for their children.'[84] In December 1949, the Kalgoorlie sub-branch teamed up with Legacy to host a Christmas party. The Kalgoorlie war widows had a mere nine shillings in their coffers and wondered at their nerve for attempting such an event. They anticipated a party for twenty children, and ended up entertaining sixty. The women were encouraged and delighted by the support of local businesses,[85] which 'lived up to their wonderful reputation' by donating decorations and a feast:

> It was an unqualified success; the hall and tree were decorated with streamers and balloons; the tables were laden with all sorts of good things to eat ... The children wore party caps and Father Xmas himself gave them presents from the tree. Quite a number of mothers arrived and were provided with afternoon tea.[86]

For the war widows, observing the children enjoying themselves was reward enough for their efforts and the Christmas party became an annual event. In Perth, Legacy held a Christmas party at Point Walter on 17 December 1949, where a number of Guild members and their children spent an enjoyable day.

Early the following year, on 21 March 1950, laughter rang out from the mezzanine floor of the kiosk as, for the first time, the Guild's monthly social evening took place in the Guild's own clubroom. The room was warm and inviting 'with its fawn and brown carpet, its polished gate-legged tables, [and] its easy chairs upholstered to match the carpet.' Bright blue tubular steel chairs added a splash of colour.[87]

On Anzac Day, the kiosk opened from 10 am until 2 pm, with a temporary closure during the service on the Esplanade. The parade began at 10 am near Anzac House in St Georges Terrace, where flags on buildings flew at half-mast. At least 20,000 people watched the Anzac Day parade in which some 4500 people marched. Legacy wards over the age of nine joined the Perth Legacy Club to lead the parade.[88] It is likely that some of the war widows' children participated that year; the children of Gwen Forsyth, Gloria MacDonald and Phyllis Thomas remember marching at various times, and would have been at least nine years old in 1950. The parade finished on the Esplanade, where the number of spectators swelled to 30,000 for a service at 11 am. Afterwards, the war widows' children walked across to the kiosk and helped serve patrons.

Although Anzac Day was busy and profitable, the Guild's first attempt at catering on a large scale was Country Hockey Week, held from 3 to 8 July 1950. The Perth City Council gave approval for the Guild to set up outdoor booths selling soft drinks during the competition. Not even 'wet weather and muddy fields'[89] prevented the event from being a successful one for the Guild, and Country Hockey Week continued to be one of the Guild's busiest periods for the next fourteen years, made possible by volunteers, some of whom were war widows' children. Gwen Forsyth's son Alan remembers:

Even as an older primary and high school student I would go and be manning one of [the booths,] opening coke bottles and taking money. It was just extraordinary. Hundreds and hundreds of people at each booth, just wanting cool drinks all the time.[90]

Initially the war widows served only tea, sandwiches and cakes at the kiosk but, by August 1950, they were offering a variety of light lunches, including a hot meal in winter. They produced brochures advertising the lunch menu, and circulated these to the offices along St Georges Terrace, and sent promotional letters to the large firms in the area. The demand for cut lunches grew considerably, and the kiosk began catering for small afternoon tea parties and special suppers.[91] As word spread, organisations such as the RSL Band, the Kindergarten Union, League of Home Help and the Suburban Hockey Club sought to hire the kiosk for meetings and social functions. An orchestra used it on

Friday evenings, and the Young Liberal Movement held dances there.[92]

From time to time, Rose Heath and her kitchen staff served some of the city's more eccentric characters who were down on their luck, including Percy Button, a well-known vagrant. Another unusual visitor, described as the kiosk's 'cheekiest customer' by a journalist for the *West Australian*, became a regular. Each morning the willy-wagtail appeared, dancing under the lawn sprinkler, fossicking in the flowerbeds for worms and waggling its tail at the magpies. Around midday, the wagtail would fly up the steps and into the kiosk, seemingly unafraid of Tommy, the cat who had taken up residence in the kitchen. The feathered customer then bounced its way between tables, dropped crumbs becoming its private banquet.[93]

The Esplanade Kiosk, standing on the corner of the Esplanade and Barrack Street in Perth, was visible to all who made their way from the Barrack Street jetty into the city centre. A sign reading 'Esplanade Kiosk, War Widows' Guild Headquarters. Morning and Afternoon Teas. Lunches' made it clear who was running the business. Flowerbeds, a green expanse of lawn and the view of the Swan River made it an attractive setting in which to take a break from work or shopping. Winifred Fowler's vision and a team effort in obtaining, renovating and opening the Esplanade Kiosk had turned into a promising business venture.

CHAPTER 4

HOUSING PLANS AND A ROYAL VISIT

In the midst of establishing the Esplanade Kiosk, president Winifred Fowler and vice-president Gwen Forsyth travelled to Sydney for a conference (6–11 June 1949) to discuss issues pertinent to the War Widows' Guild at a national level. On the opening day, Jessie Vasey suggested that the various state Guilds adopt a common motto. She proposed the use of an extract from the King's 1941 Christmas message, given just weeks after the bombing of Pearl Harbor:

> *We all belong to each other. We all need each other. It is in serving each other and in sacrificing for our common good that we are finding our true life.*[1]

Conference delegates agreed that the King's words encapsulated the ideals and aims of the War Widows' Guild of Australia, and would be a wonderful motto.[2] From then, these three sentences appeared on Guild circulars and, to this day, members recite it whenever they meet.

Issues relevant to war widows all over Australia were raised, including pensions, the Canteens Trust Fund, educational benefits and anomalies in medical benefits which meant First World War widows were unable to obtain the medical care now afforded to Second World War widows.[3] What took the greatest amount of discussion and caused an explosion of media attention was Section 43 of the Repatriation Act, which read:

> *A Board may reject a claim for a pension by a dependant*
> *of a member of the Forces, or may terminate any pension*
> *granted to such a dependant, if the Board is satisfied that*
> *the grant or continuance of the pension is undesirable.*[4]

The War Widows' Guild had heard several stories of war widows who lost their pension because the Repatriation Department had determined them to be living 'irregular lives'.[5] One widow with seven sons asked her brother-in-law for assistance when some of the children reached adolescence. Together with his mother and sister, he moved in with the war widow, whereupon she was reported to be 'living in sin', and lost her pension.[6] In another case, a war widow with three children was employed as a housekeeper for an unmarried man. When officials from the Repatriation Department visited the home, the woman's pension was cancelled.[7] Jessie Vasey acknowledged that the 'morality clause' only affected a small number of women, but it was disturbing nonetheless:

> *This section of the Act is an unwarranted intrusion*
> *on the personal liberty of the individual and is unfair*
> *discrimination against women. Men never lose their*
> *pension on moral grounds.*[8]

Additionally, the Repatriation Department already permitted de facto wives and their children to receive a pension. The delegates unanimously passed a motion that demanded Section 43 be repealed. Off the record, Jessie commented, 'If a woman is fond of her children and brings them up all right, then I do not care if she sleeps with ten men a night.'[9]

Her words were a 'foolishly absurd remark'[10] intended as a private joke amongst the delegates and not for the public arena.[11] Nevertheless, they made good headlines for newspapers across the country, and were recorded in parliament when the Opposition used them during the discussion of the Supply Bill, which determined the government's expenditure for the first four months of the next financial year. Minister Barnard reportedly 'lifted his hands in horror'[12] and said:

> *This is a terrible thing for a woman in charge of an*
> *organisation to say. If there has been any wrong done*
> *or any miscarriage of justice as far as war widows are*
> *concerned, it can be resolved without repulsive statements*
> *being made.*[13]

Jessie Vasey's statements may have been outlandish, but the *Australian Women's Weekly* gave its sympathy to the war widows' cause. Its editorial called Jessie an 'avenging angel' and claimed that without her 'ardent crusading' Australia would have remained 'complacent about the welfare of the women and children those dead men had bequeathed to their country's care.'[14] Jessie continued to campaign for the abolition of Section 43, and in September, she wrote to Minister Barnard about the matter. The Department of Repatriation made a statement that war widows whose pensions were threatened would be given an opportunity to defend themselves against any allegations of immorality, but Section 43 would remain.[15]

When the nation went to the polls on 19 December, the Liberal Party defeated Labor. Robert Menzies became prime minister for a second time and Walter Cooper replaced Herbert Claude Barnard as repatriation minister. Would the change in government bring with it greater benefits for war widows? Would Senator Cooper be more sympathetic to the request to abolish the morality clause? Only time would tell. One thing was assured: the War Widows' Guild of Australia would continue to put pressure on the government for change, no matter who was in power.

Certainly, the injustice of the morality clause refused to fade away quietly and it was not only the War Widows' Guild protesting. At its state congress in Western Australian, the RSL declared its disapproval,[16] as did the Legion of Ex-Servicemen and Women, which held its annual conference in Canberra during the first week of March 1950. Delegates alleged that Repatriation Commission investigators were 'calling on war widows late at night to check on their morals.' Lady Stanton Hicks, an artist and singer who had grown up in the Perth suburb of Peppermint Grove and now lived in Adelaide with her husband Sir Cedric Stanton Hicks, told the conference, 'The widow has no means of appeal. If her pension is stopped because of alleged immorality, the first she knows about it is when she goes to collect it [at the post office], and is told in front of other pensioners'.[17]

Lady Hicks's comments, reported in the press, coincided with the publication of an article by Jessie Vasey criticising the morality clause. If she were minister for repatriation, Jessie wrote, she would abolish the current act and construct a new one.

> *The new act would recognise that the control of people's private morals has never been one of the functions of a democratic government and that the use of security police to hound down a few widows whose mistaken conduct is as war-caused as a wound in battle, smacks very dangerously of the Fascism we set out to destroy.*[18]

❀

The recently appointed Minister for Repatriation, Senator Cooper, responded immediately and publicly that he would investigate the allegations. As far as he was concerned, 'immorality was not considered a ground for the withdrawal of the war widows' pension rights'[19] and he reported that 'not one investigation had been ordered' in the past nine months.[20] Jessie Vasey was not satisfied, arguing that the only way to offer war widows security and certainty was the removal of the clause altogether. As far as the War Widows' Guild was concerned, the fight was far from over, but it would have to wait some time before further progress was made.

In the meantime, Jessie weighed into another debate, this time about whether Anzac Day should continue to be a public holiday, and whether the day should be one of celebration or mourning. Jessie believed the march should occur in the morning and people should be free to enjoy the afternoon and evening.[21]

> *Anzac Day should surely be a day of national rejoicing – a day of exaltation, not of gloom and misery. Mourning, sadness and heartache must always be there, but only as an undercurrent to a tremendous upsurging pride that such men have been.*[22]

If I Were Minister For Repatriation

(For "The Duckboard")

By MRS. G. A. VASEY.

If I were Minister for Repatriation, I know, dear Editor, that I would not be Minister long. This Cinderella of Departments could never be really popular with either Prime Minister or Treasurer or the rest of the Cabinet. This is the Department which asks for money and does not make it, because no one has assessed the value of human lives, still less have they worked out what it means to Australia to preserve the lives and opportunities of one of her finest groups of citizens.

Surely the time has come when we stop talking about "pensions" for disabled servicemen or the families of dead ones. Pensions are something offered as a bounty, but men whose sufferings or whose lives have preserved the Australian nation and its thousands of millions of income might well be recognised as people who have "bought the show" — people who should receive a fair share of its assets. Remember how terrified so many of our fellow citizens were at the thought of an air raid in 1942? Would these same people have changed places with a serviceman for lower wages? As Minister, I would start out with the feeling that not one serviceman should suffer in comparison with a civilian because of his service and that men who were incapacitated should not only be given the right to live with decency, but should be rewarded for their sufferings and compensated for their lost opportunities. I would see to it that the men who gave their lives died in the full knowledge that their families would be able to live just as well as the families of the civilians who stayed behind and that every unit which must face bereavement with its tremendous handicaps for wife and child should have all the compensation a grateful nation could give them. I would not regard my people as "serfs" who could live at half the Australian standard. Responsibility for so many maimed lives must be a heavy burden and one only to be faced in fear and trembling.

It should be possible to put this Department above Party politics. Party leaders must look for votes — they must look for revenue; but surely at some time a generous nation could say that those maimed in its service should receive compensation at a standard which guaranteed them freedom from want. These people are not criminals to be punished, but faithful servants who should be treated with justice, if not mercy.

Very early I should set to work to find another description for the people in my charge other than "pensioner," with all its suggestion of patronage and inferiority, condescension to the unfortunate and its demand for gratitude from the recipient. It should surely be the first aim of a Repatriation department to restore to the community a very valuable group of citizens who have been injured in its service. These people cannot be restored without their full self-respect.

Today we realise that an under-privileged group drags down the whole nation and for that reason our Arbitration Courts have decided that there shall be a figure below which no Australian wage earner must go — the basic wage. As Minister for Repatriation I would have many very uncomfortable moments when I realised that thousands of the families in my care are brutally punished for the service their breadwinner gave the nation by being reduced to something less than the legal minimum wage for the Australian worker. Human life has a value to the dead or maimed serviceman, for the life of service he gave the country should be assessed at the rate of his potential earnings if he had remained a civilian.

After surveying my department and adding up its responsibilities and the tremendous part it must play in the Australian nation I would, as Minister, feel impelled to ask that the Cabinet set aside the present Act with all its amendments and "ifs" and "and" (the patchwork of years) and set up a Commission to reconsider the Department's aims and objects and work out its value to the community in terms of citizens and potential citizens. This Commission should be largely made up of the people who have to live under the Act. In war these men and women were trusted with millions of pounds and thousands of lives. In peace are they not likely to be as trustworthy? And who more interested or experienced? Peace has not turned these men into "morons." They should speak and think for themselves if their self-respect is to be maintained; if they are to feel full responsibility for the new Act.

I would ask that the Commission take into account the full sum of social knowledge we have today and all the wisdom that could be gathered concerning wise treatment of men and women and to take also a little heed of the philosophy of one

Jessie Vasey's article 'If I were Minister for Repatriation' appeared in the *Duckboard* (the RSL magazine), as well as the *Argus* newspaper.
(VFP, MS3732, NLA)

For many war widows, Anzac Day was one of emotion and memory, something Jessie recognised.

Many of you may feel that you have not the courage to face such a service but we think ... all those who have attended in the past will agree that it is a heartening experience to attend with the other widows. We also feel that it is another way of reminding the public of the large number of women whose lives have been broken by the war.[23]

❀

Within months, a new generation of women would join the ranks of the bereaved. In May, Robert Menzies decided that the remaining occupying forces in Japan would return home, but they were still there when North Korea invaded South Korea on 25 June 1950.[24] Following a request from General Douglas MacArthur, Menzies agreed to send the Royal Australian Air Force (RAAF) No. 77 Squadron, which joined the war on 2 July.[25] On 9 September, Wing Commander Louis Spence was killed when his Mustang fighter was shot down. His widow, Vernon, was originally from Perth, although the couple and their two children had lived in Canberra for a number of years prior to his joining the occupying forces in Japan.[26]

The 3rd Battalion, Royal Australian Regiment (3RAR) reached Pusan on 28 September 1950,[27] with its first casualties on 3 October, including Private Kenneth Sketchley of Collie.[28] Newspaper reports suggest that the first Western Australian war widow of the Korean War was Betty Fitzpatrick, who lived in Moora, although it is not known whether she joined the Guild. She had only been married for about six months before her husband, Sergeant Everett Fitzpatrick, joined the occupying forces in Japan, prior to being sent to Korea. Sergeant Fitzpatrick died on 26 October 1950 from wounds received in a clash between Australians and North Korean communists.[29]

A letter by Jessie Vasey, which acknowledged the new war widows on behalf of the War Widows' Guild, was published in papers across the country, including the *West Australian* on 18 December 1950. In it she wrote:

In a new shadow world, far below the minimum standard of living, exist the war widows of two world wars. Now other sad and bewildered women, the widows of Korea, are coming to join them.[30]

Between 29 September 1950 and 3 January 1951, thirty-eight members of 3RAR were either killed in action or died from their wounds, with another 108 wounded.[31]

⚛

In February 1951, as the war in Korea continued, the press announced that Their Majesties King George VI and Queen Elizabeth, and their younger daughter Princess Margaret, were to tour Australia. Western Australia would host the first leg of the tour from 1 to 7 March 1952.[32] The Guild was to be allotted a section along the route of the royal progress on Fraser Avenue in Kings Park, to be shared with Legacy, and another on the Esplanade for the parade of ex-servicemen and women, where Winifred Fowler would represent the Guild on the dais. Winifred would also meet the royal family in Winthrop Hall, at the University of Western Australia, where her husband had been head of the psychology department and a scholarship had been established in his memory.[33] After having to cancel his proposed 1949 tour due to ill health, the King was finally coming, and Winifred Fowler would have the opportunity to meet the man whose 1941 Christmas message had become so significant to members of the War Widows' Guild.

A few months later, crowds of people lined Perth city streets to farewell Sir James Mitchell as state governor on Friday 29 June 1951. Scores of smiling schoolchildren cheered and waved flags as his car wove its way through the city to the Capitol Theatre.[34] The Guild felt a great deal of respect and affection for him, not the least because his wife had been their inaugural patron until her death on 13 October 1949. But a month after the honour parade, Western Australians were shocked by the news that Sir James Mitchell had died unexpectedly in his sleep, after a day's shooting at his son's farm.[35]

Sir Charles Gairdner was sworn in as Western Australia's new governor on 6 November 1951.[36] Winifred Fowler and several other members attended a reception organised by the RSL. The Guild wasted no time in writing to Lady Evelyn Gairdner about the possibility of her patronage, a role she accepted.[37]

Further unfortunate news arrived, this time from abroad. King George VI had suffered further illness and in September 1951 he underwent lung surgery. Doctors had not cancelled the tour prior to the operation because the King was eager to visit Australia. Subsequently, however, it was deemed inadvisable to risk his health further by travelling. Rather than cancel the tour altogether, Princess Elizabeth and her husband the Duke of Edinburgh agreed to visit in the King's place.[38]

On 5 February, the executive committee discussed the allotment of tickets for war widows to view the royal progress, both in Kings Park on 1 March and on the Esplanade on 3 March. Winifred Fowler indicated her wish to resign from the position of state president at the next AGM, but after much persuasive discussion, she agreed to be nominated for another year.[39] As part of her role, Winifred was invited to represent the Guild on the dais on Monday 3 March, and at a reception in Winthrop Hall on Thursday 6 March.[40]

The plans would be to no avail. The following evening, 6 February 1952, Prime Minister Robert Menzies' voice cracked as he made a sombre announcement in parliament: 'It is my melancholy task to inform the House that news which ran in rumour a few minutes ago is now officially confirmed, and His Majesty the King is dead.' The Prime Minister suggested that the House should adjourn until the morning. He then 'slumped into his chair, pressed his elbows on the table, and pressed the knuckles of his clenched fists into his mouth.'[41]

It was scarcely believable. The King was dead at the age of fifty-six. Princess Elizabeth and her husband were in Kenya, en route to Australia and New Zealand. The royal couple returned to England immediately, and the Australian tour was cancelled as the palace made plans for a funeral and a coronation.[42]

The King's funeral was held in St George's Chapel, Windsor, on Friday 15 February 1952.[43] In Perth, thousands attended services at various churches, including St George's Cathedral.[44] Many women wore violets as a mark of respect, and two minutes' silence was observed in the city at midday.[45] The day coincided with the tenth anniversary of the fall of Singapore. Madge Anketell, whose husband had died in Singapore, laid a wreath at the State War Memorial on behalf of the War Widows' Guild, although the commemorative service was postponed until Sunday out of respect for King George VI.[46]

On Anzac Day, Muriel Jones made and laid a wreath at the State War Memorial, although the War Widows' Guild was still not part of the official wreath laying ceremony. As in previous years, the Esplanade Kiosk opened for a busy day, which included catering for a Church of England Boys' Club breakfast.[47] The kiosk closed temporarily for the service on the Esplanade, at which Frederick Charles Chaney, acting state president of the RSL, acknowledged the death of King George VI and alluded to public apathy towards the Korean War.[48]

Although the RSL had not invited the War Widows' Guild to participate formally on Anzac Day, it did ask whether the Guild wished to participate in National Flower Day – Silver Chain's major fundraising event. Various RSL branches were making floral replicas of their colour patches, and it was thought that the Guild might wish to contribute a design in the shape of its new badge.[49] National Flower Day was only in its third year in Perth, but Silver Chain had borrowed the idea from South Australia, where National Flower Day had been held annually since 1938.[50]

On Friday 12 September 1952, the city was a mass of colour. The day attracted a great deal of attention from members of the public, with an estimated 19,000 visitors to the Town Hall alone. Wishing wells were set up around the city centre, and some of the larger floral arrangements were sold, but most of the money raised was by selling badges and buttons.[51] Businesses and department stores such as Fauldings, Elders, Alliance Assurance, Perpetual Trustees and Shell hung flower displays on the outsides of their buildings. The designs were intricate and varied: a woman in a ball gown, Little Bo Peep, dancers, and a model of an atom bomb, as well as emblems of organisations such as the Red Cross and the Florence Nightingale Society. These floral exhibits provided a vivid spectacle as people made their way to the Town Hall, where the central display was a merry-go-round, constructed out of pale blue and yellow flowers, with splashes of other bright colours.[52] The Guild's display of its badge was modest in comparison with some of the larger designs, but it was pleased with its contribution, and Winifred Fowler congratulated those involved, including Mrs R. Moyes, Muriel Jones, Mrs V. Smith and Mrs Wortley. The South Australian Guild liked the initiative so much they decided to replicate the design for their own Flower Day.[53]

From 29 September to 3 October 1952, Winifred Fowler attended a federal conference in Adelaide, as Western Australia's only delegate. Again, the morality clause was raised and, frustrated at waiting for reform, Jessie Vasey sent a telegram to Senator Cooper: 'Keep door open arriving next week. Federal Conference Adelaide asks complete removal of Section 43. VASEY.'[54] Jessie and three other delegates flew to Canberra for a meeting with Senator Cooper. At the meeting, Jessie pointed out the incongruity of pensions being provided for de facto wives and their children, while penalising a war widow should she step out of line. This time, Jessie's words proved persuasive.[55] Senator Cooper promised to amend Section 43 so that there could be no misunderstanding. He remained true to his word and changes to the Act were made in July 1953.[56] The triumph over the misuse of what was intended to be a 'harmless section of the Act' deserved celebration. 'We have fought and won a very big battle for women to be recognised as human beings with a right to their own lives,' said Jessie Vasey.[57] The victory certainly highlighted what was possible when war widows refused to take no for an answer.

As the Guild waited for Senator Cooper's promise to take effect, Jessie Vasey attended Queen Elizabeth's coronation on 2 June 1953 on behalf of the War Widows' Guild of Australia. She was a late inclusion on the official guest list, and only after Prime Minister Robert Menzies was made aware of the lack of a war widow representative. Jessie departed Melbourne on 29 April aboard the *Oronsay*. En route was a visit to the Guild at the Esplanade Kiosk when the ship docked in Fremantle on 4 May. Jessie arrived in London just a few days prior to her first social engagement – a garden party held at Buckingham Palace on Thursday 28 May.[58]

When Queen Elizabeth announced honours for people who had contributed greatly to the community, twelve Western Australians were among them, including Guild member and matron of Hollywood Hospital, Jean Ferguson. After her war service, Jean Ferguson worked

Left: Jessie Vasey's invitation to the coronation of Queen Elizabeth II.
(VFP, MS3782, NLA)

Right: Jessie Vasey prior to her departure for the coronation.
(Guild archives, WA Branch. Photo by News and Information Bureau,
Department of the Interior)

at the 110th Military Hospital, becoming its matron in 1947 following its transfer to the Repatriation Department. In the same year, she organised the Royal Australian Army Nursing Corps in Western Command. Now, she was made an associate of the Royal Red Cross for her contribution to nursing.[59] Winifred Fowler was presented with a coronation medal for her services to war widows.[60]

Jessie Vasey was still abroad when an armistice to end the Korean War was signed on 27 July 1953. Altogether, 339 Australians had been killed in the conflict and 29 taken prisoner of war.[61] Articles in the *Guild News* and notes in Guild minutes mention nothing of this, and instead focus on Vasey's trip, the Queen and commemoration services attended by members of the War Widows' Guild.[62] In October, Jessie Vasey and fellow Victorian Guild member Connie Hoffman were among 25,000 people who witnessed the unveiling of the Runnymede War Memorial. Beneath a grey English sky, the newly crowned Queen Elizabeth II, accompanied by her husband, unveiled a memorial to the 20,000 Commonwealth airmen who died in the Second World War and had no known grave. Among the names were 1403 Australians, including Connie Hoffman's husband, Owen.[63] Connie's presence was significant, as the War Widows' Guild had only won the right to representation at such dedications the previous year, after repeatedly approaching the Australian War Graves Commission.[64] That same month, memorials to those killed in Papua New Guinea were unveiled in Port Moresby, Lae and Rabaul. Matron Jean Ferguson, who served in Papua New Guinea and whose husband died in Port Moresby, and Mrs O'Neil, represented the West Australian war widows at the services.[65] Despite this, there was a long way to go to see war widows officially recognised at such commemorations, as would be evidenced during the Queen's Australian tour the following year.

❀

As the nation looked forward, finally, to a royal visit, founding member and weaver Phyllis Thomas was planning a wedding. Between caring for her young daughter and elderly parents and her involvement with the Guild, she had little spare time to socialise, but through a mutual friend, she had met Jack McLoughlin, who had served on the anti-aircraft guns in Darwin. Phyllis married Jack at the beginning of 1954 and, with her daughter Patricia, moved to Jack's home in Mount Lawley. The new house was too small to fit her precious weaving loom. Reluctant to lose it, Phyllis searched for a place to store the loom, but to no avail, and she was forced to make the difficult decision to part with it.[66]

While Phyllis farewelled the Guild, West Australians were otherwise preoccupied. Perth city was covered in a sea of red, white and blue. Shields, Tudor roses, Union Jacks and large portraits of the Queen and Duke appeared in city workplaces. Flowers were planted, timed to bloom during the visit. Huge archways along the length of St Georges Terrace lit up the night, and thousands visited Kings Park to view them.[67] School children collected pictures and wrote projects about the Queen.[68] They learned patriotic songs and practised cheering.[69] People lined the streets wherever the Queen would pass by. Not even the polio epidemic, at its height in Western Australia with 215 cases recorded for March 1954,[70] could dampen the excitement, although several precautions were established. Organisers placed conditions on presenting bouquets, banned handshaking, and held functions outside wherever possible. Meals for the royal couple were prepared on board their ship SS *Gothic*, which berthed at Fremantle.[71]

Eagerly anticipating Queen Elizabeth II's arrival, the War Widows' Guild of Australia sent Her Majesty flowers and a hand-woven scarf. In Perth, the Guild was formally represented on several occasions during the royal visit. Winifred Fowler and Rita Kuring were invited to the civic reception and to a women's reception at the University of Western Australia.[72] Wearing the coronation medal she had been awarded for her Guild work, Winifred Fowler was also presented to Her Majesty on Saturday 27 March, at a parade of ex-servicemen and women on the Esplanade.[73]

While in Melbourne, Queen Elizabeth dedicated additions to the Shrine of Remembrance. It was a ceremony designed to honour the war dead, and a number of war widows felt slighted and marginalised by their treatment. According to Jessie Vasey, some widows 'had a distant view of the ceremony' and saw just enough of it to feel as though they had taken part, but other widows and mothers were heartbroken because they 'were pushed round to the east steps and could neither hear nor see.'[74] Jessie Vasey believed that war widows should be chief mourners at such services.

> *I watched my husband's juniors and barracks soldiers and their wives ushered into seats. Officials of all service organisations and their wives received invitations also, but not one came to the Guild.*[75]

So distressed and angry were some of the widows that Jessie Vasey declared that the Guild would not attend Anzac Day services at the Shrine of Remembrance in an official capacity that year.[76] This response sparked controversy in Victoria. The presidents of the Soldiers', Sailors' and Airmen's Widows' Association and the War Widows and Widowed Mothers Association (WWWMA) disagreed with Jessie. Although some members of the WWWMA supported Jessie's views, its president Muriel Ebeling announced that her organisation had no intention of boycotting the Anzac Service at the shrine.[77]

Jessie took her protest one step further and organised a Remembrance Day commemoration specifically for war widows.

Despite wet, stormy weather, hundreds of widows attended a midday service at the Shrine of Remembrance on Sunday 7 November 1954.[78] In Western Australia, there was not the controversy over Anzac Day and Remembrance Day that troubled Victoria, but the Guild nevertheless lobbied for recognition at commemoration services. Following Anzac Day in 1954, a 'spirited discussion arose' among the executive committee because the Guild had not received a formal invitation to lay a wreath at the war memorial, although executive member Muriel Jones did so unofficially each year. Nor were war widows officially recognised at the service on the Esplanade.[79] The Guild wrote a letter of protest to the RSL. The RSL promised to consider the matter, but the following year there was little change.[80]

It is not clear when attitudes did change in Western Australia, but in 1956, Rita Kuring, who had resigned as state treasurer at the end of the previous year, travelled to England with Madge Anketell and laid a wreath of mauve and white irises and carnations at the tomb of the Unknown Soldier in Whitehall on behalf of the War Widows' Guild of Western Australia.[81] While in England, Madge and Rita met the Guild's national patron, Princess Marina, Duchess of Kent, who held a reception for them at Kensington Palace.[82] Some progress was made at a national level that same year when the War Widows' Guild of Australia was afforded the privilege of laying a wreath at the Australian War Memorial on Anzac Day. Jessie Vasey laid a wreath of roses, yellow carnations, and white chrysanthemums.[83] The governor-general's wife was the only other woman to lay a wreath, and this set a precedent to be repeated every Anzac Day thereafter.

❀

Jessie Vasey had long held the belief that the best way to help war widows was to build homes for them.[84] She had visited the Western Australian Guild in November 1950 to rouse interest in the idea. At a special executive meeting, she spoke in some detail about establishing a housing scheme for widows who, for any number of reasons, wished to sell their home and move into a flat, either bought or rented.

In Victoria, Jessie attempted to persuade state and federal governments to build flats for older war widows. When this failed, she resolved to raise funds to do it herself. In late 1951, she set her sights on a two-storey house on a large block in Hawthorn that had the potential to be divided into flats. The Victorian Guild needed £7000; they had £10.[85] Guild members were worried about where they would find the money, but Jessie Vasey refused to let the financial situation hinder her goal. 'Think big!' she exhorted them. 'Write to everyone who has promised to help.'[86] Two hundred handwritten letters were posted, and the money was raised.[87] With government subsidies for such projects still three years away, Jessie's vision was ahead of its time.

In Western Australia, the Guild was interested in investing in a similar scheme, but a more pressing concern was the Esplanade Kiosk's finances. At a meeting on 4 December 1951, the treasurer, Rita Kuring, had reported that, in contrast to the previous year, the situation was serious, with a loss of £55 for the previous month alone. The crisis had eased by February the following year, helped by cutbacks to paid staff and Rita Kuring's administrative assistance,[88] nevertheless, the idea of building affordable housing for war widows was put on hold until the kiosk loans could be repaid.[89] This came about in 1955, when Rotary chose the Guild as the annual beneficiary of its wishing well in Kings Park. By the end of May, the Guild was finally out of debt. Despite this, its financial position continued to be shaky, threatening the viability of the handcrafts section despite a successful fete on the Esplanade in September. Reluctant to fold, the handcraft group continued for another year, paying a commission to use a corner of the kiosk.[90]

Rose Heath had continued to manage the kiosk until May, when she began work as a clerk at the Taxation Department.[91] She was followed by two short-term managers, and further discouraging financial statements, before Sheila Barron agreed to take on the role, assisted by Flo Best, who was already working in the kitchen.[92] Aside from her family, the Guild became Sheila Barron's primary interest. Sheila had previously worked in the canteen at her children's school; managing the kiosk meant resigning from that role, as well as forgoing sports days and other school functions.[93] On weekdays, the kiosk opening hours were now roughly the same as a school day, and Sheila often travelled home on the same bus as her daughter Gwen. On weekends, Gwen regularly assisted in the kiosk, selling ice creams.[94]

Sheila Barron (far right) at a family wedding.
(Courtesy of Florence Gordon)

Under Sheila Barron's leadership, kiosk finances improved, showing a profit for the second half of 1956 into 1957 and beyond into 1958 and 1959.[95] Anzac Day 1957 saw a record £100 in takings, followed shortly after by another profitable day on Empire Youth Sunday, when children and young people were encouraged to remember they were part of the Empire.[96] Staffing, however, was still an issue because of high labour costs. Sheila pleaded for more volunteer assistance from members, particularly on Saturday and Sunday afternoons.[97]

One of the regular helpers was Gloria MacDonald, who worked full time during the week as a ledger keeper at Drabbles, a Claremont hardware store. Nicknamed Snow due to the colour of her hair, Gloria volunteered faithfully at the Esplanade Kiosk every Sunday afternoon, accompanied by her son Alex. It was often presumed that her hair had turned white with the shock of her husband's death, but apparently it had been that colour from an even earlier age. Gloria maintained a positive outlook on life. 'I'm lucky. I've got a son,' she commented. 'Some people don't even have that to remember their husbands by.'[98]

At the AGM in May 1957, five years after first attempting to give up the state presidency, and following further sick leave, Winifred Fowler stepped down from the position she had held for almost a decade. Gwen Forsyth accepted a nomination for the role, and was elected unopposed. Initially, Winifred remained on the council and executive committee but, in October, she resigned from all official duties. The Guild was reluctant to accept her resignation; Gwen Forsyth asked her to reconsider. Winifred relented, and instead took leave of absence.[99]

In February 1958, Jessie Vasey returned home from Rome, where she had attended an international conference on the subject of fatherless families. Her ship docked in Fremantle en route to Melbourne, and she took the opportunity to visit the Perth Guild. A large number of members met at the kiosk on 7 February to hear Jessie speak about the conference and the housing projects in Victoria. The Victorian Guild now owned three houses which they had turned into flats.[100] Jessie urged the Perth members to consider, urgently and seriously, their own project to build homes for elderly war widows.

Her visit propelled the Guild into putting housing back on the agenda, but not, for the moment, the building of flats. When Robert Menzies' government was returned to power in 1954, it had fulfilled an election promise by introducing the *Aged Persons Homes Act* to subsidise approved organisations on a pound for pound basis.[101] In 1957, the subsidy was doubled, meaning that the government now contributed two pounds for every pound raised by an organisation.[102] The following year the Guild heard that the RSL planned to build a War Veterans' Home. The government had allocated 11½ acres of the former Scadden Pine Plantation in Mount Lawley for the project, which qualified for the two for one subsidy. Would it be possible for the Home to have a wing to accommodate war widows who had no home and were too old or infirm to live independently, the Guild wondered.[103] Gwen Forsyth contacted the RSL president, Bill Lonnie, to enquire about the possibilities of the venture.[104]

The reaction was positive. While the detail was unclear, the RSL was amenable to a war widows' wing at the proposed War Veterans' Home. To gauge interest, the Guild distributed a state-wide circular in April 1959. According to Gwen Forsyth, the response was 'successful beyond our dreams'. More than seventy widows registered their interest, and the Guild enrolled scores of new members. Even when the RSL indicated that the cost of board and residence might be quite high, 27 widows remained eager for inclusion in the scheme.[105]

At a meeting at the Esplanade Kiosk on 3 September 1959, RSL representatives informed the Guild executive they could have their wing built provided they met the capital cost of £21,000.[106] With the government's £2 for £1 subsidies, the Guild needed to raise approximately £7000 plus another £2000 for furnishings.[107] Even with the subsidy, it would take every penny the Guild had saved over the years to see their dream become reality. Nevertheless, the executive agreed to the RSL's conditions.

The Guild sent letters to anyone it thought might assist them. The result was encouraging and included generous donations from Red Cross, Legacy, Boans and the Soldiers' Dependants Appeal Committee. Further funding came via the *Sunday Times* Timeswords.[108] The Anzac Day Trust Fund, Rotary, RSL Women's Auxiliary and a number of small firms also donated funds.[109] The Guild organised a much larger fete than it had on previous years, which was held outside on the Esplanade on 7 November 1959.[110] The kiosk's £580 profit was added to the fundraising efforts, as were individual contributions. One member, Mrs Frederick, raised £16 by making and selling jams; another widow donated £6 anonymously.[111] The amounts may not seem a great deal by today's standards, but for these widows, any amount was significant and could make a difference, as had been seen when they raised the 'key money' for the kiosk in 1949.

The foundation stone of the War Veterans' Home was laid on 21 July 1960, and Jessie Vasey visited Perth for the occasion.[112] Eight months later, on 11 March 1961, approximately one thousand people attended the official opening by Premier David Brand.[113] The War Widows' wing was named Vasey House in honour of the War Widows' Guild founder and it comprised twenty bedsitters, each facing north and opening onto a common verandah and garden.[114] Other facilities included a communal kitchenette, laundrette, two ablution blocks and a sitting room. The Soldiers' Dependants Appeal Committee made an additional donation to furnish the sitting room with wall-to-wall carpet, pictures, a television and a radiator.[115] Major Owen Howes, the superintendent of the War Veterans' Home, treated them with 'unfailing courtesy and care.'[116] Vasey House was a significant achievement for the Guild, and this was the first time in Australia that war widows had been included in an RSL War Veterans' Home.[117]

CHAPTER 5
END OF AN ERA

With the wing at the Veterans' Home open and seventeen war widows happily settled there, the Guild explored again the idea of building its own flats for elderly war widows who were able to live independently. With such projects already established in Victoria, New South Wales, South Australia and Queensland, a similar scheme was long overdue in Western Australia.[1] But, just as they began to search for suitable sites, they were forced to put their plans on hold, as difficulties at the kiosk once more dominated the Guild's time and energy.

Gwen Forsyth had been cautiously optimistic about the kiosk in July 1960.

> *It has been an excellent year. Days in the tearooms have been quiet and wages go up periodically and frankly we were a bit worried about what the yearly balance would show …. [but] the auditor was unsparing in his praise [of Sheila Barron and Flo Best] this morning. He said he was quite amazed when he found the profit that had been made … this profit would not exist without the voluntary workers, they just make the difference and without them we could not carry on.[2]*

A year later, though, the business was barely breaking even. Despite keeping paid staff to a minimum, a rise in the basic wage and a drop in trading dramatically affected profit margins. Business was also lacklustre elsewhere in the city, where a number of small eating-houses had already closed down.[3] Furthermore, some banks had opened their own cafeterias, and coffee houses had grown in popularity, drawing customers away from tearooms.[4] The future of the kiosk looked decidedly grim, but Gwen Forsyth and other members were still reluctant to relinquish it. Gwen wrote in the *Guild News*:

> [W]ithout the Kiosk we would have no Guild as we know it; no place to meet, no office, no hall, no headquarters for interstate visitors or country members to come to. Even if we had a little office somewhere in the city and hired a hall for meetings, it would not be at all like this ... It is for this reason we ask for voluntary help for weekends and holidays. We could not keep going without voluntary helpers, the wages bill would be quite impossible and the Kiosk would have to be given up.[5]

Unfortunately, 1962 saw little change. 'We are out of the way down here,' Gwen Forsyth reported in August that year, 'particularly since Repatriation has moved, the R and I Bank has opened a cafeteria and the Orchestral Shell has taken concerts away from the Esplanade.'[6] The Guild persevered, but it continued to be a struggle. On Thursday 21 February 1963, Gwen Forsyth and Sheila Barron accompanied two Perth City councillors on an inspection of the kiosk. From the Council's perspective, the building was in a poor condition. Additionally, 'the lack of care taken by the Clubs who use the dressing room [was] deplorable.' Shower roses were stolen almost immediately they were installed, and walls and ceilings were damaged by bouncing footballs and other equipment.[7]

'The Council will have to seriously consider the future use of the kiosk and the dressing rooms,' Councillor Florence Hummerston told Gwen and Sheila.[8] With characteristic honesty,[9] Gwen admitted the kiosk had been running at a financial loss. 'Perhaps under those circumstances,' said Councillor Hummerston, 'it would not be a great loss to the Guild if the tenancy was terminated.'[10]

'From the Guild's perspective,' Gwen said, 'the main advantage is that the kiosk provides a very convenient meeting place for our members.' She added that she would not be surprised if the Council terminated the lease. 'But please give us sufficient time to make alternative arrangements.'[11]

Shortly afterwards, in a letter dated 19 June 1963, the Guild received official word that the Perth City Council would terminate the lease;[12] the Guild was finally losing its headquarters of fourteen years. In view of the mostly successful partnership with the RSL over the War Veterans' Home, Gwen Forsyth hoped the RSL could offer assistance.[13] It did. In July, the Guild secured a small office at Anzac House, in which to hold executive meetings.[14] The Lower Hall in the basement was available for concerts, the handcrafts group, and the member meetings held on the third Monday of every month.[15] And so, on 30 September 1963, the War Widows' Guild closed the doors to the Esplanade Kiosk for the final time.[16]

The following day, 1 October 1963, the executive committee held its first meeting in Anzac House, although Vera Judge had already hosted a bridge afternoon there on 27 September.[17] Just a fortnight after the move, Gwen Forsyth attended a federal conference in Melbourne, lamenting the fact that high travel costs made her the sole representative from Western Australia. 'I am sorry that Western Australia is so far away that we can only afford to send one delegate,' she said. 'I think this is really unwise; we should look to the future and always have younger people coming on to hold responsible positions.'[18]

Hearing about the developments in other states provided Gwen with a snapshot of Guild work nationally, as well as giving her further ideas for Western Australia. She arrived home just in time for an office warming party at Anzac House on 21 October 1963.[19]

Four days later, Sir Douglas Kendrew was sworn in as the new governor of Western Australia. During a long military career that included the Second World War and Korea, he had risen to the rank of major general and had been awarded the Distinguished Service Order (DSO) four times.[20] As other governor's wives had done before her, Lady Kendrew consented to being the Guild's patron. One of her first engagements as patron was to visit Vasey House while attending a fete at the War Veterans' Home, and war widows living there were impressed by her charm and friendly interest in them.[21]

With the closure of the kiosk, Sheila Barron made the decision to move interstate in January 1964. She had contributed so much to the running of the kiosk and, in turn, the Guild had been her lifeline, but she missed her children and grandchildren, most of whom now lived in Melbourne. It was time to move to Victoria to be closer to them. There, she purchased a sandwich bar which she ran with the help of one of her daughters. By December, however, Sheila was homesick for the west, and returned to Perth and the Guild.[22] Before long, she was co-opted back onto the executive committee.[23]

Clockwise from top left: Jessie Vasey was well known for her beautiful hats; Jessie Vasey in a more serious moment; Delegates of the 1963 National Conference – Jessie Vasey is fourth from the left and Gwen Forsyth is fifth from the right. (All three photos courtesy of John Forsyth)

The Guild was happy to welcome her home. The year had been tinged with sadness for the organisation. In March, foundation member Patricia Connor died aged only sixty-two. Patricia had been on the executive committee and represented the Guild on the Soldiers' Children Education Board for fifteen years. Then, on 16 May, at the age of seventy-two, Rita Kuring passed away in her sleep.[24] At the AGM, Gwen spoke of Rita's 'constant care and thought' and her 'years of devoted book work.' Rita had been a 'capable treasurer and business advisor through all [the] worry and struggle at the Esplanade Kiosk.'[25] It must have been difficult saying goodbye to women who had become such valued friends.

⚙

In 1965, fifty years after the first Anzacs landed at Gallipoli, long-time member Elsie Ketterer was selected to represent the Western Australian Guild at the Anzac Day Jubilee ceremony in Canberra. Her husband, Victor Ketterer, had embarked from Fremantle with the 16th Battalion on 22 February 1915 and served in Egypt, Gallipoli and the Western Front before returning to Australia in 1918. He was mentioned in despatches twice and received a Military Cross for 'gallantry and initiative as an intelligence officer.'[26] Elsie became a war widow when his death on 31 July 1936 was attributed to war causes. As well as being involved in the Guild, Elsie had been actively involved in the RSL Women's Auxiliary. The Guild considered Elsie to be an ideal representative for the Jubilee commemorations in Canberra.[27]

In addition, a group of around three hundred Australians and New Zealanders travelled to Anzac Cove. Among them were seventy-one men who had landed at Gallipoli on 25 April 1915. Now, in 1965, they alighted there again, this time in a Turkish lifeboat. Instead of sniper fire, they were greeted by some one hundred people, including journalists, cameramen, villagers, soldiers from the Gelibolu army base and four Australian hitchhikers. According to historian Ken Inglis, the veterans welcomed the hitchhikers as 'unexpected living evidence that *some* young people cared about the Anzac tradition.'[28]

As Anzac Day commemorated those who had fought in previous wars, conscription was about to see a new generation of young men sent into battle. The first lottery, in which men whose birthdates were randomly selected were conscripted, had been drawn on 10 March and, on 29 April 1965, Prime Minister Robert Menzies announced that Australia would 'provide an infantry battalion for service in Vietnam.' Australia had entered the Vietnam conflict in 1962, but the men involved were regular soldiers and the public paid little attention to their involvement. Opposition leader Arthur Calwell objected to the troop deployment, although there was not a strong negative reaction from the public. There was even some support due to the perceived threat of Communism.[29]

This changed after Harold Holt succeeded Robert Menzies as prime minister on 26 January 1966 and announced the expansion of Australia's involvement in Vietnam. A task force of 4350 was to be sent and would include national service conscripts. On the night of 1 April, a large wooden cross was set alight at the Kings Park State War Memorial. A second cross was burned at the war memorial on 8 June. Three days later, more than five hundred people gathered in Forrest Place to oppose conscription. Three young men burned their draft cards. 'One, two, three, four, we don't want another war!' the crowd chanted. Demonstrators hurled abuse at police and the confrontations intensified as police used force to make arrests. Members of the Communist Party picketed the US Consulate on St Georges Terrace for several days, and the Youth Campaign against Conscription organised a march in the city on Sunday 6 August, culminating in a rally on the Esplanade. This time, police did not intervene when two young men burned their draft cards.[30]

❖

The War Widows' Guild, at both a state and national level, continued to fight for greater benefits and conditions for *all* war widows, whether or not they were members. Locally, the Guild gained discount cards from a number of retailers, and at a national level, Mr Reginald Swartz, the Minister for Repatriation, agreed to a reduction in telephone rentals for war widows.[31] The Guild also set out to gain fare concessions on public transport. It canvassed members of parliament to garner support, among them Dr Guy Henn, the Member for Wembley.

Dr Henn had served as a medical officer in the merchant navy in 1941 before enlisting in the RAAF as a surgeon flight lieutenant. After the war, he worked as a general practitioner before taking a position at the Repatriation General Hospital (RGH), later known as Hollywood Hospital.[32] It is likely that he had worked with Jean Ferguson at the RGH, and as the MLA for Wembley, Dr Henn was Gwen Forsyth's local member. Whatever the initial contact, Dr Henn offered to introduce a proposed deputation to the state Minister for Transport, James Craig.[33]

On 7 December 1964, Gwen Forsyth and vice-president Win Greenshields took the deputation to the Minister for Transport, requesting a reduction in fares for war widows who were over the age of sixty and had a limited income. Mrs Clear, a war widow and president of the Friendly Union of Soldiers' Wives, also attended at the Guild's invitation. The women argued that until 1960, many war widows had been eligible for a partial old age pension from the Department of Social Security, and thus a concession fare certificate. With an increase in the war widows' pension, however, no war widow was currently eligible for the partial pension or its associated allowances, such as subsidies for fares, and television and wireless licences. A woman receiving the old age pension from the Social Services Department, supplemented by superannuation and investments up to a total of nineteen pounds, was eligible for these concessions. A war widow, whose sole income was her pension also received nineteen pounds, but was *ineligible* because she was paid by the Repatriation Department.[34] Gwen pointed out that Victoria, New South Wales and Queensland already had concessions to varying degrees.[35] In concluding, Gwen stated:

> *A war widow solely dependent on her pension, which is now £19 per fortnight, is suffering great hardship owing to the high cost of fares. Many of our widows now cannot afford to come in to meetings and social gatherings if they live in areas where it is necessary to catch two buses into Perth. Loneliness and isolation are the chief causes of mental and physical ill-health among our members who are now too old to earn their supplement.*[36]

The deputation impressed Guy Henn, although the Guild waited ten months, until October 1965, before hearing the campaign had been successful.[37] Travel concessions were granted to West Australian war widows sixty years and over, provided their only income was the pension they received from the Repatriation Department. The concessions took effect in February 1966, and, according to Gwen Forsyth, provided 'much relief to many people, particularly those who lived a long way from the city.'[38]

While the Guild continued to campaign for greater benefits, it did not neglect the social needs of war widows. With one of the major aims being the prevention of social isolation, monthly get-togethers were held on the third Monday evening of every month and various events were organised, such as concerts by the Masonic Men's Choir and picnics.[39] Vera Judge coordinated the picnics, attended by approximately sixty war widows, as well as bridge and card afternoons, which had become more popular since the move to Anzac House. Some widows were unable to attend the Monday evening meetings but the executive committee was keen to include these women in the 'Guild circle' and so Bertha Denton hosted a Saturday afternoon group, until a pending eye operation forced her to step down. At that time, Vera Judge, Mrs E. Miller and Olive Hancock shared the role.[40]

Bertha Denton had also assisted Mrs J. Rowan and May Hiatt in visiting war widows in Hollywood Hospital, where Jean Ferguson was still matron. May Hiatt also stepped down from the role due to ill health, but Mrs Blackmore joined the team of weekly visitors. Once a week, the women visited both the medical and surgical wards, each of which contained thirty-two beds, and helped war widows with shopping, letters, messages and advice. A number of women joined the Guild after being visited in hospital.[41]

❦

Western Australia was home to one of the smaller state Guilds, with only 2500 war widows in the entire state; in 1963 approximately 600 of these were Guild members, double the membership of 1959.[42] The NSW Guild had a much larger membership base of 7500, with thirteen clubs in Sydney, a further eight sub-branches in the country, and a financially sound housing scheme. In South Australia, the Guild had also made progress with respect to housing. It had purchased a block of land and built eleven units. In Tasmania, the smallest of the state guilds, the focus was on friendship building and, while the Launceston branch was temporarily inactive, a branch had recently formed in Devonport. The Victorian Guild had a large focus on social work and visiting the ill, as well as developing its own housing projects, now under the umbrella of the Vasey Housing Auxiliary (VHA), and valued at £1,000,000.[43]

Jessie Vasey had been struggling with ill health for some time, and was concerned about how it might affect her Guild work. Doctors had warned her to reduce her workload as early as 1955, and she had hinted at the need for a new leader at the 1963 conference. More recently, she had spent a brief period in hospital in December 1965 and another in March 1966. In February 1966 Lois Hurse began working for the Victorian Guild in the role of deputy president, in the hope of reducing Jessie's work load. The plan was that Jessie would retire in 1967, beginning with a world trip funded by the War Widows' Guild, as a form of long service payment.[44]

Although her failing health was becoming more noticeable to those around her, Jessie found it difficult to take a back seat. While this is understandable given her passionate commitment to the organisation she had founded, it caused some conflict within the Victorian Guild. When the state branch became a limited company in March 1966, and a board of directors replaced the existing executive committee, it appears that Jessie agreed to hand administrative control to Lois Hurse, but remain as chairman of directors.[45] But at a subsequent board meeting, Jessie refused to allow Lois Hurse be elected as vice-chairman and managing director. According to one board member, Jessie insisted on retaining the role, arguing that Lois was not 'capable of running the show.' Board members refused to pass Jessie's motions, because the proposals were not on the meeting agenda, and nor had she consulted anyone prior to the meeting.[46]

Jessie finally agreed to take a rest after accepting an invitation to holiday with Queensland president Billie Hughes at Surfers Paradise. Jessie spent time with her sister in Noosa before she joined Billie to enjoy ten relaxed days in the tropical climate, reading, shopping and swimming.[47] She visited a number of old friends, including Ruth McLennan, who had nursed General Vasey back to health during the Second World War. Jessie contemplated travelling north to Cairns to see her husband's grave for the first time, but for reasons unknown, that leg of the journey never eventuated.[48] On Wednesday 21 September 1966, Jessie and her sister packed the car and set off on their return journey to Melbourne. They drove as far as Grafton, where they stayed overnight. The following morning, Jessie woke with a severe headache. Within an hour, she was dead following a cerebral haemorrhage.[49]

CHAPTER 6
'CARRY ON THE MAGNIFICENT WORK'

Although Jessie Vasey had been unwell for some time, her death shocked the members of the War Widows' Guild.[1] Gwen Forsyth flew to Melbourne to attend the funeral held at Toorak Presbyterian Church on Tuesday 27 September 1966. Gwen sat with the other state presidents in the pew immediately behind Jessie's family. Among the two hundred mourners were Repatriation Commissioner Brigadier Chilton; Mr Stephens, General Secretary Services, Canteens Trust Fund; General Rowell, a friend of both George and Jessie Vasey; and other representatives from government departments and ex-service organisations.[2] Sympathy telegrams were sent by Princess Marina, Lady Casey, wife of the governor-general; former repatriation minister Sir Walter Cooper; and Sir Roden Cutler, the New South Wales governor.[3]

The general feeling in the War Widows' Guild was that Australia had 'lost an outstanding and noble woman.'[4] Gwen Forsyth held her in the highest esteem. Although the two women had not agreed on everything, the respect and affection was mutual.[5] Gloria MacDonald admired her too, and had enjoyed meeting with her on both a social and business level. Coincidentally, when Gloria's son Alex landed his first job with Golden Fleece, his sales manager was Jessie's son Robert, which provided a common interest.[6]

The day after the funeral, the state presidents convened an emergency meeting in Melbourne. With 'memories and sorrow'[7] they determined to 'carry on the magnificent work she started.'[8] They decided to commission a portrait in oils of Jessie Vasey as a memorial, but agreed that the best memorial would be to 'continue with the utmost vigour the struggle for benefits and housing that she began.'[9]

Portrait of Jessie Vasey, commissioned by the
War Widows' Guild and painted by Alma Figuerola.
(Guild archives, WA Branch)

A new national[10] president, Janet Mayo, was elected. Janet Mayo had been twenty-six and pregnant with her second child when she received news that her husband Eric had died when the German ship *Kormoran* sank the HMAS *Sydney* in 1941.[11] Janet had joined the Guild on its inception in South Australia, and became its state president four months later.[12] In her first letter to war widows nationally, she wrote:

> *I am most humbly aware that I have assumed my new office*
> *as successor to a woman who was, and rightly so, known*
> *all over Australia to the general public, and who was (and*
> *rightly so) loved and admired by thousands of war widows*
> *all over Australia. I do not think that my shoulders are*
> *broad enough to wear Mrs Vasey's mantle; she was one*
> *of whom we say 'We shall not see her like again.' But I do*
> *promise you all that I shall do my very best to be worthy of*
> *the position entrusted to me.*[13]

The War Widows' Guild of Australia celebrated its 21st birthday in November 1966. Each state hosted its own commemorative event. In Western Australia, the Guild held a buffet dinner in the Anzac House Ballroom on 17 November. According to the *Guild News*, 'a band of enthusiastic workers transformed' the ballroom into a 'delightful party setting with pot plants and masses of flowers.'[14] Gwen Forsyth opened the evening with a welcome speech, and later the Guild patron, Lady Kendrew, blew out the twenty-one candles on the two-tiered birthday cake before cutting it. Members were delighted when Lady Kendrew chatted freely among them. The executive committee thought the dinner an appropriate occasion on which to acknowledge Gwen Forsyth's enormous contribution to the Guild. Jean Ferguson paid tribute to Gwen's leadership, and vice-president Ethel Bird presented her with an Omega gold watch.[15]

Newly appointed national president Janet Mayo travelled to Western Australia in 1967 as part of a publicity campaign and to meet war widows in all states. Jessie Vasey had been such a public figure that Janet Mayo's tour was intended to prevent the War Widows' Guild fading from view without the commanding presence and influence of its founder. The Guild was pleased, therefore, that the visit received attention from the local press.[16] In Perth, Janet's activities included visiting the War Veterans' Home, where she planted a tree at Vasey House, met war widows in Hollywood Hospital, and attended a reception at the Repatriation Department. She spoke at a Legacy luncheon and met with Lady Kendrew, Premier David Brand and the newly appointed lord mayor, Thomas Wardle.[17]

❀

The average age of Guild members was rising and their needs were changing. Those who had been young women in the 1940s were now middle aged. Their children were grown, some with families of their own. Locally, a number of women who had played key roles, such as Vera Judge, Winifred Fowler, Rita Kuring, Elsie Ketterer and Patricia Connor, had passed away; others were unwell or frail. Supporting aging war widows, especially in the area of housing, had never been more important.

Winifred Fowler had raised the issue of chronically ill war widows as early as July 1954, believing there was a need for a ward, preferably in an existing nursing home, to be reserved for war widows.[18] Her awareness may have been influenced by her own ongoing health problems, as she had suffered from recurring stomach ulcers and other health problems that necessitated extended stays in hospital.[19] More recently, Gwen Forsyth had attempted to address the issue by writing to then federal Repatriation Minister Reginald Swartz in July 1963 about the need for a home for sick war widows.[20] Initially, he had indicated that hospital care for the chronically ill would be investigated but, in early 1964, he wrote to the Guild again, saying that the war widows would need to look into their own future care.[21]

The Guild refused to give up. At a national level, delegates at the 1967 conference lamented 'the fact that Repatriation Medical Benefits cease just when war widows really need them most, that is when they are aged and infirm or actually chronically ill.'[22] They raised the issue with the Minister for Repatriation when he visited the conference.

'My aim is to give greatest benefit to those in need,' he responded. 'If, in giving you this, it means cutting out someone in greater need, this would have to be weighed.'

'The need is desperate for chronically ill war widows. They cannot meet the cost of a convalescent home,' said New South Wales delegate, Una Boyce.[23]

Delegates also voiced their dissatisfaction over low pension rates, although some progress had been made in that year, with war widows over the age of sixty becoming eligible for a partial age-pension if their total income was less than $23 per week. This brought with it added benefits such as reduced rates on television and wireless licences, reduced land rates and concession fares on public transport.[24] Those attending the conference also spent time drafting an updated national constitution.

Upon her return from the 1967 conference, Gwen Forsyth pursued the possibility of building flats for those who could live independently. In May 1966, she had raised the question of building flats for war widows on the site of the War Veterans' Home. The Guild had advertised for expressions of interest but within a year Gwen had to inform members that plans were once more on hold as the RSL had rejected the Guild's request.[25] Despite this, Major Owen Howes, superintendent of the War

Veterans' Home, accompanied Gwen when she met with the Minister for Lands, William Stewart Bovell. There is no record of what Gwen Forsyth said to the minister but it appears she was very persuasive. In a letter dated 14 November 1967, Stewart Bovell wrote:

Dear Mrs Forsyth

Since you called to see me with Major Howes to discuss a site on which the War Widows' Guild could erect homes for the aged, I have considered the points raised by you in support of such a worthy cause.

I explained at the time there was virtually no Crown land left within a reasonable distance of the city centre which could be used for the purpose and that the one or two blocks left in the Scadden Pine Plantation would be required for purposes other than aged persons homes.

You mentioned an area of approximately 2 acres as being required to erect homes for the aged within the limited funds available to your Guild and, because of this, I have had a closer examination made of the remaining small blocks at Scadden Pine Plantation.

There is one on the corner of Freedman Road and Plantation Street ... It contains just over 1¼ acres and being a corner block is accessible from both streets.

Because of the very special cause which you have submitted, I would be pleased to offer this site to you on the understanding that no further land can be made available in the area for aged persons.

Yours sincerely

Stewart Bovell
Minister for Lands[26]

The land at the Scadden Pine Plantation in Mount Lawley[27] was conveniently located, due to its close proximity to Vasey House. The Guild planned to build a small block of rental flats in the form of bedsitters. It secured a Commonwealth subsidy and employed architect company Kenneth Broadhurst, Ryan and Evans to draw up plans.[28] The housing dream which had been thwarted for years was finally becoming a reality.

Past president Winifred Fowler, who had been an advocate of affordable housing, passed away on 12 April 1968, before the Guild could fully realise its vision. Gwen Forsyth spoke about Winifred Fowler's contribution to the Guild at the AGM:

> *Mrs Fowler was a wonderful person, so ready to help and advise, so gentle, kind and understanding. I worked with her a great deal on Guild affairs and owe her a tremendous debt for her example and guidance ... we were fortunate to have her to lead and guide us for so long.*[29]

At that meeting, Ethel Bird resigned from her position as vice-president, citing ill-health, although she agreed to stay on the council. Gwen Forsyth paid tribute to her, too: 'Mrs Bird has always been by my side ready and willing to do anything I asked for myself or the Guild.'[30] Amy Pereira and Mrs Crompton, two more active members, died shortly after the AGM.[31] Next came unexpected news that the War Widows' Guild national patron, Princess Marina, had died.[32]

Recognition for the work of two Guild members came in 1969. Gwen Forsyth was awarded a British Empire Medal (BEM) in the New Year's honours list for her untiring work on behalf of war widows and their children. Accompanied by her sons Alan and John, and Guild secretary Win Greenshields, Gwen attended a ceremony at the Government House Ballroom, which looked magnificent with its draped flags and masses of flowers. After the ceremony, John and Alan escorted Gwen and Win to lunch at the Savoy Hotel.[33]

In May, Jean Ferguson, who had retired as matron of Hollywood Hospital the previous year, was awarded the Florence Nightingale Medal, the Red Cross's highest international honour, for her long and distinguished record of army and repatriation service.[34] Matron

Ferguson had already been awarded the Associate Royal Red Cross in 1953 and her commitment to serving and training others was again acknowledged when she was appointed MBE in 1963.[35] Guild members had long appreciated Jean Ferguson's care of war widows in hospital and were proud to say, 'Matron is also a war widow.'[36]

Ellen Peck never received such an award, but her generosity was to be remembered and appreciated by the Guild for many years. A First World War widow and long-term member, Ellen Peck died on 29 May 1969, leaving the main part of her estate to the Guild. Aside from fortnightly allotments paid to a friend and to her son-in-law (her daughter Frances had died in 1965, aged forty-five), Ellen specified that the annual interest from her estate was to be paid to the Guild for a minimum of twenty years. After that time, the Guild could access the principal.[37]

Ellen's husband, Lieutenant Colonel John Henry Peck, participated in several of the battles commemorated today. Embarking at Fremantle on 2 November 1914 with the original members of the 11th Battalion, he was adjutant of this battalion at the Gallipoli landing. Wounded the same day, he was evacuated, but recovered and returned to his unit. He later went to France where he was made Brigade Major of the 4th Brigade on the Somme and then promoted to Lieutenant Colonel of the 14th Battalion. He was present at Messines, Polygon Wood, Passchendaele and Villers-Bretonneux. He was mentioned in despatches five times, awarded a Distinguished Service Order and appointed to a Companion of the Order of St Michael and St George.

The details of Ellen's life are less public. It is known that she grew up in Perth, and met John Henry Peck when he was posted there as an army instructor prior to the First World War. They married on 22 July 1913. After her husband returned to Australia in May 1919, she and her daughter Frances joined him when he was posted to Melbourne and later Brisbane. She became a war widow on 2 September 1928 when John Henry died from chronic nephritis, a condition attributed to war injuries.[38] Ellen eventually returned to her home town of Perth, where she joined the Guild. Her generous and substantial bequest gave the Guild a financial security it had never previously experienced.

All wills, other than those whose beneficiary was exempt under the *Administration Act*, were subject to probate duty. The exemption applied in cases where the entire trust was 'for the benefit of a charitable organisation.'[39] As Ellen Peck had also bequeathed a small amount to two individuals, the exemption was not applicable. Thus, the Guild was 'not prescribed under the Administrations Act as an organisation entitled to have probate on bequests waived,'[40] meaning that approximately $16,000 in probate duty was to be paid. The money would come from the estate and not Guild funds per se; however, over the next twenty years, it would equate to a loss in interest of more than $23,000. The Guild's solicitors sent a detailed submission to the Commissioner of Probate Duties, arguing that the Guild should be considered exempt. In March 1970, Gwen Forsyth received the welcome news that the commissioner was prepared to allow the exemption. This set a precedent for the other state Guilds should they have money bequeathed to them in the future,[41] illustrating yet again both the independence and interdependence of the state Guilds and the national body.

❀

By 1969 there were 48,000 war widows and 6000 war orphans in Australia,[42] with some 22,000 of the women involved with the War Widows' Guild at some level.[43] But the Guild worked to assist all, regardless of whether or not they were members.

In October, the South Australian Guild hosted a national conference in Adelaide. Sir James Harrison, governor of South Australia, opened the conference, saying that 'the work of the Guild was well known, as it should be, and the nation has cause to be grateful.'[44] A new major issue had appeared, with delegates acknowledging that the Vietnam War had brought a new group of women to join the ranks of the bereaved. The main issue discussed was that of vocational training, which many war widows had undertaken following the Second World War. In 1969 there were approximately one hundred Vietnam War widows, but very few had applied for vocational training. To be eligible, a war widow needed to apply for training within five years of her husband's death or before her youngest child turned seven. Yet, as some foundation members knew from personal experience, training could be difficult with young children at home. It was suggested that war widows be encouraged to apply for training even if they were not ready for it, and that it be held over until they were ready.[45]

While consideration of this younger group of widows was on the agenda, so, again, was care of the chronically ill, aged and infirm, which was considered the 'most important recommendation' that could come from the War Widows' Guild. Gwen Forsyth agreed wholeheartedly, and expressed her belief that the Repatriation Department should take responsibility for these people. She reported that in Western Australia the Repatriation Department had made ten beds available for war widows at Edward Millen Convalescent Home in Victoria Park. Win Greenshields added that Gwen had campaigned for many years to acquire this amenity. Delegates congratulated Gwen on her efforts and agreed that the WA Department of Repatriation had established a precedent that might be useful in other states.[46]

The project of building the bedsitter flats at the former Scadden Pine Plantation in Mount Lawley continued. Gwen Forsyth, Gloria MacDonald and other members spent many hours poring over plans, budgeting costs, and applying for subsidies before building could begin. They deliberated on safety features such as bathroom rails, non-slip surfaces, shower recesses with stools and hand-held shower-heads.[47] Official approval was granted on 30 April 1969, and the first nine flats were ready to occupy by the end of the year.

Lady Kendrew officially opened the flats on 6 December 1969. Such occasions entailed a certain protocol which, in this case, included a blessing by the chaplain general of the armed forces. Invitations should also be extended to the chaplain general of the individual services – army, navy and air force. As a number of these men were bishops, their respective chaplains should also be invited, as well as their Anglican or Catholic counterparts. When the executive committee discussed this, they realised there would be more clergy than flats. 'It's nine flats in the middle of grey sand,' said Gwen. Her elder son John, an Anglican priest, was suggested as an alternative. John was unavailable, so Gwen called her younger son Alan.

'Al, can you bless flats?'[48]

Alan was a deacon in the Anglican Church, but not yet a qualified priest, and technically unable to bless anything. Meaning to turn down the invitation, he replied, 'No, I can only ask God to.'

'Oh, good,' Gwen said, 'would you ask Him on Saturday?'[49]

The Guild named the flats Forsyth Gardens as a way of acknowledging

Gwen's commitment and contribution to the Guild since its inception in 1946. According to her son, Gwen was mildly embarrassed at the honour, but also rather pleased.[50] And there was much about which to be pleased. Finally, eighteen years after Guild members had first discussed the possibility of flats for war widows, the vision had become a reality.

The following year a block of six flats was built and, by February 1971, all fifteen flats were occupied, the grass was flourishing and sixty shrubs had been planted.[51] Due to the initiative of one resident, Mrs Paisley, Forsyth Gardens had a visiting baker, butcher, milkman and greengrocer. Across the road was Carinya Village, a Church of Christ home, and the women were able to shop at the village canteen, attend handcraft classes and even call the resident nurse should an emergency arise.[52]

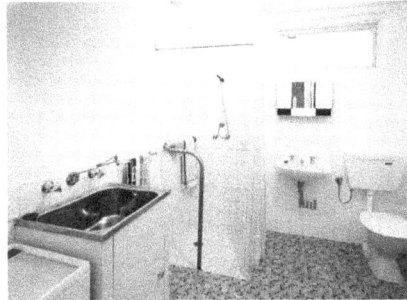

Clockwise from top left: One of the recently built units at Forsyth Gardens, 1971; The living room and kitchen of one of the units; Combined bathroom and laundry; Looking across Plantation Street at Forsyth Gardens, 1971. (All four photos by A.J. Nutt & Associates)

❀

Despite the success of the building project at Forsyth Gardens, the larger problem of caring for the aged, frail or chronically ill war widows remained largely unsolved. Gwen Forsyth was determined to find a solution and, at her suggestion, this became the theme of the 1971 biennial conference, held in Adelaide from 12 to 14 October.[53] Gwen Forsyth and Win Greenshields attended as the WA delegates, with May Hiatt accompanying them as an observer. Those present expressed 'grave concern ... at the ever increasing gap between the cost of accommodation in nursing homes and the income of a war widow.' Rendle 'Mac' Holten, Minister for Repatriation, and Richard Kingsland, Chairman of the Repatriation Commission, attended the meeting and listened to the delegates. They reassured the War Widows' Guild that they would do 'everything possible to devise a system which may alleviate the very complex and difficult situation.'[54]

Following the conference, all states, including Western Australia, wrote letters to members of parliament and talked to anyone they felt could be influential in the matter.[55] National president Janet Mayo also travelled to Canberra to present the Guild's concerns. On 15 August 1972, the federal budget was announced. The war widows' persistence had paid off. Repatriation Minister Mac Holten announced:

> As from 1st January 1973, funds for nursing home care for War Widows will be provided by the Repatriation Department ... When the Department establishes that nursing home care is necessary, and arranges admission, the patients mentioned will be admitted on the basis of a patient contribution of $18.00 a week.[56]

The minister publicly acknowledged the dignity and clarity with which Janet Mayo had presented the war widows' case.[57] The war widows received the news with relief, thankfulness and 'tremendous joy' as the funds would contribute greatly to 'overcoming the heavy financial burden of chronic care.'[58]

❀

In September 1972, a third block of flats was completed at Forsyth Gardens. Reflecting on the achievement, Gwen stated:

Our Forsyth Gardens has now taken on the air of a little community. I remember that when the first nine flats were built they looked rather comical perched, as they were, all by themselves on the corner of our block, surrounded by sand. Now with the lawns and trees thriving the site presents a different picture.[59]

Additionally, the RSL planned to build a Frail-Aged Centre at the rear of the Veterans' Home, and war widows living at the Home would be eligible for admission. The Guild believed this would provide a wonderful feeling of security, and so, at a special meeting, the Guild committed $10,000 towards the building of the centre, provided the eligibility for admission widened to include residents of Forsyth Gardens.[60] The Frail-Aged Centre was officially opened on 10 March 1974, and named Howes in honour of Major Owen Howes, the inaugural superintendent of the War Veterans' Home. Nine war widows were offered rooms. Together with nineteen living in Vasey House, twenty-three in the self-contained flats at Forsyth Gardens and fifteen at Clifton House, another wing of the Veterans' Home, sixty-six war widows were now accommodated through the work of the Guild.[61]

Forsyth Gardens in 1973, the lawn and shrubs flourishing.
(Guild archives, WA Branch)

CHAPTER 7

STILL FIGHTING

The Guild's building projects had occurred against a backdrop of social and political changes. In the state's north, mining discoveries resulted in new towns springing up from the red dirt, while across the country, Aboriginal people had finally won the right to vote, although stereotypes and prejudice remained, and the women's liberation movement was gaining momentum.[1] In 1947, women had formed 22 per cent of the work force; in 1971, they made up one third, and half of these were married. Yet there was still little provision for childcare,[2] and despite the granting of equal pay for equal work in 1969, the average woman still earned only about two-thirds of the male wage.[3]

Between 1967 and 1974, the nation had been led by five prime ministers, with Gough Whitlam assuming the role after a federal election on 2 December 1972. His deputy, Lance Barnard, son of the repatriation minister who had sparred with Jessie Vasey twenty-five years earlier, immediately announced the abolition of national service and the release of gaoled draft resisters. The remaining Australian troops in Vietnam would also return home to complete the withdrawal which had started two years earlier. The war itself would continue until 1975.[4]

These significant changes had not, however, reached the repatriation system, which remained much the same as when it began in 1920 after the First World War. Originally seen as generous, repatriation compensation 'no longer compared favourably with civilian compensation.'[5] At the time, the war widows' pension, including a domestic allowance, was worth only about half the Commonwealth minimum wage.[6] Thus, in 1971, the federal government appointed Justice Paul Burcher Toose, a NSW Supreme Court judge, to conduct an independent inquiry into the repatriation system. The War Widows' Guild made a written submission at a national level, which stated in part:

> *The Guild's chief desire has always been that a war widow should receive some sort of practical compensation for her husband's life. We have, year after year reminded succeeding governments that our men's lives were war material. All other war materials were paid for in hard cash; had they not been so warships would not have sailed, guns would have stayed silent, aircraft would have remained on the ground – and so on, down to boots and bully beef and billy cans. All war materials were paid for, all except the human lives that were used.*[7]

Janet Mayo then appeared before Justice Toose on 14 June 1972. When asked if she would like to address the issue of pensions, she replied:

> *Well, for one thing we dislike the word 'pension'. We have always preferred that the moneys we receive should be regarded as compensation. We are quite aware that nothing can compensate for what we lost; there is no way of valuing a man's life and the potential, particularly of a young man who was killed, was limitless probably … the widow of a man who was killed on active service or whose death was due to his war service should receive enough for her to live on decently and with dignity.*[8]

Janet Mayo's comments parallel those expressed by Jessie Vasey and other foundation members years before, an indication that although progress had been made and benefits won, the struggle for recognition and compensation continued. Justice Toose appears to have supported the views expressed by the War Widows' Guild, as his final report states:

*the nation is specially indebted to those who have
voluntarily given service to it in time of war by enlisting
in the Armed Forces, thereby endangering their lives and
health and probably suffering economic loss.*[9]

He noted that this also applied to those who had been enlisted
compulsorily and continued:

*The nation therefore has a duty to ensure that those who
have thus served, together with their dependants, are
properly cared for to the extent that they should never have
to beg or rely on charity.*[10]

This statement echoed the original intent of the War Pension Bill,
introduced into the House of Representatives in November 1941,
which had called for a pension that would 'keep the wolf from
the door of any of those who are unfortunately bereaved of their
breadwinners.'[11] Justice Toose also recommended that the term 'war
widow pension' should be replaced by 'war widow compensation'[12]
and noted that 'compensation and other benefits should be available
as a matter of right and not as a welfare hand-out,'[13] further resonating
with the convictions long expressed by the War Widows' Guild.
Although Justice Toose completed his report in June 1975, it was not
tabled in parliament until February the following year, several months
after Whitlam's dismissal by the governor-general. Mrs MacMaster,
who shared the state secretary role with Gloria MacDonald, studied
the report and 'decided that the conditions and benefits concerning
War Widows were satisfactorily taken care of.'[14] But two years later,
the government and the Repatriation Department (now known as
the Department of Veteran Affairs) were still considering Toose's
recommendations, with little action taking place.[15]

While the review was still in process, Gwen Forsyth was summoned
to a special meeting of the national executive. The state Guilds may have
been united under the banner of the War Widows' Guild of Australia,
but they were not always of one mind. The NSW Guild proposed a no
confidence motion in Janet Mayo as the national president because it
did not feel she was doing enough for that state. This was despite her

representation at the repatriation inquiry and her work in achieving government subsidies for nursing homes during the same period. Gwen was unable to attend because she had travelled to London to visit her son and attend the International Congress of Home Help Organisations as the sole Australian delegate.[16] She did, however, write a letter indicating that 'the WA Guild entirely supported the National President in what she had done on behalf of war widows.'[17] At the meeting on 7 April 1973, nobody seconded the no confidence motion; instead, a vote of confidence was passed, with the NSW delegates abstaining from the ballot.[18]

It is likely that some tension remained after the meeting, as Guild minutes record that 'there was dissension between some of the states' prior to the national conference in October. As a result, Gwen Forsyth and Win Greenshields travelled to Adelaide a day early to 'sort out some pre-conference matters.'[19] In the event, Janet Mayo retained her national presidency, and Gwen Forsyth and Victoria's Lois Hurse were appointed vice-presidents.[20]

One of the issues discussed at the conference was that of concessions on public transport. To date, Queensland and the ACT were the only states to receive subsidies on local transport, although Western Australia had won discounts for war widows who were over sixty and

Janet Mayo, far left, with Joan Hogben (Nat. Hon. Sec.), Senator Bishop (Minister for Repatriation), Billie Hughes (Qld) and other delegates at the 1973 national conference in Adelaide. Gwen Forsyth is ninth from the left.
(Courtesy of John Forsyth)

on a limited income in 1965. Delegates resolved to ask for interstate rail concessions that were not subject to a means test, and aimed to campaign for reduced fares at state level.[21] When the Liberal Party won the state election on 8 April 1974, the Guild gave the new premier, Charles Court, what it thought was enough time to 'settle in' before Gwen Forsyth wrote to him in early May. She congratulated him on his election win, and requested travel concessions for *all* war widows.[22] According to executive minutes, Premier Court replied that he was unable to grant the request.[23]

About the same time, the Department of Social Security wrote to war widows over sixty who also received a part old age pension, requesting the return of medical cards. This caused great confusion, with many war widows 'upset at the inference that they would be losing their medical entitlements.'[24] Gwen Forsyth, who was acting national president while Janet Mayo and Lois Hurse travelled to London, spent considerable time clarifying the issue with the Repatriation Commission, Social Security and the other state Guilds. She ascertained that the cards in question were the Pensioner Medical Service (PMS) entitlement cards issued by Social Security, and not the Repatriation entitlement cards war widows used when seeking medical treatment.[25] Thus, war widows were not in danger of losing their hard-won Repatriation medical benefits. However, the women could no longer use their travel concession passes, or receive a reduction on television and wireless licences, which were only available to those in possession of a PMS card.[26] One source of these anomalies was that eligibility boundaries remained the same while pensions rose beyond them. Thus the relatively small pension rises resulted in a loss of benefit rather than the intended increase.

Gwen Forsyth met with the newly appointed federal Minister for Repatriation and Compensation (previously the Repatriation Department),[27] Senator John Wheeldon, on 4 July 1974, to discuss the difficulties associated with the loss of benefits. She then wrote to Senator Reg Bishop, Postmaster General, and Bill Hayden, Minister for Social Security, arguing for the reinstatement of these concessions:

The widows affected are elderly and very often desperately lonely. Participation in community welfare is essential for their mental and physical well-being. The rise in pension does not keep pace with the rise in living costs and the whole situation becomes daily more difficult. To lose concessions on fares and TV licences is catastrophic.

We earnestly ask to consider our proposal to allow all war widows over 60 years of age to be issued with PMS cards.[28]

Bill Hayden responded to Gwen's letter, making it clear that the government would not shift its position, and pointing out that the transport concessions were in fact a state matter.[29] Refusing to concede defeat, the Guild wrote to the State Minister for Transport, Ray O'Connor, requesting his assistance in appealing for the re-issue of travel concessions.[30] The Guild also sent a written submission to the chairman of a state government inquiry into pension anomalies, and on 14 January 1975, Gwen Forsyth attended a hearing to elaborate on the submission. Gwen apparently presented a very strong case concerning travel passes for war widows on public transport[31] but the Guild was forced to wait more than a year for the state government to make its decision.[32]

Shortly after the 1976 AGM, the Guild finally received news that war widows were about to enjoy travel concessions, some for the first time. Discounts on fares for *all* war widows were granted on metropolitan transport in July 1976, and rebates on country transport became available from 1 November, including one free trip each year to anywhere in the state and half fares on all other country journeys. The Guild's hard work had once again paid dividends, with Western Australia the only state to be granted such comprehensive concessions.[33]

Marjorie Hassett had been directly affected by anomalies in transport concessions. Marj had met her husband Fred in Northam before the war and they married in 1939. Already a member of the Civilian Military Forces (CMF), Fred had enlisted in the AIF in September 1942, and joined the 2/23rd Battalion for service in Lae and Tarakan in New Guinea. Marj remained in Northam with their baby daughter. After the war, Marj and Fred stayed in the country for a time before moving to the Perth suburb of Maylands, where they raised their children. Following her husband's death many years later, Marj received a civilian widows' pension, which entitled her to reduced fares on public transport. When her husband's death was eventually deemed to be war related, she qualified for a higher pension, but lost her travel concessions until the Guild's successful campaign.[34]

Although Marj's husband, Fred, passed away in 1973, she did not join the War Widows' Guild until 1975, after attending a Legacy Camp. The friendships she made at the Guild secured her long-term involvement, but her first day was almost her last. 'We need somebody to help with the circulars. Will you come in?' her friend Ena Keeley asked her.

'What do you have to do?'

'Just write people's names and addresses on a piece of paper.'

Marj arrived at Anzac House and walked down the narrow stairs to the Guild rooms in the basement. Constructed in 1934, the building was now forty years old and in need of substantial maintenance. A 'tatty old place', it reminded Marj of a dungeon. Ena Keeley glanced up from her task and indicated a chair. 'Just sit over there, Marj, and when I'm not busy, I'll find you a seat.'

Marj followed Ena's instructions, until another member entered the room. 'That's my seat,' the woman grumbled. 'I've always sat there.'

'Don't worry,' Marj replied. 'I'm only sitting here until Ena tells me what to do.' Silently she told herself that if *this* was the War Widows' Guild, she would not be returning.

'I'm so sorry,' Ena apologised. 'I didn't expect her so soon.'

For the rest of the day, Marj helped address magazine wrappers, but afterwards, she told her friend, 'I'm not coming back.'

'Oh, yes, yes. Come back next time. I'll meet you.'[35]

Marj was not alone in her experience. Despite the firm friendships that could be made, newcomers quickly learned that there were women who preferred to sit in the same seats week after week.[36] At least one war widow was unhappy with these dynamics and complained about the 'unfriendly atmosphere of the Guild at a social afternoon.'[37] Gwen Forsyth responded to criticisms in the August 1975 issue of the *Guild News*:

> *Inevitably there must at times be differences of opinions or clashes of personalities, it would be dull without these and*

we all should be free to express our views. But the large
numbers attending our monthly meetings, our increasing
membership and the large number of appreciative letters
received ... give ample evidence of the overall harmony and
goodwill present ...[38]

A number of war widows responded in writing. Three of the responses are included here:

How sad was I to hear, or rather read, there is criticism
of the Guild, when there is much done for us all, and all
so freely and voluntarily given ... I have only been a War
Widow for nine years, but I have been so happy to come to
the meetings and I have made lovely friendships there.

I am sure that the number of members who do criticise
must be in the minority. We all realise the amount of work
entailed in running an organisation as large as the War
Widows' Guild and knowing that it is all done by voluntary
workers, many of whom are probably older than ourselves,
we should say a very big thank you to them all ...

I would like to thank you and your helpers, for the lovely
party you arranged for us last week. I enjoyed myself
immensely as did the ladies who were seated near me ...[39]

Despite her initial misgivings, Marj did return, and became good friends with the member who had spoken rudely to her.[40] Just months later, Marj was nominated for the Guild council at the 1976 AGM. The following week, when the council met to elect office bearers, she found herself co-opted onto the executive committee.

❀

The low-cost housing at Forsyth Gardens assisted members socially and financially, and the various meetings and outings helped the organisation fulfil its aim to prevent social isolation. However, this was limited to city members. The Guild did have some rural members, and welcomed them when they visited Perth, but no country branches existed in the state, despite the Guild's desire to see them established. A branch had formed in Kalgoorlie in 1949, but was no longer active. In 1967, the Guild had attempted to organise meetings in Albany, Northam, Narrogin and Bunbury. Gwen Forsyth visited a gathering in Busselton, but nothing eventuated.[41]

On the goldfields, the discovery of nickel in the late 1960s had caused the Poseidon mining company's shares to soar. However, when the boom collapsed in the early 1970s, many suffered financial losses, not only share investors but also those who ran local businesses. Across the nation, inflation was rising, export revenue was falling and farmers had suffered through several poor seasons. Local Kalgoorlie newspaper The Miner reported:

> we have come through the most prosperous and
> transforming years of our history … yet the Australian
> mood also had changed. We go into 1973 readier to
> count for anxieties than our blessings … Inflation lives
> in every pocket.[42]

In the midst of the changing economic climate, long-time Kalgoorlie resident Alma Japp enquired about the possibility of gathering a group of war widows on the goldfields.[43] Alma's husband Gilbert had served with the 2/4th Machine Gunners and, unlike many others, survived his time as a prisoner of war. Alma and Gilbert met after the war, while both were working at The Duke, a local Kalgoorlie hotel. They married in 1946 and had one daughter Mary Ann.[44] Alma had only recently buried her husband on 17 August 1972 and received automatic war widow status in acknowledgement of her husband's horrendous experiences as a POW.

It is not known how many women initially met in Alma's Kalgoorlie home each month, but by 1976 the branch included sixteen members.[45] In her daughter's eyes, Alma was a nurturing, gracious person who enjoyed a good joke.[46] Mary Ann remembers her mother sitting on the verandah or lawn on hot summer nights with a group of war widows who listened to each other's complaints and offered emotional support.

One of those women was Laura Anderson, who has similar memories of those gatherings. Laura had been widowed twice, losing both men to war-related causes, and she appreciated the companionship and understanding provided by the small group.[47]

Back in Perth, the 1970s were shaping up to be a decade of demolition and development. In contrast to Fremantle, where many historic buildings were being preserved, the inner city skyline had changed dramatically. The Bank of NSW building had been demolished in 1971, and the AMP building, on the corner of St Georges Terrace and William Street, suffered an identical fate the following year. On the same intersection, David Jones, the Commonwealth Bank and Elder Smith Goldsborough Mort were also earmarked for destruction. In the case of the Palace Hotel, major rebuilding had taken place, leaving only its original façade remaining.[48] The Esplanade Hotel had been demolished in November 1972, even though public protests had saved its verandahs a decade earlier.[49] Now the future of Anzac House was in doubt.

As Marj Hassett had observed on her first visit to the Guild rooms, Anzac House needed considerable maintenance. The Anzac House and Club board of management discussed a number of options, including renovating or moving to other premises. Initially, due to 'promising city expansion', the board decided to wait and see whether Anzac Club patronage increased once nearby buildings were completed.[50] Architects were engaged to discuss possible improvements, but in May 1976, the future of Anzac House was again in doubt and by the end of June, the state government had convinced the RSL to 'surrender its property to the crown.'[51] It was to be demolished to make way for the new Law Courts, with plans including a remodelled, but smaller, Anzac House on the same site.[52] In the meantime, the RSL and the War Widows' Guild needed to relocate temporarily. The RSL promised to provide the Guild with premises somewhere in the city, with the understanding that the war widows would have a home in the new headquarters.[53]

With no firm date for vacating Anzac House, the Guild celebrated an early thirtieth birthday in September 1976 with a final dinner in the ballroom.[54] Then, in February 1977, the RSL found rooms at 4 Sherwood Court[55] which, until recently, had been occupied by the Perth Club, a private men's club.[56] The building, incorporating the upmarket Lawson Flats, had been built in 1937, the same year Riverside Drive had been constructed,[57] and was situated across the road from the Esplanade Kiosk, the Guild's home from 1949 to 1963.

The Guild's relocation was not as straightforward as anticipated. On Sunday 20 February, several weeks prior to the scheduled move, a severe thunderstorm hit Perth causing damage to a number of suburbs, including Mount Lawley where Forsyth Gardens was located. Its residents were:

> *startled and alarmed when the storm of wind, hail and torrential rain hit … Many tiles were dislodged and blown off roofs of the flats and a number of shrubs and ornamental trees were damaged. The middle of Sunday afternoon is not an easy time to arrange roof repairs but before dark, all had been made safe and weatherproof.*[58]

The following morning, the handcrafts group arrived at Anzac House to discover the floor of its meeting room awash in three inches of water. A recently donated carpet was afloat. Within a day or two, the odour from the now mouldy carpet was 'horrible', and by the end of the week it had become 'unendurable'.[59]

The RSL told the Guild that, provided the women did not mind being by themselves for a short time, they were welcome to move earlier than planned. The removalists were booked for Thursday 3 March and a team of volunteers dutifully arrived at Anzac House on the agreed morning. They waited. And waited. Upon phoning to inquire about the hold up, the women were informed, 'Oh, they went on Wednesday and no one was there.'[60]

The Guild eventually convinced the company that the booking was indeed for Thursday, and was assured that a truck would be sent at once. The women waited for several more hours before the removalists arrived at Anzac House looking for 'Mrs Forsyth of the Women's Service Guild who wanted carriers on the eighth floor.' As the Guild had been located in the building's basement for all fourteen years of its tenancy, such an error seemed absurd. Gradually, the Guild's furniture, refrigerator, crockery and other goods were heaved up to street level and into the truck. Sherwood Court had thirty steps from street level up to the new Guild rooms, and no lift, so the removalists had their work cut out for them. Finally, at about 5 pm, everything was ensconced within the new rooms.[61]

Despite the frustrations of relocating, the Guild initially felt comfortable in the new office. Although small, it was bright, airy and a considerable improvement on the Anzac House basement, which had become 'horribly run down and shabby'.[62] The handcraft group, unable to meet since the storm, settled in well until the RSL arrived and used the room for storage. However, the women continued to knit, crochet, macramé, sew flowers and, most importantly, make friends. Marj Hassett remembers the handcraft group with affection. In contrast to her first Guild meeting, several women, including Pearl

Dorothy Spiers' granddaughters present Janet Mayo with flowers at the Handcrafts Exhibition in October 1975.
(Courtesy of John Forsyth)

Inaugural state president Marjorie Le Souef (left) shows her ongoing
support by attending the 1975 Handcrafts Exhibition, with national president
Janet Mayo (centre) and state president Gwen Forsyth (right).
(Courtesy of John Forsyth)

Handcraft party 1978. L–R: Marj Hassett, Phil Goldsmith,
Olive Palmer, Beattie Hammond and Pearl Bowers.
(Courtesy of Marj Hassett)

1975 national conference. L–R: Billie Hughes (Qld),
Janet Mayo (national president), Gwen Forsyth (WA).
(Courtesy of John Forsyth)

Bowers, Margaret Dower and Millicent Speake, welcomed her warmly at the craft sessions.[63]

On 21 March 1977, 140 members gathered for a meeting in the large room near the Guild office, which had previously been the Perth Club's billiard room.[64] In May, approximately one hundred people attended the AGM, including national president Janet Mayo and national secretary Joan Hogben.[65] The meeting marked Gwen Forsyth's twentieth year as state president and she took the opportunity to highlight what she believed to be the Guild's primary role:

> *I feel that the main purpose and functions of the Guild is just to BE here, to be a place where war widows can bring problems ... where loneliness or difficulties, joys or sorrows can be discussed and shared without embarrassment and ... we are among friends. We share worries about our children and grandchildren, we discuss pensions and allowances, taxation and the cost of living, we help one another with trust and confidence ... As the years roll by we all get more wrinkles and grey hairs but we can still help one another and although sometimes we grumble we really enjoy it all, at least most of the time.*[66]

This was to be Janet Mayo's final visit to Perth as national president. At the national conference in October, she decided against renomination, although she remained the state president of South Australia. Joan Hogben and Joyce Mosbey, also from South Australia, resigned from their positions on the national executive. Conference delegates elected Gwen Forsyth to be their new national president, only the third in the organisation's history. Fellow West Australians Gloria MacDonald and Mickey Parker accepted the roles of national secretary and treasurer respectively, and Billie Hughes from Queensland became vice-president.[67]

In accepting the position, Gwen paid tribute to the 'two such gifted and capable women' who had led the War Widows' Guild before her. She promised that 'the West Australian team would do their best to follow the example that had been set.'[68] Now, along with issues affecting

Western Australia, Gwen, Gloria and Mickey were directly involved in those relevant to the War Widows' Guild as a national body.

Gwen devoted many hours to the organisation, both locally and federally.[69] And while she was often the public face, and her signature adorned correspondence to government departments and other organisations, a committed band of helpers worked behind the scenes. Gwen was especially indebted to the support and loyalty of Gloria MacDonald, who apparently coped 'willingly and cheerfully' with the president's 'odd requests and scribbled letters', as well as the additional typing, photostatting and filing associated with her role as national secretary.[70]

Hazel Carrick shared the state vice-presidency with Gloria, ran the office each Friday, coordinated the 'office girls', dealt with mail and enquiries, and attended meetings. Mrs Robertson attended the office regularly on Tuesdays, offered additional assistance on meeting days and organised the *Guild News* with the help of Mrs Sashe after Mrs Lasky stepped down. Mickey Parker, now both state and national treasurer, was an efficient bookkeeper who worked with a minimum of fuss.[71] Many others contributed too: office assistants, the group who wrapped and labelled the *Guild News*, and others who served morning tea, washed dishes, set up for meetings, arranged outings and organised fetes and exhibitions.[72]

※

The Guild continued to take 'pride in remembering the fallen soldiers' and always sent an office bearer to represent the organisation at any memorial service to which it was invited. These included the Anzac Day dawn service, remembrance ceremonies at the War Veterans' Home, and those organised by the Air Force Association. On 11 November 1977, Gwen Forsyth and Mickey Parker attended the Remembrance Day Service at the Kings Park War Memorial, notable for the presence of Prince Charles, on the final leg of his tour as patron of the Queen's Australian Silver Jubilee Appeal.[73] The following year, Gwen visited Canberra, where she laid a wreath at the National War Memorial on Anzac Day in her capacity as national president.[74] The honour was not entirely new for her, having laid a wreath there in 1974, when she had been acting national president in Janet Mayo's absence. On that occasion, Gwen had written of the experience:

> *It was a great privilege and pleasure for me to represent the War Widows of Australia at the wreath laying ceremony in Canberra. It was a most impressive and beautiful ceremony with its deep and special meaning for all widows.*[75]

Following the 1970 Anzac Day ceremony and the 'hospitality of the Canberra Guild', Gwen travelled to Brisbane, Sydney and Adelaide to visit members in those states, before arriving home for WA's AGM.[77]

Gwen received public acknowledgement for her long-standing dedication when she was named in the 1979 Queen's New Year's honours list. Accompanied by her son and daughter-in-law, Gwen attended the investiture in the Government House Ballroom on 15 March, where Prince Charles presented her with an OBE.[78] In a letter to a fellow war widow, Gwen wrote, 'So many people do so much for the Guild that I feel very humble about this award – I wish I could share it around in some way.'[79]

The WA Guild was caught up in the numerous official events that were planned to mark the 150th anniversary of white settlement in the state. Celebrations kicked off on New Year's Eve when 60,000 people crowded on to the Esplanade for a concert. Sir Charles Court gave a rousing speech about coming to an 'ancient land and making it new again' only to be rebuked by Aboriginal leader Ken Colbung, who reminded listeners that the history of this 'ancient land' stretched back much further than the arrival of Sir James Stirling. He then handed the state governor, Sir Wallace Kyle, an eviction notice for the white invaders.[80]

In March, there was a four day re-enactment of Captain James Stirling's 1827 exploration trip up the Swan River. This included a landing near the Barrack Street jetties on 10 March, where 'Captain Stirling' was greeted by Lord Mayor Chaney and presented to Prince Charles. The official party walked up Barrack Street, past the Esplanade

Gwen Forsyth (centre) visits Whitby, Guild accommodation in Dee Why, NSW. Whitby was opened in 1967. This visit was possibly during Gwen's time as national president. (Courtesy of John Forsyth)

Gwen Forsyth receives her OBE from HRH Prince Charles at Government House. (Courtesy of John Forsyth)

Kiosk,[81] which was now a nightclub,[82] and up to the Town Hall. Prince Charles then unveiled a statue of Sir James Stirling, on the same site where Mrs Dance had felled a tree to symbolise the foundation of Perth in 1829.[83]

Meanwhile, the Guild paused to reflect on its own story. The organisation had grown in number and influence since 29 November 1946, when two hundred women gathered together in the midst of uncertainty. With little money and no headquarters, the women had pitched together, lending what they could in the form of free-of-interest loans to secure the Esplanade Kiosk. They made jams and pickles for jumble stores, collected bottle tops and even rags to raise money for Vasey House.[84] And after many years of dreaming, planning and persevering, the Guild had seen the fruition of its early dream of affordable housing, and subsidised nursing care for those unable to live independently. About eighty women were now housed in hostel, frail-aged or unit care.[85]

State membership had grown to around 1300 and now, after three decades of struggling, the Guild's financial position was secure, largely due to Ellen Peck's generous bequest. But there were other contributions too, from donations, raffles, the Anzac Day Trust, monthly stalls organised by Mrs Timmel, and the annual sale of work, affectionately known as 'Mrs Greenshields' baby'. Win Greenshields obtained materials, inspired helpers and oversaw the organisation of the event. Flat rental at Forsyth Gardens also provided an income, although this brought with it the expenses of depreciation, maintenance, insurance and gardening. None of it would have been possible if not for the ongoing efforts of the members themselves, who sewed, cooked, sold raffle tickets and worked in honorary capacities.[86]

At the AGM on 21 May 1979, Gwen commented:

After 33 years we are still active and alert and it is a fact that all war widows throughout Australia have benefited through the efforts of the Guild in every state ... We have a high standing in the community and certainly live up to our stated aim 'To watch over and protect the interests of war widows and their children.'[87]

Whether it was the state's focus on its past, or simply that it had been on Gwen's mind for some time, she expressed the need for a War Widows' Guild history at the next national conference, held in Western Australia for the first time in October. The notion of a written history had first been raised at the 1969 conference,[88] then again by Gwen Forsyth in 1973 after she and two other members spent several weekends trawling through archived minutes to locate key dates and events.[89] Gwen drafted the story of the first ten years of the Guild in Western Australia, which she took to the national conference in October 1975. By then the ACT and Tasmanian branches had also compiled local histories. Now, in 1979, delegates passed a resolution that all states should collect photographs, names and dates from minutes and any other relevant information, so that a comprehensive national history could be compiled.[90]

The following April, Gwen visited her son Alan, who worked in Woomera, before travelling to the Guild branches in Sydney and Brisbane. She visited Canberra, where she once again laid a wreath on Anzac Day, and then stopped over in Adelaide for two days. There, she met with some of the 'old girls' to reminisce about the past and discuss items of interest for the proposed history.[91] Gwen stressed that it was vitally important that this be written before founding members became too elderly to assist.[92] Already the Guild in Western Australia had lost many of them, and Gwen thought it would be 'a great pity if those early hard days and those wonderful members were forgotten.'[93]

Full of memories, Gwen returned to Perth only to be met with disappointing news. The RSL informed her that although the new Anzac House was nearing completion, there was insufficient space to accommodate the Guild, despite previous promises. 'We were dismayed and shocked,' Gwen recalled. 'A worrying period followed while we consulted innumerable estate agents and inspected various city offices.'[94] The Guild eventually secured spacious rooms at Park Towers (also referred to as the Kings Hotel) in Hay Street. Thus, on 27 August 1980, the women were on the move again.[95]

The relocation coincided with an increased membership, which the Guild attributed to the cooperation of the state office of the Department of Veterans' Affairs, who had sent a printed card to all war widows inviting them to join the Guild.[96] The effort resulted in more than two hundred women becoming members for the first time.[97] There are several possible reasons as to why they had not joined previously. Some had never heard of the War Widows' Guild,[98] the card sent out to new widows presumably going unnoticed amongst a deluge of other paperwork. For others, their still-raw grief meant that joining was too difficult; they were not yet ready to reach out in that way.[99] For some women, war widow status was not granted immediately;[100] and some did not know they qualified.[101] Betty Walker, by contrast, joined almost immediately she was widowed.[102]

While many of the foundation members had been widowed after being married only a short time, Betty Walker had experienced a long marriage before her husband died of war related causes. While she wrote to 'dozens of boys' from all over Australia, she had met local boy Allen Walker through a mutual friend. Even before being introduced, she often spotted him, dressed in a white mac and waiting at the bridge for his parlour car[103] as her bus passed by on her way to work in Fremantle. Employed by a florist, Betty's duties included delivering Kentia palms to the hospital ships upon their arrival in Fremantle. One evening, as Betty and her friend Jean waited for a tram to take them home from a dance, a car pulled up and someone called out, 'Want a lift?'

'Cheeky buggers, think they can pick us up just like that,' said Jean.

The car drove away, but soon returned. This time a voice said, 'Bett, it's Jack, do you want a lift home or not?' It was her brother's mate, who lived at the top of her street.

'Yes please, Jack,' she replied this time. As the girls slid into the back seat, Betty recognised the boy sitting next to her. 'Oh, the boy in the white mac,' she said.

The meeting was the start of a twelve-month courtship, a twelve-month engagement and a wedding on 9 January 1942. Shortly after, Allen was deployed to New Guinea and served almost four years. On his return to Australia in December 1945, doctors declared him totally and permanently incapacitated (TPI). Even so, Allen told Betty, 'Wives don't work. If I can't keep you, I wouldn't have married you.' So Betty resigned from her job. She reflects matter-of-factly, 'In those days … you got married and got a house and stayed home.' Their son Robert was born in 1948, followed by a daughter Helen in 1950.[104]

Later in life, Betty and Allen travelled across Europe. Even then he was unwell, the trip only possible because they took medical supplies with them and located a hospital every Wednesday to have an injection administered. But while in Madrid, Allen said, 'Bett, get me back to England. I don't feel well at all.' So, with minimal delay they returned to the UK, staying with an English cousin for a week while he recuperated.

Upon arriving home in Perth, Allen was optimistic, declaring, 'We're saving up and going away again.' But it was not to be. He was admitted to hospital at the end of June and passed away on 10 July 1978, after thirty-six years of marriage. Betty became a Guild member two months later, on 19 September, upon the insistence of her mother-in-law: 'I'm a war widow, and you're going to be one. I'm taking you to War Widows, you're going to join.'[105]

❀

Marj Hassett was as glad to be rid of Sherwood Court as she had been to leave the rundown Anzac House. At Sherwood Court, Marj and her friend Olive Palmer typically arrived at 7.30 am each Monday morning to clean up the meeting room they shared with the RSL, which was often filthy with cigarette butts and spilled beer from the ex-servicemen's weekend activities. One of the tea ladies would have to enter the men's rest room in order to fill the urn and, after the meeting, flush the teapot dregs down the toilets. The new rooms at Park Towers were air-conditioned, quieter and more private, and included comfortable areas for office work, handcrafts and general meetings. Hotel elevators meant that many members who had been unable to cope with the stairs at Sherwood Court could now attend meetings.[106]

Satisfied with their headquarters at Park Towers, the Guild chose it for the venue of the 1981 national conference, beginning on Wednesday 16 September.[107] With Gwen Forsyth, Gloria MacDonald and Mickey Parker all part of the national executive, Hazel Carrick and Ena Keeley attended as official delegates and seven other members attended as observers.[108] Recently appointed governor, Sir Richard Trowbridge, opened the conference. His wife, and current

Guild patron, Lady Anne, also attended, as did Marjorie and Leslie Le Souef.[109] Although she had been the inaugural state president, when Marjorie remarried in 1947, the War Widows' Guild constitution required her to forgo her membership. However, she had never lost interest in its work, and had exchanged correspondence with Gwen Forsyth[110] over the years and had attended the 1979 conference as a visitor.[111]

At this 1981 conference, Gwen Forsyth, Gloria MacDonald and Mickey Parker stepped down from their roles on the national executive. Queensland president and national vice-president Billie Hughes was elected unopposed as president of the War Widows' Guild of Australia. Gwen Forsyth told the delegates that she had enjoyed the past four years, and considered it a privilege, before congratulating Billie Hughes on her appointment.[112]

Billie (born Ellen Healy) was not yet married to Major Les Hughes when he left Australia with the 6th Division in May 1940. He contracted malaria in Ceylon after Japan entered the war and Australian troops were recalled from the Middle East. Upon his return home, Billie and Les married and moved from Queensland to Victoria, where he became Chief Instructor of Artillery in Puckapunyal. When Les retired in 1944 they returned to Brisbane. However, shortly after the move, the malaria returned, and he died on 9 October 1944. Billie was herself in hospital at the time, following the birth of their son Michael a fortnight earlier. Thus, in addition to caring for a newborn, she was suddenly immersed in the sorrow and loneliness of widowhood. She attributed her ability to cope to the help of her faith, friends and the 'sisterhood of the Guild.'[113] Billie was a foundation member in Queensland, and became state president in May 1954.[114] For many years, she combined motherhood, earning an income (including managing one of Queensland's first motels, the Story Bridge Motor Inn in Brisbane) and volunteering at the Guild. She finally retired from paid work in January 1980, allowing her the freedom to accept the role of national president.[115]

Following the conference, the national executive wrote to the Department of Veterans' Affairs regarding an increase to the basic pension rate, and funeral benefits in cases where funeral cost caused financial stress to a serviceman's widow. The submissions were largely unsuccessful, with 'economic stress' cited as the primary reason. Gwen Forsyth responded to this news by writing, 'Very little seems to have been achieved.'[116] However, one matter was resolved. Some war widows had experienced difficulty when applying for passports as they could not produce a death certificate for their husband, because he had died overseas, or because he had no known grave. The passport authorities finally agreed to accept a statutory declaration, bringing relief to this group of women.[117]

❀

Gwen's frustration at achieving so little was not altogether justified for the widows had social and other needs that the Guild did meet. Gwen Forsyth regularly received boxes of soft furnishing offcuts, which she passed on to the handcrafts group. Although it was companionship that members such as Marj Hassett most appreciated, Gwen was adamant that the group's primary role was to make crafts. 'You must speak to those ladies,' she once told Olive Palmer and Marj Hassett. 'This is a handcraft session; they're not to … just sit and talk.'[118] Regardless of how much talking transpired, the women created many items including pillowslips, children's clothes, rugs, aprons, coat hangers and cushions. The year's work culminated in an annual stall, with proceeds contributing to the Guild finances.[119] Additionally they provided gifts for war widows in Hollywood Hospital and Kimberley Nursing Home, and together with the wider Guild, they donated hundreds of handcrafted toys and baby clothes to organisations such as St Vincent de Paul, the Civil Rehabilitation Council and Perth Emergency Housekeeping Service during a Christmas appeal.[120] By 1982, the handcrafts group had grown to sixty-four, a measure of the 'friendship and happy working conditions' amongst the women.[121]

Despite Gwen's call for greater productivity among the handcrafts group, and the time and energy devoted to campaigning for greater benefits, gathering together was in fact central to the Guild's aim of preventing social isolation among its members. During the early 1980s, the Guild held regular concert and luncheon parties at Park Towers, monthly bingo sessions and a monthly general meeting, where between eighty and ninety members listened to a guest speaker. Picnics were popular and included trips to Whitby Falls, the Swan River, Serpentine Dam, Mundaring Weir and Araluen. In 1982, a keep fit class was added into the mix. The best attended function was the Christmas Party, attracting up to two hundred members in addition to representatives from associated

Top: Handcraft party 1981. Olive Palmer presents Gwen Forsyth with the Guild motto. Bottom: The handcrafts group made a range of articles, which culminated in an annual stall.
(Both images courtesy of Marj Hassett)

organisations.[122] Also alleviating loneliness was the continuing hospital visits. Elsie Wright had coordinated a team of women to visit war widows in Hollywood Repatriation Hospital until the end of 1979, when Nell Yeoman took on the responsibility. Patients and their relatives were grateful for the visits and assistance, which included phone calls made on behalf of those confined to bed. Volunteers also visited the twenty-one war widows residing at Kimberley Nursing Home once a month and the women looked forward to seeing them.[123]

❀

According to Gloria MacDonald, Gwen Forsyth and national president Billie Hughes became 'true and close friends, with affectionate rapport' during their lengthy involvement with the War Widows' Guild at a national level.[124] Gwen welcomed Billie to Perth shortly after Anzac Day 1983, neither aware it would be the last time they saw one another.[125] Several weeks later, on 16 May, Gwen chaired the state AGM. As the meeting drew to a conclusion, Gloria addressed the gathering, announcing that this year marked the twenty-fifth anniversary of Gwen Forsyth's presidency. Gloria stated that 'a wise and competent leader was essential for the growth and success of an organisation and such a person was the President.'[126] Gwen departed the gathering smiling and holding a bouquet of flowers, but as she opened her car door, she collapsed. She never recovered, and passed away aged seventy-eight.[127]

Gwen's death stunned members of the War Widows' Guild nationwide. Many past and present office bearers had known and respected her since the early days, and appreciated her gracious and friendly presence.[128] She had been involved in the Guild for three and a half decades, and seen many changes. When she had attended the initial meeting in 1946, she had been a young woman, forced by the war to become both mother and father to two toddlers. Whether by choice or chance, Gwen never remarried, although her son Alan had encouraged her to do so. Instead she had poured her energies into her children, her church and the Guild, where she found comfort and fulfilment.[129]

In the Guild rooms at 'The Kings' on the occasion of national
president Billie Hughes's visit to Western Australia, April 1983.
L–R: Gloria MacDonald, Gwen Forsyth, Billie Hughes, Mickey Parker.
(Guild archives, WA Branch)

In the foyer of 'The Kings' during Billie Hughes's 1983 visit to Perth.
L–R: Mickey Parker, Gwen Forsyth, Billie Hughes, Hazel Carrick,
Gloria MacDonald.
(Courtesy of John Forsyth)

After visiting South Australia in 1980 to discuss a possible history
of the War Widows' Guild of Australia, Gwen had returned home
reflecting on what it meant to belong to such an organisation. She
concluded:

> *War Widows do not meet together to weep or be sad, to complain or to grumble, that has never been our way, but we have all lost much which made life dear to us and we need one another and support from time to time to fill in, in some small way, the gap left by the loss of our husbands … To me it has meant a great deal. It has been a way of life, a feeling that maybe a helping hand has helped someone through a sticky patch in life. The friendships I have made have meant much to me and the goodwill and fellowship of so many completely voluntary workers over the years has, I know, been an example and inspiration to many.*[130]

In the forty years she had been a war widow, Gwen had herself been an example and an inspiration to others; now it was time for someone else to ensure the Guild continued to fulfil its aims and support those for whom the organisation existed.

CHAPTER 8
CHANGING OF THE GUARD

Forty-six members attended a sombre council meeting on 23 May 1983. Gloria MacDonald opened the meeting and spoke of the loss of their dedicated president. She expressed her hope that members would 'continue to carry on the good work' because they 'had always been such a happy and energetic group ready to give a willing and helpful hand on all occasions'. She then called for a minute's silence.[1]

Mickey Parker nominated Gloria to be the new state president. Win Greenshields seconded the motion and the council elected Gloria unanimously. She 'very reluctantly accepted the role'.[2] Her son, Alex, had said: 'If you aren't sure, don't do it by yourself. Just call a committee meeting, and get everybody else's opinion.'[3] His encouragement reassured her. 'Yes,' she said. 'I'll do that.'[4]

Gloria and Gwen had been 'good mates. They worked together, and played together … so she lost a good friend. Took it hard.'[5] The two may have been particularly close but Gwen was not the only long-time member that the Guild had lost in recent years. Foundation member Dorothy Spiers had died suddenly on 3 July 1978.[6] She had acted as treasurer for many years and lived at Forsyth Gardens since 1970, where her 'help with the constant troubles and tribulations that occurred was invaluable' and her 'kindness and care for anyone in trouble or distress was outstanding.'[7] Early the following year, on 30 January 1979, the Guild lost another foundation member, Jean Ferguson. An active member, Jean had always been ready with invaluable advice, particularly regarding the Guild's move to the Esplanade Kiosk and furnishing Vasey House. She had also cared for many war widows while matron of Hollywood Hospital. The Guild mourned her death, too, but remembered her 'cheerfulness and courage' through a long battle with blindness and multiple sclerosis.[8]

There were not only farewells, but welcomes, too. Pearl Thomson joined the Guild just prior to the 1985 Christmas party. During the Second World War, she had trained as a signaller, and met her husband Bill through his sister, with whom she worked at the Pearce RAAF base. Her future mother-in-law had told her, 'I'd love to have you for a daughter-in-law,' and proceeded to introduce Pearl to each of her three sons as they arrived home from war. Pearl fell in love with Bill, the last son to return, six months after the war ended, and they married in 1946.[9]

For Pearl, the Guild was a 'saviour' after her husband's death. Meeting other war widows and 'being involved in something' helped her cope with her loss. She enjoyed attending the 'relaxed and friendly atmosphere' of the handcrafts group. 'You'd look forward to each week, of seeing the girls, and hearing what went on. I made a lot of friends,' Pearl reflected in 2008. 'We always looked forward to each Monday, going and seeing everybody.'[10] Pearl did not consider herself particularly gifted at sewing or knitting, but felt there was always someone to assist her.

One of those women would have been Doreen Taylor, whose love affair with sewing had begun as a child. By the age of eighteen she owned a dressmaking business in Oxford Street, Leederville. At nineteen, she married and moved to the country, but when her husband was shipped off to war, she and her toddler daughter returned to live next door to her parents. She was busy dressmaking right through the Second World War and the early post-war years. Although material was rationed, Doreen sourced cottons on the black market, and had her sewing machine serviced for the cost of a home-baked morning tea.[11]

Doreen had heard about the War Widows' Guild through her friend and long-time member Nancy Coghlan, but felt daunted at the prospect of joining a group of strangers. It took three attempts before she finally stepped into the room of war widows chatting and enjoying their morning cuppa. Her nervousness dissipated after she recognised several women she had known in her younger days and she soon settled into what she describes as her 'lovely life in the War Widows' Guild'. At first, attending meetings served simply to encourage Doreen out of the house, but over the years, she became proud of belonging to the organisation. She enjoyed the camaraderie that came with helping in the kitchen, but she was most in her element creating handcrafts. She made teddy bears, quilts and other items for the weekly raffle. She recalls that while catching the bus to one meeting, a fellow passenger enquired where they could purchase a bear like the one she carried. She replied, 'You have to join War Widows to get a raffle ticket and then you can have one.'[12]

New recruits like Pearl and Doreen lifted the attendance of the crafts group to some seventy members in June 1987. By this time, Marj Hassett had replaced Olive Palmer, who had completed ten years as coordinator.[13] She in turn was succeeded by Marie Brooker who became coordinator in 1989.[14]

Top: Christmas gifts made by Doreen Taylor.
Bottom: Handcraft party, November 1988.
(Both photos courtesy of Marj Hassett)

❀

September was supposedly the beginning of spring, and sunny daffodils brightened shop windows, but the cold winds and rain lingered.[15] Gloria MacDonald and Ena Keeley headed to Brisbane for the 1986 national conference, where, for the most part, they managed to escape the wintry weather of the west.[16] Billie Hughes resigned from the national presidency and Lucille Wallis from the ACT was elected as her replacement; Gloria MacDonald became one of three vice-presidents. At the previous conference, shortly after Gwen Forsyth's death, the idea of a national history had again been raised, resulting in writer Mavis Thorpe Clark being commissioned for the task. Unfortunately nobody could find the material Gwen had collated prior to her death, and it needed re-gathering from scratch.[17] But finally, on the opening day of this conference, Governor-General Sir Ninian Stephen launched *No Mean Destiny: The Story of the War Widows' Guild of Australia 1945–85*. The title came from the original letter Jessie Vasey had written to war widows in 1945: 'Yet it is no mean destiny to be called upon to go on for a man who has laid down his life.'[18] Across the country, newspapers published articles about *No Mean Destiny* and the War Widows' Guild, once again throwing Jessie Vasey's legacy into the spotlight.

After the celebration of the book launch, it was down to serious business. For some time, there had been discussion as to whether 'defence widows' should be permitted Guild membership.[19] The issue had first been raised more than a decade earlier in 1976 by the NSW Guild.[20] At the time, the consensus within the WA Guild was that defence widows should not be granted membership as they were not classified as war widows.[21] According to the Toose Report, a defence widow was 'a widow of a veteran whose death has been accepted as related to his defence service,'[22] whereas a war widow was:

> *a widow of a veteran whose death has been accepted as related to his service in the 1914–1918 War, the 1939–45 War, the Korean/Malaya operations, the Far East Strategic Reserve or special service in South East Asia ...*[23]

However, it came to light that, prior to August 1974, both had been termed war widows by the Repatriation Department. The change in terminology had followed the expansion of repatriation compensation to include members of the Defence Force on peacekeeping service after 7 December 1972. In February 1976, NSW Guild secretary Una Boyce had discovered that the Repatriation Department had paid full war widows' pensions to defence widows for the past four years, and so proposed that the Guild's constitution be changed to include those who qualified under the Repatriation Act. The South Australian Guild 'took it for granted that Defence Widows were eligible for membership,'[24] and executive minutes of the WA Guild dated 1 November 1976 noted that defence widows were to be accepted. However, a month later the minutes recorded:

> *Defence widows being admitted to membership of the*
> *War Widows' Guild throughout Australia was discussed.*
> *Although this is being done at present the NSW branch has*
> *raised the question of whether this can be done without*
> *altering the National Constitution.*[25]

The issue was still under discussion at the national conference in October 1977, where a motion to include them was defeated. Unsatisfied with this decision, the NSW Guild altered its constitution to enable defence widows to join. The first of these joined in September 1978 to become associate members without voting powers.[26] The NSW Guild raised the issue again at the 1979 conference in Perth, but again the motion was defeated[27] and no further progress was made until 1986, when the national Guild finally voted to include defence widows as associate members. The WA Guild accepted the decision,[28] although it was not prepared to change the organisation's name to reflect the change.[29]

As for de facto wives, the state Guild remained resistant to change, with a unanimous decision that they should not be permitted membership, even though they too received full benefits from the Department of Veterans' Affairs.[30] And when a woman wished to remain a member after remarrying, this was still deemed unacceptable,[31] despite the fact that since 1985 war widows had been entitled to retain their pension if they remarried after 28 May 1984, on the basis that the benefits received were compensation and not welfare. However, that attitude would change in future years, and today, both de facto wives and remarried war widows are eligible for membership.

These generally conservative views did not prevent the Guild from actively, and even forcefully, seeking representation on committees that discussed issues relevant to war widows. From the early days, Jessie Vasey had emphatically believed that 'help for widows could only come from among themselves' and resented men making decisions on their behalf.[32] As the senate discussed the *Veterans' Entitlements Act 1986* (VEA), the Minister for Veterans' Affairs, Senator Gietzelt, established a monitoring committee to scrutinise whether the government's intentions for the VEA worked in practice.[33] When the War Widows' Guild realised that there were no women on the committee, national president Lucille Wallis wrote to the senator to protest. He replied that 'any more members would make the committee too unwieldy.' The WA Guild minutes record the following comment in response:

> *Although the Govt supports the principle of equal status for women, in this instance we appear to be back to the conditions when the Guild founder Mrs Vasey had to fight hard to be heard. It should be easier now, but we still hear that others, meaning the men, will look after us.*[34]

❀

During the early months of 1987, Western Australia was swept up in the excitement of the America's Cup. Four years earlier, Alan Bond and his team had succeeded where many others had failed. Now, for the first time in the race's history, it was to be held outside the United States, in the port city of Fremantle. Neither the event nor the Americans winning back the cup is mentioned in Guild minutes, but Princess Anne's corresponding visit is, with Gloria MacDonald representing the war widows at a garden party held in the grounds of Government House in the princess's honour.[35]

About this time, Iris Rowtcliff, who had joined the Guild in 1983, became more actively involved. Iris had grown up on the Atherton

Tablelands in Queensland, and met Frederick James (Jim) Rowtcliff when he was evacuated out of New Guinea. They married in Cairns on 22 January 1944, before Jim was repatriated by hospital train to the 110th Military Hospital (later Hollywood Repatriation Hospital) in his home town of Perth. Wartime regulations required civilians to obtain a permit to travel south of Brisbane, and so Iris spent six weeks in the Queensland capital before she could journey across the country and embark on married life. She was a shy young woman and her mother had worried about her travelling alone, but Iris survived the train trip west. Jim met her at the station before returning to hospital to recuperate for another month while Iris stayed with her mother-in-law. Once he was discharged, Iris and Jim moved to the inner-city suburb of Mount Lawley.[36] Then, after twenty-eight years of marriage, Iris found herself alone again when Jim died on 7 February 1972 at the age of only fifty-eight. She contemplated returning to Queensland once her children married and started their own families, but the move never happened.

Iris had her application for a war widow's pension rejected twice despite the fact that Jim went to war a fit man, and spent much of his early return years in hospital. The reason, Iris believes, was that while working away from home as a wool classer, Jim missed one appointment to have his pension reassessed, and his benefits were promptly cancelled. It was only after a Legacy meeting that Iris discovered she might after all be entitled to a pension.

'Are you a war widow?' one of the Legacy members asked her.

'No.'

'Didn't your husband go away?'

'2/11th,' Iris replied. 'Served in New Guinea *and* the Middle East.'

'You should qualify. Get a form and fill it in.'

'No way. They're not going to say no to me again.'

Months later, Iris still had not reapplied for the war widows' pension. Finally Vi Smiles told her, 'Get up and get a form; we're going to help you fill it in.' After listening to Iris's story, the Legacy volunteer (known as a legatee) Joe Burton told her, 'You'll have no problems. You'll have it in six weeks.' True to his word, Iris soon received a war widow's pension, more than ten years after her husband's death.

Now, as Iris crossed the park to catch the ferry following a Legacy

Some of the executive members on the day of the Guild
Christmas party 1986. Back (L–R): Betty Smith, Vi Smiles,
Marj Hassett, Agnes Ritson, Dot Aley. Front (L–R):
Elsie Lewis, Gloria MacDonald, Jean Coleman.
(Courtesy of Marj Hassett)

meeting in South Perth, Vi said, 'When we get a spot on Friday girls, you can come and be one.' Vi was assistant secretary and coordinator of the Friday girls in the office since Hazel Carrick's resignation in November 1985.[37] She had been a member for much longer, having joined the WA Guild in 1952 after moving from Brisbane, and been involved on the executive committee since 1977.[38] Shortly after the conversation with Iris, Vi announced she was travelling to Fiji for a holiday. 'You can type, can't you?' she asked.[39]

'A bit like a woodpecker these days,' replied Iris. Nevertheless Iris, who held a certificate in business studies, took on the task of typing letters while Vi was away between February and March 1987.[40] At the time, the Department of Veterans' Affairs (DVA) was advising the Guild of twenty to thirty newly widowed women every week, and Iris would type an introductory letter to each of them over the weekend, ready to post when the office reopened.[41] Then in April, Iris stepped in to assist in the office on Mondays and Tuesdays when the Guild's secretary, Ena Keeley, resigned from that role and from the executive committee entirely, after being actively involved since 1973. The executive minutes cite 'ill health' as the cause and the *Guild News* states 'personal reasons'.[42] Although neither the minutes nor the magazine hint at disharmony, Iris Rowtcliff sensed a tense undercurrent in the office and felt like a mouse in the midst of it. At the AGM a month later, Iris 'fell' into the position of secretary. Despite the title, Iris felt her role was actually more of a clerk's job. By the time Gloria MacDonald accepted the presidency, she had been secretary for many years and continued to undertake the clerking work of writing cards, typing some letters and sorting the mail. It is possible that this blurring of job descriptions was the origins of some underlying conflict, but the tension eventually dispersed and the office settled back into a friendly routine.[43]

Ena Keeley had also been responsible for addressing and despatching the *Guild News*. Now Marj Hassett and Ada Mortimer found themselves in charge of this task. Marj recalls that preparing the quarterly newsletter for posting was a time-consuming 'work of art'. Marj hand-made the glue required to attach the address labels to the magazine wrappers, which were then folded carefully around the circular to meet post office regulations.[44] Once the magazines were wrapped and labelled, Marj and Ada hauled them down to the post office. At least, they did until doing so coincided with a heavy downpour. The last thing Marj wanted was to brave the wet weather, nevertheless they loaded the magazines onto the trolley cart, and headed off. The wind whipped its way down the street, almost knocking the two women off their feet. 'This is ridiculous!' Marj told Ada. 'I am not doing this any more.'

'But how will we get them to the post office?' Gloria asked.

'I don't care what you do, but we're not going to take them.'

The state president could be persuasive, but on this matter Marj was determined and Gloria eventually agreed to organise a courier to collect the magazines in future.[45]

The glue for the magazine labels and wrappers may have been made from flour and water, but for Marj it continued to be friendship that held the Guild together, despite the occasional undercurrent or personality conflict that arose. As she explained, 'What will upset you today has gone tomorrow, and you're ready to come back again next week.'[46]

By 1988, state president Gloria MacDonald had been involved with the Guild for more than four decades and, in this bicentennial year, she received an OAM for her commitment and ongoing work for the organisation. State Governor Gordon Reid, husband of the Guild's patron Ruth Reid, presented her with the award at an investiture at Government House on 29 September.[47] Gloria was also one of ten recipients from 1200 nominations nationally to be awarded a Bicentennial Commemorative Medal. This award recognised her as someone who 'consistently demonstrated such qualities of leadership, compassion and humanity.'[48] Margaret Southwood, a relatively new member at the time, believes that the public acknowledgment

Gloria MacDonald receiving her OAM from the
Governor of Western Australia, Gordon Reid, in 1988.
(Courtesy of West Australian Newspapers / *West Australian*)

was thoroughly deserved. Margaret 'admired and adored' Gloria and describes her as a lady who 'always held herself very well. She respected people [and believed there was] nobody better than the War Widows.'[49]

Margaret Southwood had been widowed on 8 December 1984. Her husband Bert had served at Balikpapan in the Pacific during the Second World War and sustained serious injuries when an aviation fuel tank blew up. An American surgeon successfully inserted a metal plate in his head, but Margaret comments:

> *My husband came back a broken man. And as he got older,*
> *he got more cantankerous, I think is the word. He was an*
> *old bugger at times. He was a real old bugger at times.*
> *But we had a good marriage. I look at his photo sometimes*
> *and I say, 'You miserable old sod, you said you'd never*
> *leave me.'*[50]

He was not the only family member affected by war either; their son had been permanently paralysed while training for Vietnam.

Prior to meeting and marrying Bert, Margaret had lived in Victoria, training as a telephonist and working for the *Argus* newspaper, among other employers. She met her husband in Melbourne, but had to wait some time before heading west. When she did, she was given twenty-four hours' notice to board the train. Assuming that Bert was still overseas, she was surprised to find him waiting for her on the platform in Perth. They raised a family of five in Western Australia, but for years after her move west, and even more so after Bert's death, she cried on Melbourne Cup Day, as he had been a horse trainer and they both enjoyed the races. Bert died in 1984, after Margaret had nursed him for ten years. Afterwards, she decided to become so busy that she did not have time to think about her loss, so she joined Legacy and the War Widows' Guild.

After attending Guild meetings for a couple of years, Margaret decided she wanted to move from her East Fremantle home to be closer to the city. Upon hearing of a vacancy at Forsyth Gardens, she rang Gloria MacDonald. 'Mrs Mac, I'm interested in one of your units that is available.'[51]

WA delegates Gloria MacDonald (left) and Pearl Thomson
at the 1992 national conference in Sydney.
(Guild archives, WA Branch)

'Oh, good, darling,' Gloria replied. 'I'm glad one of our girls has got it.'[52] Although Margaret eventually moved to a larger unit in a neighbouring suburb, she thoroughly enjoyed her time as a resident at Forsyth Gardens.

Fellow resident Elsie Lewis was an active member whose involvement included the role of treasurer following Mickey Parker's resignation in February 1984. In July 1988, Elsie agreed to coordinate a residents committee to facilitate the smooth running of the units, including lawns and gardens. Anything difficult or unusual could still be handballed to the office and Gloria would continue to do the accounts.[53] The following year, Elsie travelled to Darwin to visit her daughter before returning for the September meeting. After collecting the raffle money and placing it in the office for safekeeping, she rejoined the gathering to listen to a guest speaker. At meeting's end, Iris Rowtcliff, who was now the Guild's secretary, hurried to the office to start the counting, expecting Elsie to follow. When she did not, Iris stuck her head round the door to discover Elsie looking straight past her. Concerned, Iris walked over and tapped her friend on the shoulder. When Elsie failed to respond, Iris recognised the signs of a stroke. The visiting speaker phoned the ambulance and made Elsie comfortable on the office stretcher until medical assistance arrived.[54]

Gloria MacDonald accompanied Elsie in the ambulance to Royal Perth Hospital. Feeling otherwise helpless, Iris counted the raffle money with executive member and 'Friday girl' Pearl Thomson. 'How about coming in and filling in until we know how Elsie is?' Iris suggested.[55] Sadly, Elsie passed away, and Iris felt the loss keenly, as she had assisted Elsie whenever possible.[56] Gloria missed her too. Neighbours at Forsyth Gardens, Gloria considered her to be not only a 'financial genius' but a dear friend.[57]

Iris offered to take on the role of treasurer until Christmas, and Pearl agreed to become acting secretary until the next AGM, when somebody else could be elected to the role. But the vote never took place. The partnership seemed to work and, in Gloria's words, 'Why change it?'[58] For ten months of the year, secretary Pearl Thomson and treasurer Iris Rowtcliff spent two to three days every week involved in Guild work. Other regulars in the office included Gloria MacDonald, and vice-presidents Belle Leitch and Marj Hassett, as well as Vi Smiles and her Friday girls, who included Jean Coleman, Pat Doyle and Ada Mortimer. 'It was a happy place,' reflected Iris in 2008.

'A very happy office,' agreed Pearl. 'I don't know what I would have done if I hadn't been going into the office every week.'[59]

According to Pearl, the women sought ways to save every possible cent, whether it was scouring to find material at minimal cost, or catching a bus in the pouring rain instead of a taxi. It is difficult to determine whether the penny pinching was a result of the stock market crash and recession, or if it was simply the way the Guild had always operated. Gloria MacDonald undertook the banking herself, and was very proud of the money the Guild had saved. 'The pennies were looked after, and they made the pounds,' says Iris Rowtcliff.[60] According to Pearl Thomson, the money would not have been in such good shape if it had not been for Mrs Mac's economising and Mickey Parker's 'crafty investing'. Iris also gives credit to Elsie Lewis, who she describes as 'the whiz kid'.[61]

Even a treat was planned in such a way as to save the Guild a few cents. Pearl recalls heading out of the office one day after suggesting the purchase of vanilla slices for somebody's birthday, possibly Gloria's.[62] 'That's a good idea,' said Iris, 'because you can cut one of those into three.' As treasurer, Iris was thinking of the Guild budget, knowing that she must account for every dollar spent. A vanilla slice for each woman was purchased that day, but years later, Pearl still enjoyed teasing Iris about the incident.

❀

In August 1988, the federal government had announced its intention to integrate repatriation hospitals into the public hospital system under state government control. It reasoned that as the ex-service community aged, repatriation hospitals risked becoming geriatric facilities without the ability to attract the best doctors.[63] But many war widows and other members of the ex-service community feared that the proposed changes would cause a lower standard of care.[64] In Western Australia, there was bipartisan support for Premier Peter Dowding, who opposed the integration of Hollywood Hospital into the public system without the approval of the ex-service community.[65]

Prime Minister Bob Hawke attempted to allay fears at the opening of extensions to the Repatriation General Hospital at Heidelberg in Victoria on 24 April 1989. He stated that no repatriation hospital would be transferred to a state government until 'a satisfactory agreement [was] reached on such matters as priority for veterans and war widows.' He added that the hospital transfer 'was not a step to abolishing the Department of Veterans' Affairs.'[66] He gave a similar speech in New South Wales at Concord Hospital on 7 March the following year.[67]

On Tuesday 6 March 1990, national president Lucille Wallis attended a special meeting at the Perth office where she spoke about the recent Newcastle earthquake, and indicated the Guild's intention to contribute to a monetary appeal, as there were numerous war widows living in the area. This was in addition to the WA Guild's donation through the RSL's appeal. Lucille then focused on the hospital situation. She believed the takeover would 'definitely eventuate' and said it was important to have 'firm guarantees' that veterans and war widows had private status in public and some private hospitals.[68]

Despite a pledge by the DVA Commissioner, Rear Admiral Neil Ralph, that war widows would not be deprived in any way, the Guild considered it 'a very worrying situation.'[69] It was particularly concerned about whether war widows would be able to retain their lilac cards (the precursor to the current gold card), and wanted these to be recognised as a 'guarantee of priority hospital treatment by the government.'[70] On

27 June 1990, Gloria MacDonald attended a meeting of the Unit and Kindred Association, run by the RSL. Fifty-six people from thirty-five ex-service groups were present. With the hospital transfer appearing inevitable, representatives from eight organisations, including the War Widows' Guild, formed a committee to investigate what the veteran community needed and how to achieve it.[71] Four members of the committee met with the state Minister for Health, Kevin Wilson, on 13 December 1990. He told them that no negotiations over the integration would occur unless the ex-service community was satisfied.[72] David Watson, Deputy Commissioner of DVA, attended the next meeting on 27 March 1991. The main fear seemed to be that Hollywood Hospital would close altogether if it was integrated into the state system, but the deputy commissioner assured them that this would not be the case.[73]

According to one newspaper article, not all ex-service organisations were in agreement with the RSL and the Unit and Kindred Association. The *West Australian* reported that the Australian Veterans and Defence Services Council (AVDSC), which represented twenty-four organisations, including the RAAF and Vietnam Veterans, was in favour of the integration because 'aging veterans needed the extra benefits.'[74] However, RAAF and Vietnam Veterans representatives were also on the hospital integration committee, so it is unclear exactly which organisations supported the views of the AVDSC, and which approved of the RSL's resistance to proposed changes. What is certain is that the state government refused to agree to the transfer without the RSL's approval and in the absence of assurances by the federal government that adequate funding would be available.[75]

Almost a year later, Ben Humphries, the Federal Minister for Veterans' Affairs, stated that Hollywood Hospital had no place in the state government's strategic planning for public hospital services. Instead, private sector options were sought, with the aim of Hollywood Hospital becoming a preferred private hospital for the ex-service community.[76] Eight companies responded to the request for proposals in February 1993, and three were shortlisted.[77] By July, the RSL indicated their support of the tendering process,[78] but the integration committee continued to take an active interest, inviting representatives from each shortlisted company to attend a meeting to present its proposal and answer questions.[79]

Ramsay Health Care eventually won the tender, and after a few months of transition, Repatriation Hospital, Hollywood became Hollywood Private Hospital at midnight on 24 February 1994.[80] The company promised to maintain the aged and extended care department, psychiatric facility, palliative care unit and the chapel.[81] During the official opening, Paul Ramsay spoke of his personal commitment to the veteran community. As if to reassure those unsettled by the transfer, he showed the audience a piece of a Spitfire propeller blade, and spoke about his ex-serviceman father.[82] Gloria MacDonald commented on the transfer several months later:

This project was at first viewed with concern and doubts as to whether War Widows would be adversely affected health wise if and when this happened, but I'm happy to tell you that our worst fears are unfounded because all reports I have from members who have recently been treated at Hollywood Private Hospital have been excellent and satisfactory.[83]

While the Guild's fears were, in the end, unrealised, it had not been alone in its concerns. It cannot be ascertained whether the outcome might have differed had the Guild and other organisations not protested. But the process does demonstrate the Guild's proactive approach, its fighting spirit to protect hard-won benefits and a determination to keep its members' best interests on the agenda.

Hollywood Private Hospital held a function for ex-service organisations in August 1994 to celebrate six months as the 'New Hollywood'. Guild members attending included (L–R) Mary Flint (standing), Doreen Taylor, Vi Stack, Florence Gordon, Gloria MacDonald and Belle Leitch.
(Guild archives, WA Branch)

CHAPTER 9

LEAVING A LEGACY

Gloria MacDonald had alluded to the possibility of retiring in 1993, and offered to train anyone who might be interested in succeeding her.[1] Possibly no one was willing to accept the challenge, or perhaps nobody wanted to wrest the role from her, for Gloria remained state president after the 1994 AGM.[2] However, that year delegates at the national conference in Hobart voted to limit a state president's term to three years. This motion forced Gloria to retire from her leadership at the following AGM on 15 May 1995, a position she had held since Gwen Forsyth's unexpected death in 1983.

Gloria's final months as state president coincided with the start of Australia Remembers, a series of events commemorating the 50th anniversary of the end of the Second World War. In her final address, Gloria MacDonald spoke of the many functions she had attended thus far, including a display at Anzac House and a wreath laying service at the War Veterans' Home. Meanwhile, Iris Rowtcliff had laid a wreath at the Anzac Day dawn service in Kings Park.[3] Gloria commented, '[They were] impressive, very moving, and I was proud of the men and women whom we loved and lost long ago and have never forgotten.'[4]

As Gloria stepped down from her position, but not her involvement, Iris Rowtcliff became, reluctantly, the Guild's fourth state president. Iris stated firmly that she would remain so for two years only, even though a further year was permitted under the new guidelines. A quietly spoken woman even today, Iris never imagined herself in such a role, and she wondered about her husband's reaction had he been present to witness the moment.[5]

One of Iris's first tasks was to organise a Guild service at the Kings Park War Memorial in conjunction with Australia Remembers. She conceived the idea that at 11 am on Tuesday 8 August, each war widow should lay a flower on the war memorial. Although a wonderful idea, the wind and rain meant the gesture was not so easy in practice. As each woman placed her flower down, it was whipped up by the wind.

An outside observer asked, 'How often do you do this?'

'Every fifty years,' Iris quipped.[6]

Not only was it fifty years since the end of the Second World War, the War Widows' Guild also celebrated its 50th birthday nationally. To honour the milestone, members attended a church service at St Stephen's Anglican Church in Serpentine on 28 September 1995. Then, Gloria MacDonald, Iris Rowtcliff and seven other members travelled to Melbourne for another church service, and a visit to Jessie Vasey's grave in Lilydale, on which national president Eileen Watt placed a sheaf of wattle. The group attended a morning reception at Government House, followed by the unveiling of a plaque dedicated to Jessie Vasey in the shrine area of the botanical gardens.[7] Also significant was the launch of a set of stamps by Australia Post to honour 'four individuals whose service to their country and their fellows was outstanding.' Jessie Vasey's achievements were recognised when her portrait appeared on one of the stamps, alongside Sir Edward Weary Dunlop and Victoria Cross recipients Tom Derric (AIF) and Rawdon Hume Middleton (RAAF).[8]

A year later, the Guild celebrated the formation of the organisation in Western Australia with an ecumenical church service at St George's Cathedral on Monday 2 December 1996. The service began with the ringing of the cathedral bells. Gloria MacDonald recited the motto, followed by readings of selected Bible passages by Ruth Reid, the Guild patron, and Marjorie Le Souef, who as Marjorie Learmonth had been the inaugural state president. Then Jim Dalton, Deputy Commissioner of the DVA, addressed the congregation, focusing on the Guild motto. A luncheon followed, with Doreen Taylor contributing 'wonderful gifts and decorations that continuously flow[ed] from her work basket', while long-time member Hazel Carrick had the honour of cutting the cake.[9] This completed two years of commemoration and remembrance.

Australia Remembers: War widows gather on a wet and windy day
to commemorate 50 years since the end of the Second World War.
(Courtesy of Marj Hassett)

War widows battle the wind in August 1995
to lay flowers in commemoration of VP Day.
(Courtesy of Marj Hassett)

Several weeks later, and just three days after Christmas, Marjorie Le Souef became a war widow for a second time when her ninety-six year old husband Leslie passed away after a long illness. According to the *West Australian*, he was a 'kind and brilliant man who treated people as equals.' Marjorie commented that he had been 'committed to his work and dedicated to improving the way of life of people.' During their marriage, she had become accustomed to his long working hours, which often extended into the evening with phone calls to patients or their families. And when travelling to their property in Margaret River, Marjorie learned to pack a thermos flask and food; if they came across an accident, Leslie would invariably stop to render assistance until an ambulance arrived. She remained supportive of his career, and occupied herself with golf, bridge and volunteer work as well as caring for extended family and myriad friends. A love of reading and learning continued throughout her life. According to Anne Lopez, who met with Marjorie weekly for several years, Marjorie was:

> *The kind of person who was very compassionate, she was opinionated, she knew her own mind, but she was a very loyal person with both her husbands; she was totally devoted to them. When Leslie got sick, she really looked after him. And she always cared about all the members of the family … Even though she doesn't have any children she's a real matriarch of her family and friends … She was honest, she was genuine, she was passionate and she loved people.*[10]

Marjorie rejoined the Guild early in the New Year and returned to the executive committee at the next AGM to play her part in improving the lives of others.

True to her word, Iris Rowtcliff remained president for only two years, passing the role on to Fran Aggiss, with Marjorie Le Souef accepting the vice-presidency. As she stepped down at the 1997 AGM, Iris foreshadowed changes in the staffing arrangements:

> *Our financial position is very very good mainly due to good management and the efforts of voluntary staff over the*

Marjorie Le Souef and Fran Aggiss in the Guild office at 'The Kings', May 1999.
(Guild archives, WA Branch)

*years. It must be remembered we have never ever had paid
office staff. Unfortunately this could be the last year we will
be able to say that. We must move with the times ... as most
of us were young 20 year olds when the Guild was formed
I think we have come a long way to be able to manage and
run the office and affairs of the Guild competently. Our age
and health ... is telling us it's time for change and we must
admit that a computer, electric typewriter and answering
machine – as much as we dislike them – are the way to go.
So changes are on the way like it or not.*[11]

In September that year, the Guild employed Marilyn Nelligan, who
worked for a short time as an office secretary. Corrie Sweeny replaced
her in April 1998, at which time Robyn Braccia was employed as a
bookkeeper. When Robyn resigned twelve months later, Jenny Knight
joined the organisation for two mornings a week to enter the accounts
and update the database.[12] Initially, all administrative work was
done by hand, but Fran Aggiss was keen to see the Guild enter the
computer age, and Jenny possessed the necessary skills to facilitate
this technological change. Jenny's work hours and job description
gradually expanded to include other tasks such as taking minutes of
meetings due to lack of available volunteers. In the words of Guild

member Doreen Taylor, the Guild 'bloomed' under Jenny's care, as she proved to be not only a capable employee, but a committed advocate for war widows.[13]

❀

Fran Aggiss was born and raised in the farming community of Harvey in the state's south-west. She left school at fourteen to work as a cashier for the local butcher, and it was there she met John Aggiss, who had moved from Albany after completing an apprenticeship. But when John turned eighteen, he was called up for war service and sent to Northam before travelling to Queensland for jungle training. Fran and John wrote most days, and when the mail became more irregular, Fran knew he had departed for an overseas posting. They married on 5 January 1945, while he was home on leave. When he returned to duty three weeks later, Fran moved to Perth to work as a bookkeeper in the navy office. One morning she picked up the paper to read that the 9th Division had landed in Borneo, with many dead or wounded. She now knew her husband's whereabouts, but not whether or not she was a widow. She was one of the lucky ones. Several months after the war ended, Fran awoke at 5.30 am because the navy boys had told her a ship was due; her husband was aboard. Fran and John returned to Harvey until they purchased a butcher's shop in Albany, where they lived with their four school-aged children for eleven years.

They later retired to Perth until John's sudden death on 13 November 1985, but Fran's ongoing connection to Albany would prove fortuitous when it came to reaching out to rural war widows. Although Alma Japp had restarted a sub-branch in Kalgoorlie in 1973, it no longer operated, and so no country branches existed in Western Australia. Fran Aggiss aimed to change that. She still knew people in Albany, and in 1998, after placing an advertisement in the *Albany Advertiser*, she travelled to the southern coastal town, hoping for a positive response. One of those who read the ad was Ruth Moir who, until recently, had been unaware she qualified as a war widow. She only discovered the possibility after phoning the DVA about having her husband Keith's name engraved on a plaque in the Karrakatta memorial rose gardens. The man answering Ruth's call informed her that she needed a pension number.[14]

'I don't have a pension,' Ruth replied.

'Well, I'm afraid we can't do much about it.'

'Do you mean to tell me,' Ruth said crossly, 'that my husband, who was a veteran of the Desert Campaign, can't have a plaque put to his memory without me having a pension number?'

'I'm afraid that's the case.'[15]

When DVA representatives visited Albany, Ruth's war widow friend, Norma Barr, encouraged her to attend the meeting and clarify the issue. An RSL member listened to Ruth's story, read her husband's death certificate and said, 'Oh, you're going to apply for a war widow's pension.' Soon after, Ruth received both her pension *and* a plaque honouring her husband's war service.[16]

Thus, when Ruth saw Fran's advertisement, she was keen to attend the initial meeting on 8 August 1998, where she met five other women and reconnected with Fran – Ruth had been a customer in John Aggiss's butcher shop. The small group resolved to start a branch of the War Widows' Guild. As a result of further advertising in the local paper, word of mouth and the DVA contacting all war widows in the area, thirty-three women gathered in Ruth's home on 7 September. They elected office bearers, including Ruth Moir as president. 'I suppose they thought, she's always talking so dob her in,' Ruth laughs when recalling the day.[17] Ruth then approached the RSL, who agreed to let them have the use of a hall for future meetings at no cost. Membership had risen to fifty by April 1999, and in July that year it was agreed to include widows of all ex-servicemen as members.

Although Mandurah was no longer considered 'rural' – it obtained city status in 1999 – a branch soon began there in a similar way.[18] Rene Anderson was elected president of this group, with Roma Blair taking on the role of vice-president. Clarice Stewart became secretary and Bobby Bevan the treasurer.

⚜

Back in Perth, the Guild rooms were proving less satisfactory. Rent was expensive and some members felt unsafe when accessing the Guild office on the second floor. Fran Aggiss, who usually arrived by 8 am, recalls stepping out of the lift into a dark and dingy passageway, and having to walk its length before reaching the light switch.[19] One morning, office staff discovered a man's coat and a newspaper in the passageway, intimating that someone had slept there. The rooms had been broken into and money stolen at least three times[20] and a couple of members were victims of attempted bag snatches. Fran Aggiss remembers:

> *A couple of times I had blokes going along trying to get …*
> *handbags. One bloke tried to get mine one day. Luckily a*
> *couple of policemen were walking past. They skittled off. It*
> *became quite dangerous up that end.*[21]

These incidents coincided with an overall increase in the crime rate in the city centre during the 1980s and early 1990s, with the general public becoming reluctant to visit at night.[22] Furthermore, the courthouse was situated next door, and the women felt intimidated when some of its clientele accosted them for money.[23] Even with plain clothes detectives occupying offices on the same floor, and an increased police presence generally, some members remained uneasy.

A venue change was deemed necessary. But it was only after Fran discussed the concerns with DVA Deputy Commissioner Jim Dalton that moving became possible. When he heard of the Guild's safety concerns, Jim Dalton offered the women rooms at DVA headquarters, on the 9th floor of the AMP building on the corner of William Street and St Georges Terrace.[24] The Guild gratefully accepted the offer, though members had mixed reactions to the news. Many welcomed the change, but some were sad to move. Doreen Taylor contemplates that with age comes a resistance to change; the Guild had been based at the Kings Hotel for almost twenty years, and it was natural some wanted to remain with what was familiar.[25]

The Guild's move occurred on 4 October 1999. A week later, members bussed out to Forsyth Gardens, where they dedicated the rose garden in memory of Jessie Vasey and the library in Gloria MacDonald's honour.[26] Gloria, who had resided at Forsyth Gardens for many years, had passed away in February after devoting much of her life 'to the work she loved best.' She had kept her age a closely guarded secret and some members were surprised to discover she had been ninety-three when she died.[27] According to Marj Hassett, Gloria was 'War Widows through and through.' Iris supports this assertion, reflecting that 'Mrs Mac was a perfect lady ... people had their different opinions of Mrs Mac, but she was always Guild minded.'[28]

As the Guild farewelled one founding member, another returned to the helm. After more than half a century, Marjorie Le Souef resumed the position she'd relinquished in 1947. 'It seems so long ago,' she reflected when she replaced Fran Aggiss as president in May 2000:

> *There were no perks. In fact, there were no hospital benefits and war widows were poorly treated. The pension in 1946 was two pounds and ten shillings. You got 17s 6d per week for the eldest child and 12s 6d for every other child.*[29]

She reminded members about the early achievements of the War Widows' Guild, including winning access to repatriation hospitals and the accrued leave pay due to their husbands.[30]

Shortly after her election, Marjorie fractured her ankle and was forced to postpone speaking invitations until the New Year.[31] Nor was she able to travel to Canberra for the national conference. But with the assistance of a taxi and a wheelchair, she managed to attend the Guild office[32] and her broken bone did not keep her from formulating several ideas she felt would build into the community and ensure the Guild's longevity.

Long-standing and dedicated Guild members. Back (L–R): Marjorie Le Souef, Florence Gordon, Iris Rowtcliff. Front (L–R): Joy Smith, Pearl Thomson. (Guild archives, WA Branch)

The first issue under discussion was how to use the organisation's significant savings. In May 1997 the Guild had received word that the other remaining beneficiary of the Peck estate, Ellen Peck's son-in-law, had died. The Guild, who already earned the interest on the estate, now inherited the principal amount as well, and it wanted to manage this in a way that honoured Ellen Peck's generosity.[33] One possibility was to invest in a nursing home, an idea first raised at an executive meeting in 1979.[34] The Guild contributed $50,000 to the refurbishment of Vasey House in 1984,[35] but nothing further eventuated until 1993, when Gloria MacDonald attended a TPI meeting at Veteran Affairs. TPI hoped to build a forty-bed nursing home on its estate in Como, and the Guild had considered contributing financially to this project, provided war widows were guaranteed accommodation there. According to Guild minutes, the government refused the application, stating that there were already two thousand empty beds in Western Australia.[36] 'I wish I could find where they are,' commented Gloria MacDonald. 'I must say I was extremely disappointed at the failure of this worthwhile and necessary project.'[37] Executive committee member Mrs Shaw suggested one of the reasons may have been a 1986 decision to build cottage homes in preference to nursing homes.[38] Personally, Mrs Shaw believed this was unwise as war widows were growing older and would require increasing levels of care.[39]

Then, in 1995, the state president, Iris Rowtcliff, was informed that it would be 'virtually impossible' for the Guild to ever have its own nursing home.[40] And even if the organisation invested in beds in an existing home, there was no guarantee one would be available for a war widow.[41] An offer from the RAAF Association was considered, but deemed unsuitable for financial and geographical reasons. With dreams of a nursing home all but dashed, Iris had declared that the money should be saved for 'something concrete to show that the Western Australian War Widows' Guild passed this way.'[42] The executive committee had agreed to leave the money in the hands of the trustee managing the Peck Estate until it found a worthy cause.

Marjorie, who was deeply concerned about the number of relatively young women dying from breast cancer, suggested that the West Australian Guild set up a scholarship for research into the disease.

There was a national scholarship, the Jessie Mary Vasey Scholarship, established in 1993. Worth $5000 per annum for two years, it had been awarded to UWA postgraduate architectural student Annette Condello in 1997.[43] Now, with the executive committee's approval, Marjorie contacted the University of Western Australia to arrange the donation of $314,000 for a perpetual postgraduate scholarship.[44]

The scholarship was launched at an afternoon tea at UWA on 23 November 2000. Marjorie spoke on behalf of the seventy war widows who attended:

> *We lost our husbands in battle ... a battle that was*
> *successful in protecting our country. We hope this*
> *scholarship is successful in winning the battle against*
> *breast cancer.*[45]

The University thanked the Guild for its generosity and concern for others. 'Genes associated with the risk of breast cancer are being identified every day,' said Professor Landau, Executive Dean of Medicine at UWA. 'With this scholarship, we can continue that work.'[46] The scholarship's first recipient was PhD student Helen Currie, who planned to study the role of protease activated receptors in immune cells and tumour biology.[47]

Guild members enjoying afternoon tea at UWA for the launch
of the War Widows' Guild WA Breast Cancer Scholarship.
(Guild archives, WA Branch)

Top: Marjorie Le Souef speaking at the
launch of the Breast Cancer Scholarship.
(Guild archives, WA Branch)

❧

Early in 2001, Marjorie Le Souef and four other members visited
Kalgoorlie with the view of re-establishing a sub-branch of the
Guild on the goldfields, just as Fran Aggiss had done in Albany and
Mandurah. Fourteen war widows from Kalgoorlie joined them for
morning tea and agreed to form a branch that met monthly.[48] Then, on
5 June, thirty-three local war widows gathered at the Kalgoorlie RSL.
Among them were Doreen Basley and Robin Bowden, both of whom
had lived their whole lives on the goldfields.[49]

Doreen Basley's father had worked in the bush: on the railways,
woodcutting, whatever work was available. She met her husband Bill
at a dance in Kalgoorlie when he returned from serving with the RAAF
in New Guinea. They married in 1950 and together they raised six
boys and ran a *Kalgoorlie Miner* newspaper round. Her husband also
worked on the railways, at the steel foundry and as a stock controller
at Atlas Copco, with Doreen being a school cleaner for many years.
She had been widowed for a decade when she joined the Guild.[50]

Fifteen years younger than Doreen, Robin Bowden grew up on
her family's sheep and cattle property at Ora Banda before moving
to Kalgoorlie in 1959 to work on the telephone exchange. She did

In 2013 Robin Bowden (right) was awarded life membership for
her commitment to the Kalgoorlie Branch of the Guild.
(Guild archives, WA Branch)

not meet her husband Barry until he returned to Kalgoorlie in 1968
after completing nine years with the navy. They married in 1972 and
raised two children. Barry worked as a mechanic until 1981, when
they bought and operated a taxi. When Barry died in 1997, Robin
was unaware that she even qualified as a war widow. Her husband
had rarely spoken of his navy life and the Vietnam War was never
discussed. Grateful for the pension and appreciative of the assistance
and understanding she received from DVA, Robin eagerly joined the
War Widows' Guild when it started in Kalgoorlie.[51]

The Kalgoorlie war widows elected Teti Gribble to be the branch's
first president, with Doreen Basley as vice-president. Kathleen Swinton
was secretary and Robin Bowden was 'talked into' the position of
treasurer. In turn, Robin convinced Doreen Basley to become
president when Teti left in May 2002. Activities included social
gatherings, such as eating out at local restaurants, and fundraising
for various activities, for example a Mother's Day raffle. Proceeds
went to Disabled Athletics, and Edward Collick Homes (now Amana
Living), as well as to local man Jack Tinetti, who raised money to
help pensioners pay their bills. The branch is still active, and although
numbers remain small, those who do belong attend regularly and
appreciate the social connection.[52]

Soon after, the Guild invested in another project that would contribute to its long-term legacy, sponsoring one of eight new windows to be installed at Hollywood Private Hospital's chapel, which had been built in 1943–44 as a freestanding brick and tile building. All windows were donated by organisations and individuals connected to the hospital in some way. Commissioned in 2002, the caption on the Guild's window is 'Blessed are the merciful, for they will receive mercy.'[53] A descriptive explanation of the window appeared in the *Guild News*:

> *A plant grows at the base of a tree trunk and as it climbs upward it gives evidence of the strength of people, who despite their hardships continue to flower and grow.*
> *The trunk forms a cross to signify the strength many have known in the person of Jesus Christ, as they journey on into new life.*[54]

At the windows' dedication, on 4 May 2003, hospital chaplain Reverend Graeme Manolas said:

> *The new windows will be a constant reminder of the hospital's past, remembering the story of Hollywood's veteran community, our involvement in war and the need for care and healing for both veterans and the families of veterans.*[55]

Not long after the windows were installed, hospital redevelopment dictated the demolition of the chapel; mercifully, the windows were preserved and included in the new chapel, which was eventually situated inside the main hospital building.[56]

But perhaps the most ambitious project to be undertaken during Marjorie Le Souef's presidency was the redevelopment of Forsyth Gardens. The units had become run down and were in desperate need of extensive maintenance. One had been refurbished in 1996 to become a short-term rental for country visitors, but many others remained empty; the Guild had been unable to maintain a 75 per cent occupancy rate since 1997, despite advertising in the *Guild News*.[57]

Marjorie suggested renovating Forsyth Gardens, with the older units to be knocked down and replaced with self-contained, two-bedroom cottages. A letter to residents in October 2001 indicated that redevelopment was foreshadowed, although few residents would be affected in the short term, and the Guild did not 'anticipate further development for some years.' The letter also offered assistance in finding temporary housing.[58] Before long, the executive committee granted approval for architects to proceed with stage one of the project, which involved the demolition of the original ten bedsitters, now considered too small for long-term accommodation. An update in the December issue of the *Guild News* confirmed that the redevelopment would proceed with ten two-bedroom cottages to replace the existing bedsitters.[59]

This plan of action was abruptly altered when, that same month, the Guild received notice that it would need to vacate the offices at DVA headquarters within twelve months. After some deliberation, the executive voted to bring forward stage two, which included a community centre to provide amenities to residents, office space for staff and a function hall for members. Guild headquarters would henceforth be located at Forsyth Gardens. A letter dated 7 January 2002 informed residents of the additional development and proposed that they relocate by April.

Despite the benefits of the redevelopment for residents at Forsyth Gardens – tenants would no longer need to travel into town for

Guild members visit the new chapel at Hollywood Hospital, 2010.
(Photo by Melinda Tognini)

The stained glass window donated by the Guild:
'Blessed are the merciful, for they will receive mercy.'
(Photo by Melinda Tognini)

Guild meetings and office staff would be close at hand[60] – the proposed changes were not without controversy. Stage one had required the relocation of two women still living in the bedsitters; stage two affected a further seven.[61] Although they received written communication, residents complained that nobody had been to see them. Some tenants attempted to contact the office, but with little success, most likely a result of the office being closed for almost a month over the Christmas period.[62] Marjorie Le Souef was on the south coast, catching up with Albany branch president Josie Lewis.[63]

Perhaps some of the ensuing dissatisfaction might have been avoided had the timing not been over the holiday break and the Guild offices not been located offsite. But, regardless of the contributing factors, the fact remains that some residents were unhappy with what they perceived to be a lack of initial response. One woman contacted the media, including talkback radio, and an article appeared in the *West Australian* on Friday 11 January with a photograph of five residents. One of those interviewed feared 'it was only a matter of time before the rest of the widows got the eviction news' and mistakenly believed the Guild 'wanted to make a profit by selling off the land and units even though the land was donated by the state government more than 30 years ago.'[64] In fact, this was not even possible under the conditions of the original land grant.

Marjorie returned from her week away to 'face the publicity'. She thought the media attention was 'dramatic'[65] and was greatly distressed by the situation. Marjorie had never intended to upset or oust current residents but wanted to ensure that 'the future of the Guild, including Forsyth Gardens, [was] secure for both current and future members.'[66] In a press release dated 15 January 2002, Marjorie outlined the process from the Guild's perspective, including its intention to contact affected residents 'to individually discuss their accommodation options.'[67] The offer of alternate housing had not been included in the second letter,[68] but an article in the April edition of *Guild News* stated that accommodation was available at larger organisations located nearby, and residents were also offered the remaining rental units.[69]

A peace of sorts was achieved, and the Guild proceeded with the redevelopment of Forsyth Gardens. Meanwhile, Iris Rowtcliff's long-time and ongoing Guild work was recognised in the 2002 Queen's Birthday honours. Iris had now been actively involved in the Guild for almost twenty years, taking on almost every role in the organisation over that time. She had also been a resident at Forsyth Gardens, and had assisted in a caretaking role there,[70] although she found the redevelopment controversy upsetting and moved out of Forsyth Gardens, despite the fact her unit was not affected.

Hazel Donald, on the other hand, was excited about the redevelopment as it precipitated her return to Perth after twenty years away. She became a war widow in 1996 when her husband Bill died of cancer, but had her own lengthy military record. Hazel was at school when her brothers embarked for the Second World War and the women's services disbanded when the conflict ended. But in 1951 the Korean War loomed and women were once again needed to relieve the men. The Women's Royal Australian Army Corps (WRAAC) recommenced recruiting, with the first group in Perth enlisting in January 1952. Influenced by a childhood 'surrounded by khaki' and a desire to drive a truck, eighteen-year-old Hazel signed up for four years as part of the second intake on 4 February. Her friends thought she was mad, but she never regretted her decision. Four years' service extended to twenty-four, and she rose through the ranks to Lieutenant Colonel, spending time in Mildura, Sydney, Melbourne, Perth, Hobart and Canberra. Shortly before accepting a second posting to Canberra, Hazel met Bill Donald, a Melbourne

Work is underway on the Forsyth Gardens redevelopment, 2003.
(Guild archives, WA Branch)

GP who had been a medical officer during the Korean and Vietnam Wars. Two years later, Bill convinced her to marry him and return to Victoria, at which time, she left the army to work full time as his receptionist in his medical practice. Marriage was a completely new way of life for Hazel. After many years of caring for and training women, she now shared a home with a husband, two teenage step-sons and a large dog.

After Bill died, Hazel received a letter from the Victorian Guild and so sent off her subscription, although it was a Legacy meeting that she first attended. She remembers, 'The room seemed to be full of elderly grey-haired ladies and I was then sixty-two.' However, she felt welcome and enjoyed the women's stories. Two members had been Bill's patients, and they suggested that she go to a monthly War Widows' Guild meeting. She did so and within a year was invited to join both the Guild board and the Vasey Housing board. When the state president resigned several months later due to ill health, Hazel agreed to take on the role.

Hazel began to feel that the home they had shared in St Kilda had become too large to maintain. While visiting family in Perth in January 2003, her sister informed her, 'The War Widows are building a village over here. Why don't you take a look?' So, on a 42°C summer's day, Hazel inspected what was still a building site at

Work is complete on the redeveloped units.
(Guild archives, WA Branch)

Forsyth Gardens. Within an hour, she had decided to return to her home town.

Not long after Hazel paid the deposit on her new unit, Marjorie Le Souef phoned to ask her to become the state president at the next AGM. The question was not altogether out of place; although Hazel would be new to the WA Guild, she had been president of the Victorian branch. Still, 'Haven't you got anyone else?' she asked.

'No. Not your age,' replied Marjorie.[71]

Thus, Hazel arrived in Perth about ten days prior to the AGM and the official opening of the redevelopment, having agreed to become the next state president without knowing anyone apart from Marjorie Le Souef, Pearl Thomson and Jenny Knight, whom she had met at previous national conferences. 'And they just accepted me,' Hazel reflects. 'I was just accepted.'

At the AGM on 22 May 2003, which was held in the newly completed administration and community centre, Marjorie completed her term as president. Having been central to the decisions about the stained-glass window in the Hollywood Hospital chapel, the breast cancer scholarship and the Forsyth Gardens redevelopment, Marjorie joked, 'I will go down in the history of the Guild as the president who spent all the money.' More seriously she added, 'I believe we now have a valuable asset of which we can be proud and will comfortably take us into the future.[72]

Also new was the introduction of life memberships for those who had been actively involved in the Guild for twenty-five years. Pearl Thomson had suggested the idea several months before, with the executive committee agreeing that the first of these should coincide with the AGM.[73] National president Kath Ross presented the inaugural life memberships to Marj Hassett, Vi Smiles, Betty Walker, Rose Walker and Jean Tapping in recognition of their service and commitment.

At the conclusion of the AGM, Danna Vale, Minister for Veterans' Affairs, officially opened the new administration and community centre, paying tribute to Marjorie for both her current role, and for her work in establishing the WA Guild in 1946:

National president Kath Ross (left) presents
Marj Hassett with a life membership, May 2003.
(Guild archives, WA Branch)

*Marjorie has given so much to the Guild and has provided
care and support to countless war widows. She also played
a major part in the decision to redevelop Forsyth Gardens
and establish the Guild's administration and community
centre on site.*[74]

Minister Vale continued by speaking of the significance of the centre:

*The redevelopment of Forsyth Gardens means that at long
last the War Widows' Guild actually owns their Guild
centre ... The War Widows' Guild brings together those
whose loved ones have made the ultimate sacrifice for their
country, ensuring that our war widows need not carry on
alone. This is a most worthy goal and I hope that this centre
will become the heart of the care and support of war widows
in West Australia.*[75]

The minister then unveiled the plaque as she declared the centre
officially open. The plaque read:

MARJORIE LE SOUEF
ADMINISTRATION AND
COMMUNITY CENTRE
WAS OFFICIALLY OPENED BY
THE HON. DANNA VALE MP
ON
22 MAY 2003

Marjorie initially failed to register the name written on the plaque,[76] but recovered to acknowledge the work of the War Widows' Guild founder, whom she had known personally through her early involvement: 'Where would we be today if it were not for Mrs Jessie Vasey and the inspiration she gave to the War Widows' Guild?' In appreciation of the honour bestowed upon her, Marjorie commissioned her friend Mary Jane Malet to paint a watercolour of the Guild's emblem, the kookaburra, which now hangs in the foyer of the administration and community centre.

Though some residents remained offside during the redevelopment process, and increased travel distance prevented some members from attending meetings, many remained undeterred. Overall, the redevelopment has been a positive decision. Forsyth Gardens now consists of fourteen independent living units, office space and

Opening of the Marjorie Le Souef Administration and Community Centre, 22 May 2003. L–R: Hazel Donald, Kath Ross, Danna Vale MP, Marjorie Le Souef. (Guild archives, WA Branch)

a community centre, while retaining twelve of the original one-bedroom units for rent. The Guild has up-to-date accommodation and facilities, providing opportunities for members *and* residents to meet regularly, as well as financial security for the organisation as it looks to its long-term future and ongoing viability.

CHAPTER 10

REMEMBRANCE AND RECOGNITION

For members of the War Widows' Guild, remembrance and commemoration have been significant since the organisation's early days, when Jessie Vasey encouraged all war widows to attend any ceremony that remembered their loved ones and the sacrifice they made. 'We must never allow this country to forget the debt owed to its war dead,' she had said. 'Not only do we remember, we must be seen to be remembering.'[1] As early as 1948, the War Widows' Guild had lobbied the Australian War Graves Commission and the RSL for official representation at Anzac Day and other such occasions.[2] Only after continued and insistent 'badgering' was the organisation invited to lay a wreath at the Australian War Memorial in Canberra on Anzac Day from 1956, and the WA Guild would continue to lobby the state RSL until it was afforded the same privilege and recognition at the dawn service in Kings Park.

While the War Widows' Guild fought for official representation during the 1950s and 1960s, Anzac Day had been perceived by many in the wider community as a 'boozy veterans' reunion that had little relevance for other Australians.[3] This perception was encouraged by the anti-war movement of the 1960s and 1970s;[4] more recently, historians, politicians, writers and the media have all contributed to renewed interest in Anzac Day and the Anzac tradition.[5] However, the collective memory of Anzac Day continues to be problematic for those who returned home from war and died at home, referred to as the 'post-war dead',[6] for some migrants, for Australian Aborigines, for Armenians[7] and for many war widows, as well as revisionist historians. Despite this, such remembrances had, and continue to hold, great meaning for many war widows, even though they have felt excluded from such narratives and occasions in the past. In 2011, Guild member and Forsyth Gardens resident, Florence Gordon, commented that laying a wreath at the State War Memorial on Anzac Day held particular significance for her:

> *They are the events that absolutely had me gobsmacked ...*
> *because it was wonderful to think of what these men went*
> *through, and that they were being remembered.*[8]

But Guild members consider other commemorative services important, too. In 2001, representatives attended services for Victory over Japan on 15 August and Remembrance Day at Kings Park and in Fremantle, with a war widow laying a wreath at each service. In November, Marjorie Le Souef, accompanied by vice-president Pearl Thomson and executive member Florence Gordon, travelled to Geraldton, where they attended the dedication of the HMAS *Sydney* memorial with its 645 seagulls symbolic of each sailor lost. A woman who reportedly had an excellent memory,[9] Marjorie would surely have recalled the day the *Sydney* disappeared; her first husband Charles Learmonth had been part of the initial search party, and spent several days scouring the West Australian coast for any sign of it. Neither the wreck nor the crew were recovered, and despite several attempts to locate it, and a 1997 parliamentary inquiry, there had been no sighting at the time of the memorial service.

Early the following year, Guild member Shirley Hands was selected as one of four war widows to visit Singapore and Malaysia from 10 to 18 February 2002 to remember the 60th anniversary of the Fall of Singapore. She saw the trip as:

> *an opportunity to remember and honour their comrades*
> *who had died at the hands of the Japanese and see the*
> *changes which had taken place since they struggled through*
> *the marshes and jungle sixty years before.*[10]

Ironically, as Shirley remembered the war service of her husband and those he fought alongside, Australian soldiers found themselves

HMAS *Sydney II* Memorial, Geraldton.
(Photo by Stuart Adams)

involved in a new conflict. When hijacked planes had smashed into the World Trade Centre on 11 September 2001, killing some three thousand people, US President George W. Bush began talking about attacking Afghanistan on the supposition that the Taliban was sympathetic to al-Qaeda. In October, US and British forces began airstrikes on Afghanistan as part of Operation Enduring Freedom, and the following month marched on Kabul; however, it was thought that al-Qaeda leader Osama bin Laden had escaped to Pakistan. In January 2002, foreign peacekeepers arrived in the country, but the hostilities were far from over.

On 16 February 2002, SAS Sergeant Andrew Russell died when his patrol car hit a landmine. His wife, Kylie Russell, a young West Australian with an eleven-day-old daughter, became the first war widow of a soldier killed on active service since the Vietnam War. And as she struggled privately to comprehend that her husband was never coming back, the nation was collectively shocked by an act of terrorism close to home. Eighty-eight Australians were among the 202 killed on 12 October when bombs exploded outside popular tourist nightclubs in Bali, in avowed retaliation for Australia supporting the 'war on terror'.[11]

Australian troops pulled out of Afghanistan shortly after the bombings, although about five hundred soldiers remained to help coalition forces fight the Taliban and assist in reconstruction.[12] Attention then shifted to Iraq and Saddam Hussein's purported concealment of 'weapons of mass destruction'. On 10 January 2003, Prime Minister John Howard informed Australian troops of potential operations in Iraq. Anti-war demonstrations culminated in major protest rallies in each capital city on the weekend of 14–16 February. A month later, Bush declared that diplomacy had failed. John Howard agreed to Bush's request for troops, and Australia joined the United States and Britain in invading Iraq, with the objective to find and destroy the weapons stockpile that was supposed to exist. Several weeks later, on 10 April, US troops took Baghdad.[13]

※

By this time, the repatriation system was eighty-five years old and in need of reform. In February 2002, the Minister for Veterans' Affairs, Danna Vale, had announced an independent review into 'perceived anomalies in access to veterans' entitlements and of levels of benefits available to disability pensioners.'[14] Chairman of the enquiry, Queen's Counsel John Clarke, and his colleagues Air Marshal Doug Riding and Dr David Rosalky, consulted members of the ex-service community, which involved more than 3000 submissions and many meetings between May and September 2002.[15] As in previous reviews, the War Widows' Guild ensured its voice was heard at a national level by writing a submission and attending a meeting in Canberra during the first week of June.

The *Report of the Review of Veterans' Entitlements*, known as the Clarke Review, was published in January 2003, although when the

National Council of the War Widows' Guild met on 17 October, the women were still awaiting the outcomes of the report, as it had not yet been tabled in parliament. As a result, many motions discussed at that meeting were placed 'in abeyance pending the outcome' of the Clarke Review, especially questions pertaining to the income support supplement (ISS) and domestic allowance.[16] These were addressed several months later, in March 2004, when Danna Vale announced that some eleven thousand war widows and widowers would receive increased rent assistance in addition to the ISS, as per the report's recommendations. To receive the added benefit, a war widow or widower had to be receiving the ISS from DVA, and renting privately, with the adjustment to occur from March 2005.[17]

These were not the only improved benefits won in recent years. Until 1984, war widows who remarried saw their pension cancelled, although there had been a suggestion that they should retain it, especially as a woman in a de facto relationship did not lose her entitlements. A 1976 Department of Repatriation minute paper had previously proposed two options: allow a war widow to keep her pension upon remarriage, or widen the definition of marriage in Section 40 of the Repatriation Act so that a woman in a de facto relationship also lost her pension. The Department of Social Security had already begun doing this in preceding months, only to be accused of 'snooping'. The minute paper had concluded that adopting this option would 'rekindle the problems and criticisms which existed up to 1949' over the so-called morality clause, which the Guild had fought hard to have removed.[18]

The state executive had discussed this issue in October 1977, with a 'majority in favour' of retaining war widow status after remarriage,[19] but it was not until May 1984 that the Minister for Veterans' Affairs, Senator Gietzelt, announced that new benefits were likely, and a further eighteen months before it was confirmed that war widows who remarried after 28 May 1984 would indeed retain their pension, domestic allowance and other benefits. The reasoning was that their pension represented compensation not welfare, a view the War Widow's Guild had asserted for many years.[20] However, it was only after the 2001 federal budget that those who had remarried prior to May 1984 would also see their war widow status reinstated.

In that same budget, the federal government announced a $25,000 ex-gratia payment to Second World War veterans who had been captured by the Japanese. Where an ex–prisoner of war was deceased, his widow would receive the payment. The Guild was grateful for the attention given to the severe suffering and deprivation these men and women had experienced, but felt that compensation should be extended to other POWs. Marjorie Le Souef, whose second husband Leslie had spent four years in German camps, wrote to the Minister of Veterans' Affairs, Danna Vale, outlining her husband's experiences, and querying why the payment excluded such men. While Marjorie did not particularly need the financial assistance, she pursued the issue on principle, seeking awareness for those who had been POWs alongside her husband.[21] According to a reply from Vale's office, the government had based the decision on the higher death rate of those imprisoned by the Japanese and the precedents set by New Zealand, Canada and the United Kingdom who had compensated former Japanese POWs but not those imprisoned by other countries.[22] Marjorie pursued the issue further, and in 2006 she wrote to Bruce Billson, who had replaced Vale as the Minister for Veterans' Affairs. She lamented the lack of compensation:

> *Recently I sat next to a man who flew during the time of the 'Battle of Britain' and eventually was shot down over the English Channel and spent nearly five years as a POW. He remarked, 'We are forgotten men.' My husband and many of his unit later became POWs in Greece and Crete and spent four years behind bars.*[23]

At the War Widows' Guild conference in Tweed Heads in October that year, delegates from Western Australia and New South Wales raised the issue again. The WA branch proposed a motion that 'the Special Ex-Gratia Payment of $25,000 for ex-Prisoners of War, or their widows, is extended to Ex-Prisoners of War in Europe, or their widows' because 'all prisoners of war have suffered from privation and hardship and have lost their liberty.'[24] The motion was carried, and added to a 'priorities list' to be forwarded to the relevant government minister. The War Widows' Guild was not alone in its request; other organisations such as the ex-POW Association and the RSL also campaigned on the matter.[25] Finally, on 8 May 2007, the Australian government announced that Australians held as POWs by Germany, Italy or their allies, would now be eligible for the ex-gratia payment of $25,000 'in recognition of the unique hardships they suffered.'[26]

❀

During this first decade of the 21st century, paid staff in the WA office began to take on more and more of the work previously seen as the domain of honorary office bearers. When the Guild employed Jenny Knight as office manager in 1999, her main role had been to keep the membership database and accounts up to date, although the treasurer Beth Lindsey had still signed the cheques. The workload gradually increased after Marjorie Le Souef became president and delegated tasks such as writing letters, organising outings and guest speakers, and the work associated with the Forsyth Gardens redevelopment.[27] Subsequently, Sally Carver was employed to manage the residential village from April 2003, and Anita Atkin joined the team in September 2004, replacing Chris Paton as receptionist and personal assistant to Jenny Knight.[28]

Jenny observed that many ex-service organisations displayed a flag or colour patch at commemorative services and thought it appropriate for the national War Widows' Guild to have its own flag. Delegates of the 2004 national conference in Hobart supported the concept, and Jenny worked on a draft design, which incorporated the kookaburra logo in white on a royal blue background. The other state guilds embraced the design, and since then, this flag has been flown outside the Marjorie Le Souef Administration and Community Centre during Monday meetings and at half-mast when a member passes away. It is also used at the Guild's annual November service at the State War Memorial, and during visits to Gallipoli and the Western Front. In 2013, five war widows marched with the banner in the Anzac Day parade through Perth. It was the first time, anywhere in Australia, the Guild had been permitted to march in the parade, so this was a particular achievement for the WA members.

2013 Perth Anzac Day march. For the first time,
Guild members march under their own banner.
(Photo by Beryl Gilbert)

Coinciding with the 2005 national Guild meeting were celebrations to commemorate sixty years since the foundation of the War Widows' Guild in Australia. Twelve women from Western Australia, including staff members Anita Atkin and Jenny Knight, travelled to Melbourne for the occasion. Hazel Donald and Pearl Thomson attended meetings as official delegates, and all twelve joined in a 'lovely service at Mrs Vasey's tree' and a special anniversary luncheon.[29]

That year was also the 60th anniversary of the conclusion of the Second World War. In Perth, Marjorie Le Souef was a special guest at the Len Hall Anzac AFL game on Saturday 23 April between the Fremantle Dockers and Carlton at Subiaco Oval. And in September, Hazel Donald's brother, Bert Woodhouse, fulfilled a long-held dream to return to the country in which he had served. He was one of ten Australian veterans selected to travel to Papua New Guinea to commemorate the formal surrender of the Japanese army.[30] Although Bert was officially representing his old battalion, Hazel Donald used her sisterly influence to ensure he wore a War Widows' Guild badge,[31] something he was eligible to do because he was one of two war widowers who were Guild members.[32]

As Bert travelled to Papua New Guinea, and Australia commemorated the end of the Second World War, the media announced that Australian troops had returned to Afghanistan in the form of a Special Forces Task Group, whose role was to conduct combat patrols, reconnaissance and surveillance operations.[33]

The following year, the WA Guild turned sixty, sparking further commemoration. On Monday 27 November 2006, members attended a river cruise along the Swan River, and the following day, participated in a 'moving remembrance service'[34] at Kings Park. Hazel Donald laid a wreath along with Kate Rhodes, state president in South Australia, and June Healy, president of the ACT branch, who were visiting for the occasion. Then, each member laid a poppy at the eternal flame as they remembered their husband's life and war service. 'I was feeling close to tears as I watched them do this,' reflected Hazel Donald.[35]

An informal lunch followed at Forsyth Gardens, where Sally Carver had organised a display of memorabilia. Two days later, on the anniversary of the Guild's inaugural meeting in 1946, there was a service at St Andrew's Church in St Georges Terrace. The St Edmund's Anglican Church Choir sang, with member Gloria Lygne accompanying them on the organ. Jill Hodgson, one of the 'younger widows group', gave the first Bible reading, Hazel Donald read a second scripture and the motto, and the Very Reverend Dr John Shepherd addressed the gathering, using the motto as the basis for his talk:

> *The Guild motto sums up the two most critical aspects of our Christian faith – belonging and serving – being part of a community and working for the good of the community. And these are the two critical aspects which constitute the foundation of the War Widows' Guild of Australia. Today we ... give thanks for the community, and sense of belonging they have provided throughout this time, and for the selfless service they have offered to those women bereaved in time of war.*[36]

At the conclusion of the service, members and invited guests enjoyed a luncheon at the Novotel Hotel. Marjorie Le Souef cut the cake, baked by member Heather Fairhead and depicting the kookaburra and wattle.

As Hazel Donald's term as state president drew to a close in 2007, she and Marjorie Le Souef approached Florence Gordon about

Guild members attend a river cruise to mark sixty years
of the Guild in Western Australia, November 2006.
Top (L–R): Peggy Blain, Marjorie Le Souef, Fran Aggiss.
Centre (L–R): Shirley Sames, Laurel Taylor, Myrtle Hiatt,
Val Stickland, Gladys Hartzer, Val Cvitan, Alma Taylor.
Bottom (L–R): Dora Anderson, Florence Gordon, Marj Hassett, Alma Ardagh.
(All three photos: Guild archives, WA Branch)

nominating for the position. Florence had been a member since 1989, but had known about the Guild for many years before that. As a young woman, her best friend was the daughter of Sheila Barron, who had managed the Esplanade Kiosk in the 1950s and 1960s. Florence had grown up in Walcott Street, Mount Lawley, and was nineteen when the Second World War broke out. She worked as a manager's secretary at T & G Mutual Life Assurance Society, and volunteered for the Women's Australian National Service (WANS). In addition to packing socks, cakes and other items to send to servicemen overseas, she underwent first aid training and learned to operate the switchboard

Top: Gloria Lygne playing the organ at a service at St Andrew's Church in St Georges Terrace to commemorate sixty years of the Guild in Western Australia. Bottom: Guild members inspect memorabilia collected for the 60th anniversary. (Both images: Guild archives, WA Branch)

at the North Perth Fire Station, to enable firemen to attend their posts in the event of an air raid. Florence found it all rather exciting, failing to appreciate the seriousness of war until she witnessed its impact on those returning from combat.[37]

Florence had met her husband Kevin in May 1946, after he was discharged from the army, and they married on 15 October 1949. After raising four children and sharing almost forty years of marriage, Kevin died on 23 September 1988. Her neighbour, Guild member Pearl Thomson, encouraged Florence to join the Guild. 'Come down and I'll introduce you to everyone,' Pearl told her. Florence immediately felt

Top: Celebrating sixty years of the War Widows' Guild in Western Australia, 2006.
Bottom: Marjorie Le Souef, state president from 1946 to 1947 and then again from 2000 to 2003, cuts the cake.
(Both images: Guild archives, WA Branch)

welcomed by the other women, including long-time members Norma Roberts and Marj Hassett.[38] Florence became a regular at meetings and card games and joined the executive committee in 1993. But even though she had shared the role of vice-president with Pearl Thomson since 2002, she never considered herself to be presidential material. 'I could never do that,' she said. 'I haven't got the confidence.'

'Yes, you have,' Hazel and Marjorie replied. 'We'll give you all the help you need.'[39]

After much discussion and persuasion, Florence reluctantly accepted the nomination and, despite her initial reticence, ended up thoroughly enjoying the role and grateful for the privilege. When asked why she remained involved in the Guild for such a long time, Florence replied that it was the potential to help others. 'Some of them had a terrible time.' The Guild, she added, 'means the world to me. I just love it.'[40]

Sue Wilson expresses similar sentiments, saying, 'I just love being in it and I am very proud to be in it.' In contrast to Florence's long personal connection to the Guild, Sue was a war widow for almost two decades before she discovered its existence, quite by accident, when she enquired about rental accommodation at Forsyth Gardens in 2009.

Until then, Sue had always been a country girl, growing up on properties in the Riverland area of South Australia, and later bringing up a family in the Pilbara. She met her husband Merv while working as a farm cook and housecleaner; she married at eighteen and was raising three children by the time she was twenty-one. When he went to Vietnam, Merv did so as part of the regular army rather than as a conscript, but even before then, he had often worked away on large engineering projects, including travelling to Borneo and Sabah with 21 Construction Squadron to build the road from Sarawak to Sabah. Merv's absence took its toll on Sue. 'It affects the woman, too, you know, the one that's home,' she says. 'You know you've got to be the father as well as the mother to the children.' Sue was also on the receiving end of those protesting Australia's involvement in Vietnam:

> *They spat on you, and didn't talk to you … You'd say your husband's in Vietnam and [the response would be], 'Oh, a*

war you shouldn't be at.' … Yes, we got abused sometimes …
so none of us mentioned they were in Vietnam. It was the
easiest way to get around it.[41]

Merv experienced little direct action in Vietnam, as his job had been to build roads and helipads, but he had seen many bodies and 'saw the boys coming back devastated and a mess.' He only talked about it when he met up with the men he'd served alongside, but Sue knew the experience had deeply affected him. In bed, she frequently had to duck as he fought in his nightmares; the next morning, he would have no idea his wife had been dodging his fists during the night.[42]

When Merv died, the undertaker, who was also a Vietnam Vet, offered Sue understanding, support and the forms necessary to apply for a war widow's pension. He also contacted a legatee on her behalf, who then visited regularly to check whether she needed anything. But nobody mentioned the War Widows' Guild. Sue supposes that there may have been information amongst the paperwork she received at the time. 'You get stacks of paperwork … could have been something about War Widows, but I don't remember reading anything.'[43]

In fact, she did not hear of the Guild for another seventeen years. After several years travelling, she contemplated settling down again, and in the process learned of Forsyth Gardens and, subsequently, the War Widows' Guild. Not long after her move into one of the rental units, she was enticed onto the executive committee.[44] She was vice-president for two years, before becoming president in 2012, after Hazel Donald completed a second term in the role.

Sue's experience typifies the continuing difficulty of how to inform war widows of the Guild's existence, and the benefits to which they are entitled.

> *New war widows are advised through DVA about the Guild.*
> *This is usually at a very raw, early stage of becoming a war*
> *widow … Many times we hear from a new member that she*
> *did not know anything about the Guild. Such members hear*
> *about us through friends, following hospitalisation, media*
> *articles or through sheer co-incidence.*[45]

The Guild also recognises the practical realities of younger widows' lives that prevent them from being more actively involved.

> *It is increasingly hard to find younger members to take*
> *on Executive Committee positions … a lot of the younger*
> *widows have to work to pay off a mortgage and some still*
> *have children at home or are involved with grandchildren.*[46]

In 2003, researcher Marie Cooke published a journal article, based on her case study of a Vietnam War widow, in which she argued that some younger women did not identify themselves as war widows because that symbolised dependence, was perceived to be past rather than future focused, and was seen as a label for older women. In contrast, the Second World War widows Cooke interviewed identified proudly with the term war widow.[47]

Sue Wilson offers a different response. 'If I had known about the Guild, I would have joined straight away, seventeen years ago,' she says.[48] And fellow Vietnam War widow Robin Bowden eagerly joined the Guild when it began in Kalgoorlie because she had been so grateful to receive her pension.[49] In Hazel Donald's case, she did not initially think she deserved a war widow's pension, believing that it was simply normal to care for the man she loved without requiring a reward. But friends told her, 'You have earned it for your dedication in looking after Bill.'[50]

These diverse responses make it clear that there is no simple way to draw in such a range of widows as has resulted from the various conflicts involving Australians. Yet the Guild continues to seek ways to address the needs of existing members while reaching out to new widows. Information evenings, 'handyman' workshops and 'girls night out' events aimed at younger women have helped, but there is undoubtedly more that can be done.[51] As one young war widow expressed, the Guild must:

> *embrace these new members and reach out with the hand*
> *of experience to revitalise the whole organisation or risk*
> *having such an enigmatic group gradually lose its long held*
> *and well justified power and influence.*[52]

De'Arne Prosser was searching for such a supportive 'hand of experience'. De'Arne is healthy, full of ideas and unafraid of expressing her opinion, yet she understands the grief, loneliness and vulnerability that accompany the recent loss of a partner. During her husband Tom's long army career, which included service in 1RAR, the first group of Australian men to serve in Vietnam, De'Arne endured frequent absences, sub-standard housing, and the snobbery of rank distinctions. But she also experienced the richness of camaraderie when disaster or tragedy struck, such as the time Tom contracted hepatitis while she was heavily pregnant. Everyone rallied around. 'There were challenging times, but there were good times,' she says.[53] Although being an army wife had its difficulties, none of it compared to losing Tom suddenly in September 2010.

> *This is my toughest challenge. Getting through without him. I've always – I have a survival mechanism, you know, and I reckon I've always met all the challenges pretty well. This is the only one I'm having a battle with.*[54]

De'Arne describes her own grieving process, and imagines it would be similar for others, too:

> *You've got everybody with you at first and then they go home. But the family, they all kept a close eye on me, so in the first twelve months, you are in this haze and just allow life to go by you. Then the second twelve months, I thought, oh yeah, I am paying bills, I guess I better look at all this stuff and start working my own life and getting organised.*[55]

People assumed that she was strong, De'Arne says, 'But you're not. You put on a façade but you're not. You're vulnerable.' She adds that, 'the loneliness is the killer. And the night-time is the worst … all of a sudden you're on your own and you need to create this new life.'[56]

After an army friend mentioned the War Widows' Guild, De'Arne contacted Jenny Knight. She initially found it difficult to attend Guild meetings, but chatting to fellow member Cecily Wright made a huge difference. One day, Cecily told her, 'I know how you feel, but it will get better.' De'Arne says, 'It felt good to be able to talk and know the other person understood.'[57]

Hazel Donald adds, 'It doesn't matter whether you lost your husband … sixty years ago or ten days ago. You've got a common bond. You're a war widow. Your husband's done something for this country.' Sue Wilson encourages other widows, of all ages and conflicts, to join. 'They don't know what they are missing, I reckon. They should come and join us … even if they stay for ten minutes just to hear what's going on. And just to meet the older ones. There's experience from the older ones … we have been there. We can help them.'

❀

A number of war widows enjoyed travelling but lacked the confidence or desire to do so alone. State executive officer Jenny Knight had also heard many of them express an interest in military history, not only because of their husband's service, but also that of other family members. With these elements in mind, Jenny designed a trip to Istanbul and the Gallipoli Peninsula to coincide with Anzac Day 2008, and extended invitations to members in other states. Fifteen war widows and two war veterans responded, and the group arrived in Turkey in the early morning of 18 April.

2008 Gallipoli tour members.
(Photo by Jenny Knight)

The Gallipoli Peninsula is crowded at this time of year, but at other times it is an isolated, lonely place. The group visited cemeteries and walked between the graves, reading the names of the young men who lost their lives. Many of the women were close to tears as they did so; however, one of the most poignant moments of the trip occurred not in a cemetery, but during a visit to the village of Bigali, the headquarters of the Turkish general Mustafa Kumal, who later became Ataturk, the first president of modern Turkey. The group toured his simply furnished home, now a museum, and meandered down the narrow, cobbled street to where locals sat on their front steps, hoping to sell a few souvenirs. Unable to resist a street stall, the war widows stopped to browse and were welcomed with strong, sweet tea.

One of the stalls was run by a thirty-eight year old widow, who supported herself and her daughter by selling doilies she has crocheted. Norma Harmsworth, whose father and uncle had fought at Gallipoli, spoke with the widow, tour guide Kazim acting as interpreter. 'I am a widow, too,' Norma said, as she purchased several items. The similarities between the young Turkish widow and founding members of the War Widows' Guild, who learned to weave as a way of supplementing their meagre pensions, were not lost on the widows from Australia.

In the dark hours before the dawn service, thousands of people snuggled into sleeping bags at North Beach, the landing site of the 11th Battalion from Western Australia. The War Widows' Guild was among the fortunate few allocated priority seating in temporary stands, although the chill still cut through layers of clothing and blankets. Behind them, the enigmatic Sphinx rose out of the hillside, an ancient sentry. Two large screens played interviews with historians, members of the armed services and individuals whose relatives fought at Gallipoli. Documentary footage and letters from young soldiers to their families provided images of that bitter spring morning ninety-three years before.

Just before 5.30 am, the master of ceremony, Judy Bailey, a veteran broadcaster from New Zealand, stepped to the dais. Behind her, the flags of Turkey, Australia and New Zealand fluttered at half-mast. Waves lapped gently and the flagpoles creaked, but the crowd was quiet as she formally opened the service. Australian and New Zealand representatives addressed the crowd. In his speech, the Australian

Top: Preparing to head to the dawn service at Anzac Cove. L–R: Hazel Donald,
Bert Woodhouse, Harry Cable, Norma Harmsworth, Marj Wilson.
Bottom: Tour members rugged up against the cold at the 2008 Gallipoli dawn
service.
(Both photos by Melinda Tognini)

Minister for Defence, Joel Fitzgibbon, demonstrated that, despite the
efforts of revisionist historians, the Anzac legend was alive. He spoke
of 'courage, commitment and sacrifices' in a 'brutal and ugly war'
and 'the strategic mistakes of ... leaders and the high human cost of
victories and defeats alike,' then added:

Here they gave birth to the Anzac legend and gave
legitimacy to Australia's nationhood … they brought
larrikinism, irreverence and dry humour to one of
the toughest places on earth … the word mate would
undoubtedly figure most prominently. No word could be
more synonymous with the character of the Aussie digger.

The sky lightened. The service proceeded through hymns and prayers for peace, the Ode of Remembrance and the haunting notes of the Last Post. Two minutes of silence was broken by the Reveille. Dignitaries and officials from various organisations laid wreaths, although the War Widows' Guild would have to wait for the conclusion of the Lone Pine service to pay their respects. Only then could immediate-past-president Hazel Donald and Norma Harmsworth, who at ninety was the oldest person at Gallipoli that year, lay a wreath on behalf of all Australian war widows, along with any other members of the public who wished to do so.

The following year, Jenny took another group of widows to Gallipoli, and again a representative laid a wreath after the conclusion of the Lone Pine Service. But by 2010, Jenny Knight had successfully lobbied for the Guild's formal inclusion. This time Diana Bland, then national secretary/treasurer, was afforded the honour of laying a wreath during the dawn service. It is unlikely that many of those watching would have realised the significance of this moment. Nevertheless, this was indeed a milestone for the War Widows' Guild.[58]

The next year this privilege went to Hazel Donald, who had returned to the role of state president. And in 2012, the War Widows' Guild national president, Audrey Blood, not only laid a wreath but was invited to join the official party for two days prior to the service. Meanwhile, Hazel formally participated in the equivalent dawn service in Villers-Bretonneux, the scene of Australia's victory after 46,000 men had died on the Western Front. This was far greater than the losses at Gallipoli, and many more returned home physically and emotionally crippled.[59] Hazel's own father had fought in France with the British Army. Speaking at the service, Australian Ambassador-Designate Ric Wells said:

*When we think of the victory that was won here, we must
also remember the cost. And we must remember the fighting
here at Villers-Bretonneux was just one episode in a war
that took millions of lives.*

2008 Gallipoli tour, Lone Pine.
Top: War Widows' Guild flag displayed at the service.
Bottom: Hazel Donald and Norma Harmsworth
lay a wreath on behalf of all war widows.
(Both photos by Jenny Knight)

Nick Miller, recipient of the South Australian Premier's ANZAC Spirit School Prize, read a letter written by an army chaplain to the mother of a soldier killed on the Western Front. Then Hazel read a letter from a mother requesting information about her son J.J. Goulding. Goulding had first been reported missing at Fromelles, then as a prisoner of war and finally as killed in action, but no further details had been forthcoming. His mother wrote of her hope for news and the sense of being forgotten. She said: 'the war has just begun for mothers that dearly love their boys all over the world.'

Hazel had practised reading the moving letter many times since her invitation, yet still doubted the ability to do so without her voice cracking. But, dressed in a heavy coat and hat to ward off the below-freezing conditions, she appeared confident and calm, her voice steady and clear. Later in the service, she laid a wreath on behalf of Australian war widows. She was invited to return the following year, where she again read a letter from a bereaved mother. What a contrast to those early years of the War Widows' Guild when Jessie Vasey was obliged to urge all war widows to protest about being excluded from official participation in these services.

After all the years of struggle for public recognition and official representation at such commemorations, has the Guild finally arrived? Some would argue that it hasn't; that while much has been achieved, there is one important step yet to be taken: war widows are still not recognised as chief mourners. They are 'put way back down the bottom of the line to lay the wreath at many services,' to quote Sue Wilson. 'We are actually the main mourners,' Sue observes. 'We should come after the diggers themselves. All the same, it is nice to get invited to them all.'[60]

Florence Gordon addresses the 2008 Guild service,
held each November at the State War Memorial in Kings Park.
(Photo by Melinda Tognini)

Members attending the 2008 Guild service.
L–R: Lorna May, Pearl Thomson, Iris Rowtcliff, Marj Hassett and Joy Smith.
(Photo by Melinda Tognini)

In 2012 the Guild formally invited a representative from each conflict
to lay a wreath at the Guild service in Kings Park. Here, Skye Butler,
whose husband served in Afghanistan, sits with her young son
waiting for the service to begin.
(Photo by Melinda Tognini)

2012 Guild service (L–R): Tonya McCusker, Sue Wilson,
Governor of Western Australia Malcolm McCusker, Jan McLeod.
(Photo by Melinda Tognini)

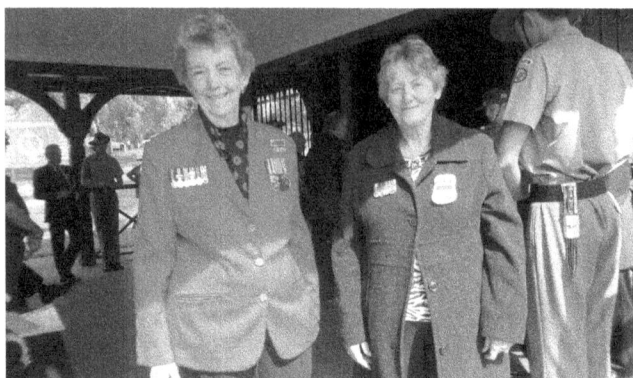

Hazel Donald and Jan McLeod attend the 2013 Vietnam Veterans Memorial Service.
(Guild archives, WA Branch)

Centre: In 2013, the Guild was privileged to have Gwen Forsyth's
sons John and Alan attend the service in Kings Park.
Bottom: Wreaths for remembrance.
(Both photos by Melinda Tognini)

EPILOGUE

Much has changed since November 1946 when two hundred war widows gathered at Anzac House to listen to the commanding voice of Jessie Vasey. The average age of those women who formed the Western Australian branch of the War Widows' Guild that day was twenty-six; today a war widow's average age is eighty-three. The needs of many current members are vastly different from the needs of women widowed during the Second World War, and from this new generation of young widows. The changing role of women, increased career opportunities and greater access to child care mean that the widows of contemporary conflicts live in a society vastly different to the one that existed in 1945. But despite the differences between the eras and generations, all war widows can identify and empathise with the myriad emotions associated with loss and the journey taken while traversing grief.

Many of the benefits war widows enjoy today are a result of the work of the War Widows' Guild. But the organisation cannot afford to be complacent; it continues to maintain a presence in Canberra to ensure that these benefits are not eroded.[1] Although war widow numbers may decrease in the future, they will never disappear completely while Australians are deployed overseas, whether to war zones or on peacekeeping ventures. Whenever this occurs, there will be loved ones waiting anxiously at home, and for some, that return journey may not eventuate. The Very Reverend Dr John Shepherd alluded to this in his address at the Guild's 60th anniversary service:

> we pray for the time when violence will cease, and wars will
> be no more. Yet we are realistic enough to know that the

propensity for war remains always with us, and so we are aware of the need for this organisation to be maintained and supported, not only for our present war widows, but against the time when future calamities may revisit us, and another generation of destroyed marriages and wounded families will be created.[2]

And as long as there are conflicts that result in the death of Australian servicemen and women, the War Widows' Guild will continue to support and advocate for war widows of all ages.

APPENDIXES

APPENDIX 1

The information contained in this appendix was compiled from Guild minutes and copies of the *Guild News*; however, some of these records are missing, and therefore some dates are only approximate. Unless an early resignation was noted in the minutes, it is assumed that terms of office began from the date of the AGM held in the year given. At times, first names are not known, as many of the early records noted only a first initial, sometimes that of a widow's husband. In a few early instances, there are some dubious spellings of names, and where it was impossible to unequivocally check these, they have been left as they appeared in the hand-written record.

In attendance at the first provisional committee meeting, 29 November 1946
Jessie Vasey, Mrs Mann, Mrs T. Collins, Jean Elsie Ferguson, Mrs E. Thompson, Mrs M. Pyke, Madge Anketell, Marjorie Learmonth, Mrs M. Dyson, Mrs G. Smith, Mrs M. McLinden, Gwen Forsyth, Muriel Jones, Mrs L. Bisiat, Mrs N. Lewis, Edna Ramage, Nell Chapman, Mrs O. Keating, Mrs J. Stewart, Mrs V. Johnson, Mrs L. Jacoby, Patricia Connor, Mrs E. Stewart, Mrs C.E. Elder, Mrs S. Tucker, Peggy Walker, Phyllis Thomas, Lucille Rickards

Interim officers elected on 29 November 1946
Chairman: Marjorie Learmonth
Vice-President: Marjorie Anketell, Jean Ferguson
Secretary: Lucille Rickards
Assistant Secretary: Muriel Jones
Treasurer: Mrs G. Smith

Inaugural Executive Committee and Office Bearers, as elected 9 May 1947
President: Marjorie Learmonth
Vice-Presidents: Marjorie Anketell, Jean Ferguson and Rita Kuring
Hon. Secretary: Muriel Jones
Hon. Ass. Secretary: Mrs M. McLinden
Hon. Treasurer: Mrs G. Smith
Executive:

Peggy Walker	Patricia Connor	Phyllis Thomas
J. Foreman	M. Dyson	Nell Chapman
Betty Thompson	Marjorie Davidson	D. Armstrong
C. Elder	Gwen Forsyth	Edna Ramage
F. Lewis	E. Stuart	M. Rodda

State Presidents
1947   Marjorie Learmonth
1947–1957 Winifred Fowler
1957–1983 Gwen Forsyth OBE BEM
1983–1995 Gloria MacDonald OAM
1995–1997 Iris Rowtcliff OAM
1997–2000 Fran Aggiss
2000–2003 Marjorie Le Souef
2003–2007 Hazel Donald
2007–2009 Florence Gordon
2009–2012 Hazel Donald
2012–2015 Sue Wilson

Vice-Presidents
1947–1948 Marjorie Anketell,
           Jean Ferguson, Rita Kuring
1948–1949 Rita Kuring, Jean Ferguson,
           Gwen Forsyth, Mrs Kelly
1949–1951 Marjorie Anketell, Jean
           Ferguson, Gwen Forsyth,
           May Hiatt
1951–1952 Gwen Forsyth, May Hiatt
1952–1953 Gwen Forsyth
1953–1954 Gwen Forsyth, Mrs V. Smith,
           Ethel Bird
1954–1957 Gwen Forsyth, Ethel Bird
1957–1958 Ethel Bird, Mrs Olden
1958–1959 Muriel Jones, Mrs Olden
1959–1960 May Hiatt, Muriel Jones,
           Mrs Olden
1960   May Hiatt, Muriel Jones,
           Bertha Denton
1960–1961 May Hiatt, Bertha Denton
1961–1963 May Hiatt, Bertha Denton,
           Sheila Barron
1963–1964 May Hiatt, Sheila Barron,
           Win Greenshields
1964–1965 May Hiatt, Win Greenshields
1965–1968 Ethel Bird, Mrs Martin
1968–1974 Mrs Martin,
           Gloria MacDonald
1974–1982 Gloria MacDonald,
           Hazel Carrick
1983–1985 Hazel Carrick, Jean Coleman
1985–1987 Jean Coleman, Olive Snedden
1987–1989 Jean Coleman, Marj Hassett
1989–1990 Jean Coleman, Isabel Leitch
1990–1992 Isabel Leitch, Marj Hassett
1992–1993 Isabel Leitch, Marj Hassett,
           Doreen Taylor

1993–1995 Isabel Leitch, Doreen Taylor,
           Mrs S. Shaw
1995–1997 Isabel Leitch, Doreen Taylor
1997–1998 Doreen Taylor,
           Marjorie Le Souef
1998–2000 Marjorie Le Souef,
           Ada Caple
2000–2001 Ada Caple, Doreen Taylor
2001–2002 Iris Rowtcliff, Pearl Thomson
2002–2007 Pearl Thomson, Florence
           Gordon
2007–2008 Joy Smith, Phyllis McMiles
2008–2009 Joy Smith, Hazel Donald
2009–2010 Shirley Sames,
           Marjorie Wilson
2010–2012 Sue Wilson
2012–2015 Jan McLeod

Secretary
1947–1948 Muriel Jones,
           Mrs M. McLinden (assistant)
1948–1949 Mollie Hayes,
           Mrs M. McLinden (assistant)
1949–1950 Wyn Spence,
           Phyllis Thomas (assistant)
1950–1951 Mrs Rosenberg,
           Phyllis Thomas (assistant)
1951–1952 Mrs Moyes (minutes),
           Yvonne Helliwell
           (correspondence), Phyllis
           Thomas (correspondence)
1952–1953 Mrs Moyes (minutes),
           Yvonne Helliwell (assistant)
1953–1954 Patricia Connor (minutes)
1954–1955 Rita Kuring
1955–1956 Rita Kuring,
           Mrs Pike (assistant)
1955–1957 Mrs R. Moyes
1957–1958 Mrs Wortley
1958–1959 Mrs Pike
1959–1960 Mrs Pike (minutes),
           Mrs Keast (correspondence)
1960–1961 Muriel Jones (minutes),
           Mrs Keast (correspondence)
1961–1962 Muriel Jones (minutes),
           Yvonne Helliwell
           (correspondence)
1962–1966 Muriel Jones (minutes),
           Gloria MacDonald
           (correspondence)

1966–1968 Win Greenshields (minutes), Gloria MacDonald (correspondence)
1968–1974 Win Greenshields, Mrs Primrose
1974–1975 Win Greenshields, Mrs MacMaster (assistant)
1975–1977 Gloria MacDonald, Mrs MacMaster
1977–1983 Gloria MacDonald, Hazel Carrick (assistant)
1983–1985 Gloria MacDonald (acting), Vi Smiles (minutes), Hazel Carrick (assistant), Ena Keeley (assistant)
1985–1986 Ena Keeley, Vi Smiles (minutes), Hazel Carrick (assistant)
1986–1987 Ena Keeley, Vi Smiles (assistant)
1987–1989 Iris Rowtcliff, Vi Smiles (assistant)
1989–1993 Pearl Thomson, Vi Smiles (assistant)
1993–1995 Pearl Thomson, Vi Smiles (assistant), Mrs N. Roberts (social)
1995–1997 Pearl Thomson, Vi Smiles (assistant)
1997–1998 Beryl Wood, Vi Smiles (minutes)
1998–2001 Corrie Sweeney (paid position)
2001–2015 Jenny Knight (paid position)

Treasurer
1947–1948 Mrs G. Smith
1948–1956 Rita Kuring
1956–1959 Enid Bird
1960–1961 Dorothy Spiers
1961–1966 Mrs Laughton
1966–1976 Dorothy Spiers
1976–1984 Mickey Parker
1984–1989 Elsie Lewis
1989–1990 Iris Rowtcliff
1993–1994 Phyl McIllree (acting)
1994   Phyl McIllree, Iris Rowtcliff (assistant)
1994–1995 Iris Rowtcliff
1995–1997 Phyl McIllree, Phyl Quartermaine

1997–1998 Phyl Quartermaine
1998–1999 Robin Braccia (bookkeeper/ accounts manager)
1999–2002 Jenny Knight (accounts manager)
2003–2008 Jenny Knight (Guild administrator)
2008–2015 Jenny Knight (executive officer)

Executive Committee
The Executive Committee consisted of the state president, vice-presidents (usually more than one), treasurer, secretary and other members. The Council was a wider group which met every three months.

Mrs Abbey	1972–1974
Mrs Fran Aggiss	1993–2003
Mrs Ahern	1957–1958
Mrs Dot Aley	1980–1989
Mrs Nellie Allan	1981–1986
Mrs Allen	1967–1969, 1987–1988
Mrs Dora Anderson	1984–2003
Mrs Angel	1978–1985
Mrs Madge Anketell	1946–1956
Mrs D. Armstrong	1947–1955
Mrs Bailey	1962–1968
Mrs J. Baker	1981–1986
Mrs Barbara Banfield	2014–2015
Mrs Bateman	1966–1969
Mrs Sheila Barron	1949–1961, 1965–1966
Mrs Ethel Bird	1952–1959, 1965–1968
Mrs Blackmore	1963–1967
Mrs Blair	1974–1982
Mrs Pearl Bowers	1979–1985
Mrs Brimmell	1987–1988
Mrs Brockman	1989–1990
Mrs Marie Brooker	1984–1997
Mrs Brooks	1993–1994
Mrs Buhler	1961–1962
Mrs Burgess	1960–1961
Mrs I. Burvill	1987–1989
Mrs Lilian Cadwgan	1972–1975
Mrs Cannon	1968–1969
Mrs Ada Caple	1990–2004

Mrs Hazel Carrick	1966–1969, 1973–1989
Mrs Carroll	1962–1967
Mrs Carson	1983–1984
Mrs B. Carter	1995–1997
Mrs Nell Chapman	1947–1948, 1958–1959
Mrs Chester	1984–1988
Mrs P. Cleland	1950–
Mrs Clifford	1968–1970
Mrs Nancy Coghlan	1986–1989
Mrs Jean Coleman	1980–1996
Mrs Coley	1985–1992
Mrs Collins	1978–1982
Mrs Colquhoun	1950–1951
Mrs Patricia Connor	1947–1954
Mrs Olive Cromb	1999–2001
Mrs Cunningham	1969–1973
Mrs D'Arcy	1977–1983
Mrs Beatrice Davey	1949–1951
Mrs Davey	1955–1956
Mrs Marjorie Davidson	1947–1949
Mrs Mary Davies	1949–1950
Mrs Davis	1970–1972
Mrs Bertha Denton	1955–1963
Mrs de Pedro	1972–1977
Mrs Diamond	1964–1970
Mrs Dick	1970–1974
Mrs Hazel Donald	2003–2015
Mrs Jean-Shirley Donaldson	2000–2010
Mrs Doran	1965–1971
Mrs E. Downe	1949–1952
Mrs Pat Doyle	1981–2000
Mrs M. Dyson	1947–1950
Mrs Easom	1969–1970
Mrs Margaret Eddy	1989–2000
Mrs C.E. Elder	1947–1948
Mrs Evans	1966–1968
Mrs Jean Ferguson	1947–1957
Mrs Fletcher	1958–1962
Mrs Marjorie Flint	1988–2000
Mrs J. Foreman	1947–1949
Mrs Gwen Forsyth	1947–1983
Mrs Winifred Fowler	1947–1957
Mrs Frederick	1957–1961
Mrs Gaynor	1957–1960
Mrs Gibson	1958–1960
Mrs Glew	1970–1971
Mrs Goddard	1971–1976
Mrs Phil Goldsmith	1975–1990
Mrs Florence Gordon	1992–2012
Mrs Elvein Gostelow	1968–1972
Mrs Gray	1960–1962
Mrs Will Greathead	2009–2014
Mrs Win Greenshields	1960–1991
Mrs Gregory	1988–1990
Mrs Grose	1966–1968
Mrs Hall	1965
Mrs Beattie Hammond	1975–1981
Mrs Olive Hancock	1958–1968
Mrs Harley	1960–1966
Mrs Marjorie Hassett	1976–1999, 2003–2007
Mrs Mollie Hayes	1949–1952
Mrs Rose Heath	1949–1958
Mrs Yvonne Helliwell	1950–1961, 1967–1983
Mrs May Hiatt	1948–1977
Mrs Holman	1962
Mrs Hume	1960–1961
Mrs Hurdle	1972–1987
Mrs Theresa Ingate	2013–2014
Mrs Gwen Isaacs	2010–2011
Mrs Muriel Jones	1947–1966
Mrs Betty Jones	2004–2007
Mrs Vera Judge	1960–1966
Mrs Keast	1958–1961
Mrs Keddie	1968–1975
Mrs Ena Keeley	1973–1987
Mrs J. Kelly	1949–1952
Mrs Kennedy	1964–1965
Mrs Kenny	1987–1988
Mrs Elsie Ketterer	1960–1963, 1966
Mrs Kevin	1970–1972
Mrs King	1960–1961
Mrs Kruger	1956–1980
Mrs Kathleen (Rita) Kuring	1950–1958
Mrs Madeline Landwehr	2004–2005
Mrs Laney	1951–1952
Mrs Langford	1972–1974
Mrs Lapsley	1966–1971
Mrs Lasky	1975–1978
Mrs Laughton	1958–1981
Mrs M. Learmonth/Le Souef	1947, 1997–2008
Mrs Leete	1987–1992

Mrs Isabel (Belle) Leitch 1985–1999
Mrs F. Lewis 1947–1950
Mrs Elsie Lewis 1983–1989
Mrs Beth Lindsey 1999–2004
Mrs Jill Longmore 2011–2013
Mrs Love 1967–1968
Mrs Lowe 1968–1970
Mrs J. Lyon 1949–1950
Mrs Gloria MacDonald 1961–1999
Mrs MacMaster 1977–1984
Mrs Maller 1984–1985
Mrs Manning 1962–1974
Mrs Marks 1979–1980
Mrs Martin 1964–1974
Mrs Lorna May 2007–2010
Mrs E. McArthur 1993–1996
Mrs McCreery 1988–1995
Mrs Phyl McIllree 1989–2000
Mrs McLeod 1967–1969
Mrs Jan McLeod 2011–2015
Mrs Phyl McMiles 1994–1996,
2003–2010
Mrs McNab 1967–1969
Mrs F. Meldrum 1997–1998
Mrs Miller 1958–1966,
1972–1978
Mrs M. Miosich 1996–1998
Mrs Morrison 1972–1973
Mrs Ada Mortimer 1981–1999
Mrs Morton 1961–1963
Mrs R. Moyes 1948–1958
Mrs Nelligan 1974–1975
Mrs N. Nichol 1983–1987
Mrs Noble 1954–1959
Mrs Olden 1953–1957
Mrs O'Neill 1965–1967
Mrs Padley 1968–1970
Mrs Paisley 1971–1972
Mrs Olive Palmer 1971–1986
Mrs Mickey Parker 1975–1984
Mrs Amy Pereira 1961–1967
Mrs Pike 1950–1960
Mrs Primrose 1965–1968
Mrs De'Arne Prosser 2013–2015
Mrs Phyl Quartermaine 1992–2001
Mrs Edna Ramage 1947–1949
Mrs Reid 1963–1966
Mrs Relf 1970
Mrs E. Reynolds 1997–1998

Mrs Agnes Ritson 1980–1990
Mrs Roberts 1961–1962
Mrs C. Roberts 1987
Mrs N. Roberts 1985–1996
Mrs N. Robertson 1969–1979
Mrs Cecily Robinson 1993–2005
Mrs M. Rodda 1947–1951
Mrs Rosenberg 1950–1952
Mrs H. Rouse 1987–1996
Mrs Rowan 1961–1965
Mrs Iris Rowtcliff 1985–2002
Mrs Salter 1954–1958
Mrs Shirley Sames 2006–2010
Mrs Sandwell 1970, 1973–1979
Mrs Vera Shawcross 1997–1998
Mrs Violet (Vi) Smiles 1977–1997
Mrs B. Smith 1984–1988
Mrs G. Smith 1947–1948
Mrs J. Smith 1971–1972
Mrs Joy Smith 2000–2007
Mrs V. Smith 1950–1954
Mrs Olive Sneddon 1983–1987
Mrs Margaret Southwood
1995–1997,
2000–2003
Mrs Wyn Spence 1949–1952
Mrs Dorothy Spiers 1948–1978
Mrs V. Stack 1989–1998
Mrs Stevens 1963–1964
Mrs Stone 1970–1973
Mrs Storey 1958–1962
Mrs E. Stuart 1947–1949
Mrs Sublet 1987–1992
Mrs Jean Tapping 1977–1993
Mrs Doreen Taylor 1992–2001
Mrs Phyllis Thomas 1947–1954
Mrs Betty Thompson 1947–1949
Mrs Pearl Thomson 1989–2007
Mrs Timmel 1968–1972
Mrs Townsend 1980–1987
Mrs Evelyn Toy 1993–1995
Mrs Urwin 1975–1976
Mrs Vander-Velde 1958–1961
Mrs Vine 1954–1955
Mrs Roma Vinneir 2014–2015
Mrs Peggy Walker 1947–1949
Mrs Walker 1971–1974
Mrs Walton 1970–1973
Mrs D. Weedon 1955–1956

Mrs G. Williams	1950–1951
Mrs Marjorie Wilson	2006–2010
Mrs Sue Wilson	2011–2015
Mrs Beryl Wood	1997–1998
Mrs Woods	1980–1983
Mrs G. Wortley	1951–1959
Mrs Elsie Wright	1974–1980
Mrs Cecily Wright	2013–2015
Mrs Nell Yeoman	1978–1982
Mrs June Young	2009–2013
Mrs P. Young	1997–1998

APPENDIX 2
Albany Branch Office Bearers
President
1998–2001 Ruth Moir
2001–2004 Josie Lewis
2004–2007 Nancy Millard
2007–2013 Ivy Wolfe

Secretary
1998–1999 Pat Curgenven
1999–2000 Liz Wellstead
2000–2001 Joan Wellington
2001–2003 Joan E'att
2004–2006 Gwen Lawrence
2007–2011 Ruth Moir
2012–2013 Nancy Millard
2013   Doris Robinson

Treasurer
1998–2000 Norma Barr
2000–2002 Nessie Hawkins
2002–2005 Dorothy Diprose
2005–2007 Nancy Little
2008–2012 Win Sprig
2012–2013 Gwen Norman

Note: At the beginning of 2014, the War Widows' Guild employed Hannah Roscoe to coordinate the Albany branch, replacing the existing committee. Vicki Clarke took over the role early in 2015.

APPENDIX 3
Kalgoorlie Branch Office Bearers
There are no records of committee members between 1956 and when the branch was re-established in 2001. Alma Japp hosted a small group in the 1970s and 1980s but it is not believed to have had office bearers. There has not been an AGM since 2011 due to diminishing numbers.

President
1949–1952 Mrs Donaldson
1952–1953 Wilmia Oliver
1954–1956 Edith Rourke
2001–2002 Teti Gribble
2002–2010 Doreen Basley
2011–2012 Gloria Doust

Vice-Presidents
1949–1951 Wilmia Oliver
1952–1953 Mrs Anderson
1954–1955 Wilmia Oliver
1955–1956 Mrs Anderson
2001–2002 Doreen Basley
2002–2011 Gloria Doust

Secretary
1949–1953 Edith Rourke
1954–1955 Mrs Anderson
2001–2004 Kathleen Swinton
2004–2012 Robin Bowden

Treasurer
1949–1950 Mrs Carrington
1950–1951 Mrs Catherine Rasmussen
1952–1953 Mrs Black
1955–1956 Mrs Oliver
2001–2004 Robin Bowden
2004–2006 Laurie Wilson
2007–2008 Kathleen Swinton
2008–2012 Peg McKenzie

APPENDIX 4
Mandurah Office Bearers
President
2000–2008 Rene Anderson

Vice-President
2000–2005 Roma Blair
2005–2006 Rosa Drage

Secretary
2000–2005 Clarice Stewart
2005–2008 Bobbie Bevan

Treasurer
2000–2002 Bobby Bevan
2002–2008 Joan Matson

Note: In 2008 Anita Atkin, who works in the Perth office, began to run the monthly meetings in Mandurah and the branch committee fell into abeyance.

APPENDIX 5
Life Members

2003	Nance Coghlan
	Marjorie Hassett
	Vi Smiles
	Jean Tapping
	Betty Walker
	Rose Walker
2005	Dora Anderson
2006	Marjorie Le Souef
2008	Pearl Thomson
	Iris Rowtcliff OAM
2009	Margaret Southwood
	Florence Gordon
	Joy Smith
2010	Hazel Donald
	Cecily Robinson
2011	Marjorie Wilson
	Edna Richardson
	Ivy Wolfe
2013	Phyllis McMiles
	Robin Bowden

APPENDIX 6
State Patrons

1947–1949	Lady Clara Mitchell
1951–1963	Lady Evelyn Gairdner
1963–1974	Lady Nora Kendrew
1974–1975	Lady Dorothy Edwards
1976–1980	Lady Mary (Molly) Kyle
1981–1983	Lady Anne Trowbridge
1984–2012	Mrs Ruth Reid AM
2012–2014	The Honourable Mr Malcolm McCusker AC CVO QC
	Mrs Tonya McCusker
2014–	Her Excellency the Honourable Kerry Sanderson AO

National Patrons

In 1948, Her Royal Highness Princess Marina Duchess of Kent CI GCVO GBE consented to being the national patron of the War Widows' Guild. She remained patron until her death in 1968. Since then, the Governor-General of Australia has consented to being the national patron.

National Presidents

1945–1966	Mrs Jessie Vasey CBE
1966–1977	Mrs Janet Mayo
1977–1981	Mrs Gwen Forsyth OBE BEM
1981–1986	Mrs Billie Hughes
1986–1990	Mrs Lucille Wallis
1990–1992	Mrs Billie Cutler
1992–1994	Mrs Marie Kays
1994–1998	Mrs Eileen Watt
1998–2002	Mrs June Healy OAM
2002–2004	Mrs Kath Ross OAM
2004	Mrs Kate Rhodes
2004–2008	Mrs Norma Whitfield OAM
2008–2012	Mrs Audrey Blood OAM
2012–2014	Mrs Anne Bonner
2014	Mrs Wendy Charlton
2014–	Mrs Meg Green

NOTES

Prologue

1. Marie Cooke, 'Australian War Widows: A Case Study to Challenge Public Policy', *Australian Journal of Social Issues*, vol. 38, no. 4, 4 November 2003, p. 465.

Chapter 1: Wartime in Western Australia

1. Charles Page, *Wings of Destiny: Wing Commander Charles Learmonth, DFC and Bar and the Air War in New Guinea*, Rosenberg Publishing, Sydney, 2008, p. 103.
2. Page, *Wings of Destiny*, p. 7.
3. Anne Heywood & Penny Robinson 'Voluntary Aid Detachments (VAD) (1914–)', *The Australian Women's Register*, 2003/2009, retrieved 21 March 2011, http://www.womenaustralia.info.biogs/AWE0491b.htm
4. Page, *Wings of Destiny*, p. 7.
5. Quoted in Page, *Wings of Destiny*, p. 108.
6. ibid., p. 117.
7. ibid., p. 124.
8. ibid., pp. 124–5.
9. ibid., p. 127.
10. 'Broadcast by King: Message to Empire', *Sydney Morning Herald*, 26 December 1941, p. 5, retrieved from http://nla.gov.au/nla.news-article17780537
11. Page, *Wings of Destiny*, p. 131.
12. 'Bombing of Darwin: Attack this Morning', *Geraldton Guardian and Express*, 19 February 1942, p. 2, retrieved from http://nla.gov.au/nla.news-article67332658
13. 'Into the Front Line', *West Australian*, 20 February 1942, p. 4, retrieved from http://nla.gov.au/nla.news-article47181712
14. Michael McKernan, *The Strength of a Nation: Six Years of Australians Fighting for the Nation and Defending the Homefront in WWII*, Allen & Unwin, Crows Nest, 2008, pp. 263–4; Bob Wurth, *1942: Australia's Greatest Peril*, Pan Macmillan Australia, Sydney, 2008, p. 143.
15. Interview with Laurel Taylor, 7 May 2009.
16. This was possibly Acme Canvas Works in Beaufort Street, North Perth.
17. Interview with Laurel Taylor, 7 May 2009.
18. Marjorie Le Souef, 'Discharge from the Army', unpublished autobiographical narrative, Perth, 2005, p. 1.
19. ibid.
20. ibid., pp. 1–2.
21. Page, *Wings of Destiny*, pp. 138–141.
22. ibid., p. 165.
23. 'Soldier Killed', *West Australian*, 4 November 1942, p. 5, retrieved

from http://nla.gov.au/nla.news-article47353682

24 'World War 2 Accident Kills 59 and Injures over 100 – Port Moresby Airfield – 7 September 1943', retrieved 24 May 2010 from www.australian-pow-ww2.com/history_24.html

25 Wendy Birman & Victoria Hobbs, 'Ferguson, Jean Elsie (1909–1979)', *Australian Dictionary of Biography*, National Centre of Biography, Australian National University, retrieved from http://adb.anu.edu.au/biography/ferguson-jean-elsie-10166

26 Alan Forsyth, personal communication, 10 March 2009.

27 Lt Col. H. Boyd Norman to Mrs Heath, 6 October 1943, private collection of David Heath.

28 *2/28 Infantry Battalion August–September 1943*, AWM52 2nd Australian Imperial Force and Commonwealth Military Forces unit war diaries, 1939–45 War, AWM, Canberra.

29 Interview with David Heath, 11 May 2011; interview with Maureen Rose, 24 May 2011.

30 Citation for Distinguished Flying Cross – REL/15999.001 – Distinguished Flying Cross and Bar: Wing Commander C.C. Learmonth, 14 and 22 Squadron, RAAF, retrieved 5 October 2010 from http://Cas.awm.gov.au/item/REL/15999.001.

31 Page, *Wings of Destiny*, pp. 293–4.

32 ibid., p. 25.

33 ibid., p. 34.

34 ibid., p. 31.

35 ibid., pp. 351–2.

36 ibid., p. 355.

37 Interview with Patricia Milne, 26 March 2010.

38 ibid.

39 ibid.

40 This conversation is quoted in Mavis Thorpe Clark, *No Mean Destiny: The Story of the War Widows' Guild of Australia 1945–85*, Hyland House Publishing, South Yarra, p. 25.

41 Quoted in Clark, *No Mean Destiny*, p. 24.

42 ibid., p. 21.

43 ibid., p. 5.

44 Mrs Vasey to Mr Forde, 4 July 1945, Vasey Family Papers, MS 3782, box 1, folder 1, NLA.

45 ibid.

46 David Horner, *General Vasey's War*, Melbourne University Press, Carlton, 1992, p. 320.

47 ibid., p. 323.

48 ibid.

49 ibid., p. 323.

50 H. Harvey to Mrs Vasey, 12 March 1945, Vasey Family Papers, MS 3782, box 1 folder 1, NLA.

51 W.L. Sinclair to Mrs Vasey, 8 March 1945, Vasey Family Papers, MS 3782, box 1 folder 1, NLA.

52 Archbishop Joseph Booth to Mrs Vasey, 14 March 1945, Vasey Family Papers, MS 3782, box 1, folder 1, NLA.

53 Jessie Vasey to Archbishop Joseph Booth, n.d., Vasey Family Papers, MS 3782, box 1, folder 1, NLA.

54 Quoted in Clark, *No Mean Destiny*, p. 29.

55 'Red Cross Sees Brides off for USA', *Argus*, 8 June 1945, p. 8, retrieved from http://nla.gov.au/nla.news-article971902

56 60th Anniversary of War Widows' Guild, radio interview, 720 ABC Perth, 28 November 2006.

57 'Red Cross Sees Brides off for USA', p. 8.

58 Page, *Wings of Destiny*, p. 357; 'Personalities', *Western Mail*, 6 July 1945, p. 31, retrieved from http://nla.gov.au./news-article38564469

59 Tom Austen, *Western Images: Western Australia in Pictures from the Colonial Era to the Present*, St George Books, Perth, 1996, pp. 138–9; 'Peace

Celebrations in Perth', *Western Mail*, 16 August 1945, p. 42; 'Joyful Perth', *West Australian*, 16 August 1945, p. 1; 'Thanksgiving: Perth's Biggest Crowd in City Tribute', *West Australian*, 17 August 1945, p. 1.

60 Page, *Wings of Destiny*, p. 356.

61 Interview with Laurel Taylor, 7 May 2009.

62 'Personal', *West Australian*, 19 February 1942, p. 4, retrieved from http://nla.gov.au/nla.news-article47181597; 'Lt-Col M J Anketell', *West Australian*, 17 January 1945, p. 4, retrieved from http://nla.gov.au/nla.news-article44994003; 'Personal', *Western Mail*, 11 January 1945, p. 21, retrieved from http://nla.gov.au/nla.news-article38559361; 'Late Lt-Col Anketell: The Manner of his Death', *West Australian*, 23 October 1945, p. 4, retrieved from http://nla.gov.au/nla.news-article44826361

63 'Personal', *West Australian*, 19 February 1942, p. 4, retrieved from http://nla.gov.au/nla.news-article47181597; 'Lt-Col M J Anketell', *West Australian*, 17 January 1945, p. 4, retrieved from http://nla.gov.au/nla.news-article44994003; 'Personal', *Western Mail*, 11 January 1945, p. 21, retrieved from http://nla.gov.au/nla.news-article38559361; 'Late Lt-Col Anketell: The Manner of his Death', *West Australian*, 23 October 1945, p. 4, retrieved from http://nla.gov.au/nla.news-article44826361

64 Les Cody, *Ghosts in Khaki: The History of the 2/4th Machine Gun Battalion*, Hesperian Press, Victoria Park, 1997, p. 171; Murray Ewen, *Colour Patch: The Men of the 2/4th Australian Machine Gun Battalion 1940–1945*, Hesperian Press, Victoria Park, 2003, p. 4. The actual date of death for Lieutenant Colonel Michael Joseph Anketell is still not completely certain. Cody states his date and time of death as 7.45pm on 14/2/42. Ewen states it as the morning of 13/2/42, and the roll of honour circular states it as 12/2/42, which is the day Anketell was wounded.

65 Peter Hoffman, *Honours Denied: The Documented Life of Herman August Kuring in Peace and War, 1895–1941*, Perth, 2005.

66 Interview with Gwen McDowell, 23 October 2009.

67 Joy Damousi, *The Labour of Loss: Mourning, Memory and Wartime Bereavement in Australia*, Cambridge University Press, Cambridge, 1999, p. 148.

Chapter 2: The War Widows' Guild Begins

1 Anne Summers, *Damned Whores and God's Police*, 2nd edn, Penguin Books, Ringwood, 1994, pp. 471–2.

2 There was a sliding scale of payment for the war widows' pension, which depended on her husband's rank. The rate of £2 10s per week was awarded to women whose husbands held a rank of lieutenant (navy), captain (army) or flight lieutenant (air force) or lower. For men whose rank was a lieutenant commander, major, squadron leader or higher, and which afforded them a higher pay rate, their widows received a pension according to his rate of pay, up to £3 8s per week. Information taken from 'Re-establishment Pamplet no. 6: War widows' Entitlements', Repatriation Commission, Adelaide, 1946; 'War Widows: Notes on War Pensions and Repatriation Benefits', Repatriation Commission, Melbourne, 1953.

3 Interview with Alan Forsyth, 12 December 2008.

4 There has been research into the effects on the families of returned servicemen, which show that life could also be difficult for them. See, for example, Tanja Luckins, *The Gates of Memory: Australian People's Experiences and Memories of Loss*

and the Great War, Curtin University Books, Fremantle, 2004. See also Joy Damousi, *Living with the Aftermath: Trauma, Nostalgia and Grief in Post-War Australia*, Cambridge University Press, Cambridge, 2001, for further exploration of the effect on women whose husbands returned from active service.

5   Clark, *No Mean Destiny*, pp. 34–5.
6   Prime Minister John Curtin to Mrs Vasey, 8 March 1945, Vasey Family Papers, MS 3782, box 1, folder 1, NLA.
7   Mrs Vasey to Prime Minister John Curtin, n.d., Vasey Family Papers, MS 3782, box 1, folder 1, NLA.
8   Mrs Vasey to Mr Forde, 4 July 1945, Vasey Family Papers, MS 3782, box 1, folder 1, NLA.
9   ibid.
10 Cyril Burley, 'AIF General's Widow on Pensions Warpath', *Mail*, 23 November 1946, p. 2, retrieved from http://nla.gov.au/nla.news-article55878114; 'War Widow's Guild: Mrs J Vasey's visit. Australia-wide Movement', *West Australian*, 27 November 1946, p. 3, retrieved from http://nla.gov.au/nla.news-article46243510
11 Vicki Court, *War Widows' and Widowed Mothers' Association of Victoria: The First 82 Years*, War Widows' and Widowed Mothers' Association of Victoria, Melbourne, 2005, p. 82.
12 Clark, *No Mean Destiny*, pp. 30, 123.
13 Clark, *No Mean Destiny*, p. 39.
14 Jessie Vasey to war widows in Victoria, dated October 1945, War Widows' Guild archives, Perth.
15 Clark, *No Mean Destiny*, p. 12.
16 Jessie Vasey to war widows in Victoria, dated October 1945, War Widows' Guild archives, Perth.
17 For a detailed discussion of this issue, see Damousi, *The Labour of Loss*; Damousi, *Living with the*

Aftermath; Pat Jalland, *Changing Ways of Death in Twentieth-Century Australia: War, Medicine and the Funeral Business*, UNSW Press, Sydney, 2006.

18 Jessie Vasey to war widows, October 1945, War Widows' Guild archives, WA Branch, Perth.
19 ibid.
20 ibid.
21 Clark, *No Mean Destiny*, pp. 38, 43–4.
22 ibid., pp. 40–44.
23 John McPhee, 'Grieve, Rachel (1885–1977)', *Australian Dictionary of Biography*, National Centre of Biography, Australian National University, retrieved 13 October 2011 from http://adb.anu.edu.au/biography/grieve-rachel-10368
24 Clark, *No Mean Destiny*, p. 41.
25 Minutes of Meeting to form the War Widows' Craft Guild, 22 November 1945.
26 Quoted in Clark, *No Mean Destiny*, p. 41.
27 ibid., p. 41.
28 Minutes of Meeting to form the War Widows' Craft Guild, 22 November 1945.
29 'War Widows' Guild: New Venture Needs Help', *Argus*, 24 November 1945, p. 2, retrieved from http://nla.gov.au/nla.news-article12154986
30 'War Widows' Guild Appeal Passes £1,000 Mark', *Argus*, 9 January 1946, p. 7, retrieved from http://nla.gov.au/nla.news-article22221335
31 'War Widows' Fund: First £1,000 in Sight', *Argus*, 21 December 1945, p. 4, retrieved from http://nla.gov.au/nla.news-article12159871
32 'War Widows' Guild, Melbourne', *Change Over*, vol. 1, no. 4, 1946, p. 5.
33 Clark, *No Mean Destiny*, p. 48.
34 Jessie Vasey to war widows in Victoria, dated October 1945, War Widows' Guild archives, Perth.

See also newspaper articles such as Cyril Burley, 'AIF General's Widow on Pensions Warpath', *Mail*, 23 November 1946, p. 2, retrieved from http://nla.gov.au/nla.news-article55878114; 'War Widow's Guild: Mrs J Vasey's Visit. Australia-wide Movement', *West Australian*, 27 November 1946, p. 3, retrieved from http://nla.gov.au/nla.news-article46243510

35 'War Widows Meet Today', *Advertiser*, 21 November 1946, p. 8, retrieved from http://nla.gov.au/nla.news-article35767878

36 Clark, *No Mean Destiny*, p. 58.

37 Clark, *No Mean Destiny*, p. 68.

38 J. Knight, personal communication, 2 February 2009.

39 Quoted in 'War Widows' Guild: Improved Status Sought', *West Australian,* 28 November 1946, p. 9.

40 ibid.

41 ibid.

42 Minutes of First Provisional Committee of War Widows' Craft Guild WA, 29 November 1946.

43 ibid.; 'Weaving Report', War Widows' Guild archives, WA Branch, Perth.

44 Minutes of First Provisional Committee of War Widows' Craft Guild WA, 29 November 1946.

45 'R.S.L. and War Widows: Mrs Vasey Seeks Cooperation', *West Australian*, 3 December 1946, p. 8.

46 'War Widows: Lightening the Shadows', *West Australian*, 5 December 1946, p. 8.

47 Clark, *No Mean Destiny*, pp. 73, 92.

48 Lorraine Wheeler, 'War, Women and Welfare', in R. Kennedy (ed.), *Australian Welfare: Historical Sociology*, Macmillan, South Melbourne, 1989, p. 178.

49 Wheeler, 'War, Women and Welfare', p. 187.

50 Rohan Rivett, 'War Widows Are Australia's Forgotten Women', *Herald*, 10 June 1947, n.p.

51 Wheeler, 'War, Women and Welfare', p. 188.

52 Rivett, 'War Widows Are Australia's Forgotten Women'.

53 Clark, *No Mean Destiny*, p. 123.

54 'All Pensions Increased', *Sydney Morning Herald*, 5 March 1947, p. 1, retrieved from http://nla.gov.au/nla.news-article18005016; 'Pensions Up 5/-', *Advertiser*, 5 March 1947, p. 6, retrieved from http://nla.gov.au/nla.news-article30515635

55 Mrs Vasey to Mr Holt, 5 March 1947, Personal Papers of Prime Minister Chifley, Correspondence 'W', part 1, 1946–1947, image 80, retrieved from http://recordsearch.naa.gov.au/scripts/Imagine.asp

56 Clark, *No Mean Destiny*, p. 78.

57 ibid.

58 'War Widows Demand Basic Wage as Minimum Pension', *Mercury*, 3 July 1947, p. 1.

59 Clark, *No Mean Destiny*, p. 82.

60 ibid., pp. 83–4.

61 Quoted in Brian Fitzpatrick, 'Why Women Must Protest', *Smith's,* 12 July 1947, p. 15.

62 ibid.

63 See, for example, Brian Fitzpatrick, 'Why Women Must Protest'; Helen Seager, 'Good Morning Ma'am!', *Argus*, 19 July 1947, p. 9, retrieved from http://nla.gov.au/nla.news-article22443701; 'War Widows Demand Basic Wage', *Canberra Times*, 3 July 1947, p. 4, retrieved from http://nla.gov.au/nla.news-article2719076; 'War Widow's Bitter Attack', *Daily News*, 2 July 1947, p. 6, retrieved from http://nla.gov.au/nla.news-article83742513

64 'Resentment at Minister's Slur', *Sydney Morning Herald*, 17 July 1947, p. 3, retrieved from http://nla.gov.au/nla.news-article18035537

65 'Minister's Reply to War Widows', *Advocate*, 18 July 1947, p. 5, retrieved

from http://nla.gov.au/nla.news-article69011812

66 Prime Minister Chifley to Mrs Vasey, 19 August 1947, Personal Papers of Prime Minister Chifley, Correspondence 'W', part 1, 1947–1948, image 103, retrieved from http://recordsearch.naa.gov.au/scripts/Imagine.asp

67 Mrs Vasey to Prime Minister Chifley, 29 August 1947, Personal Papers of Prime Minister Chifley, Correspondence 'W', part 1,1947–1948, image 102, retrieved from http://recordsearch.naa.gov.au/scripts/Imagine.asp

68 Muriel Jones, 'War Widows: Minister's "Outrageous Opinion"', letter to the editor, West Australian, 19 July 1947, p. 7, retrieved from http://nla.gov.au/nla.news-article46327089

69 War Widows' Guild, Minutes, Executive Committee, 21 July 1947, WA Branch, Perth.

70 David Black, 'Collett, Herbert Brayley (1877–1947)', Australian Dictionary of Biography, National Centre of Biography, Australian National University, retrieved 10 March 2011 from http://adb.online.anu.edu.au/biogs/A0800/3B

71 War Widows' Guild, Minutes, Executive Committee, 25 July 1947, WA Branch, Perth.

72 Minutes, Meeting of Ex-Services Organisations and the War Widows' Guild, 29 July 1947, p. 5.

73 War Widows' Guild, Minutes, Council Meeting, 8 August 1947, WA Branch, Perth.

74 War Widows' Guild, Minutes, Council, 8 August 1947, WA Branch, Perth.

75 'War Widows: Problems Discussed with Minister', West Australian, 5 August 1947, p. 3, retrieved from http://nla.gov.au/nla.news-article46330847

76 ibid.

77 ibid.; 'War Widows' Guild: Repatriation Minister's Visit', West Australian, 11 August 1947, p. 10, retrieved from http://nla.gov.au/nla.news-article46332231

78 Marjorie Le Souef, 'President's Report', Guild News, July 2003, p. 4.

79 War Widows' Guild, Minutes, Executive Committee, 5 September 1947, WA Branch, Perth.

80 'Leave Pay to Troops who Died', Argus, 18 September 1947, p. 3, retrieved from http://nla.gov.au/nla.news-article22508362

81 Transcript of radio interview, Mr Clements and Mrs Learmonth, Post War Bulletin, No. 61, 2 September 1947.

82 ibid.

Chapter 3: A Place to Call Home

1 Transcript of radio interview, Mr Clements and Mrs Learmonth, Post War Bulletin, No. 61, 2 September 1947.

2 Minutes, Meeting of Ex-Servicemen's Organisations and Departments Concerned in the Re-establishment of Ex-service Personnel held at the Ministry of Post-War Reconstruction, 11 March 1947.

3 ibid.

4 ibid.

5 Transcript of radio interview, Mr Clements and Mrs Learmonth, Post War Bulletin, No. 61, 2 September 1947.

6 War Widows' Guild, Minutes, Executive Committee, 9 May 1947, WA Branch, Perth.

7 Transcript of radio interview, Mr Clements and Mrs Learmonth, Post War Bulletin, No. 61, 2 September 1947.

8 Transcript of radio interview, Mr Clements and Mrs Gahan, Post War Bulletin, No. 53, n.d.

9 War Widows' Guild, Minutes, Executive Committee, 11 July 1947, WA Branch, Perth.

10 War Widows' Guild, Minutes, Executive Committee, 20 May 1947, WA Branch, Perth.

11 Rosa Lind, 'These People', *Western Mail*, 1 April 1948, p. 3.

12 Transcript of radio interview, Mr Clements and Mrs Gahan, Post War Bulletin, No. 53, n.d.

13 Minutes, Meeting of Ex-Servicemen's Organisations and Departments Concerned in the Re-establishment of Ex-service Personnel held at the Ministry of Post-War Reconstruction, 29 July 1947.

14 ibid.

15 Lind, 'These People', p. 3; interview with Peggy Litchfield and Graham Walker, 12 May 2011.

16 Transcript of radio interview, Mr Clements and Mrs Gahan, Post War Bulletin, No. 53, n.d.

17 Interview with Laurel Taylor, 7 May 2009.

18 Murray Ewen, *Colour Patch: The Men of the 2/4th Australian Machine Gun Battalion 1940–1945*, Hesperian Press, Perth, 2003, pp. 42, 184.

19 Interview with Laurel Taylor, 7 May 2009.

20 Transcript of radio interview, Mr Clements and Mrs Learmonth, Post War Bulletin, No 61, 2 September 1947.

21 War Widows' Guild, Minutes, Executive Committee, 8 August 1947, WA Branch, Perth.

22 Interview with Peggy Litchfield and Graham Walker, 12 May 2011.

23 War Widows' Guild, Minutes, Executive Committee, 21 July 1947, WA Branch, Perth.

24 War Widows' Guild, Minutes, Executive Committee, 25 July 1947, WA Branch, Perth.

25 War Widows' Guild, Minutes, Executive Committee, 19 September 1947, WA Branch, Perth.

26 Noel Stewart, 'Lady Mitchell: A Governor's Wife' in *As I Remember Them*, Artlook Books, Perth, 1987, p. 35.

27 War Widows' Guild, Minutes, Executive Committee, 17 October 1947, WA Branch, Perth.

28 Leslie Le Souef, *To War Without a Gun*, Artlook Books, Perth, 1980; Page, *Wings of Destiny*, p. 359; interview with Anne Lopez, 18 March 2009.

29 Wheeler, 'War, Women and Welfare', p. 178.

30 Jenny Knight, Eulogy for Marjorie Le Souef, 18 April 2008, private archives of Jenny Knight.

31 War Widows' Guild, Minutes, Council, 7 November 1947, WA Branch, Perth.

32 'Dr Fowler Dead', *West Australian*, 29 May 1946, p. 6, retrieved from http://nla.gov.au/nla.news-article50343613

33 Interview with Margaret Hateley and Beryl Haneman, 22 October 2010.

34 'Fowler Hugh Lionel: Service number V148157', NAA, Canberra, retrieved from recordsearch.naa. gov.au/NameSearch/Interface/ItemDetail.aspx?Barcode=6274968

35 'Dr Fowler Dead', *West Australian*.

36 Interview with Margaret Hateley and Beryl Haneman, 22 October 2010.

37 War Widows' Guild of Australia, Minutes, Federal Conference, 17–24 November 1947, Melbourne.

38 ibid.

39 ibid.

40 *Guild News*, September 1968, p. 2.

41 War Widows' Guild of Australia, Minutes, Federal Conference, 17–24 November 1947, Melbourne.

42 War Widows' Guild, Minutes, Executive Committee, 14 November 1947, WA Branch, Perth.

43 'War Widows: Treatment of TB Victims', *West Australian*, 25 February 1948, p. 8, retrieved from http://nla.gov.au/nla.news-article46892486

44 War Widows' Guild, Minutes, Executive Committee, 13 February 1948, WA Branch, Perth.

45 War Widows' Guild, Minutes, Executive Committee, 27 February 1948, WA Branch, Perth.

46 War Widows' Guild, Minutes, Executive Committee, 21 May 1948, WA Branch, Perth.

47 War Widows' Guild, Minutes, Executive Committee, 4 June 1948, WA Branch, Perth.

48 Mark Lyons, *Legacy: The First Fifty Years*, Legacy Co-ordinating Council in conjunction with Lothian Publishing Company, Melbourne, 1978, pp. 150–52.

49 War Widows' Guild, Minutes, Executive Committee, 17 October 1947, WA Branch, Perth.

50 War Widows' Guild, Report of Secretary, AGM, 4 May 1949, WA Branch, Perth.

51 War Widows' Guild, Minutes, Executive Committee, 16 July 1948 and 26 November 1948, WA Branch, Perth.

52 Interview with Peggy Litchfield and Graham Walker, 12 May 2011.

53 ibid.

54 ibid.

55 Interview with Helen Treloar, 4 June 2010.

56 War Widows' Guild, Minutes, Executive Committee, 17 October 1947, WA Branch, Perth.

57 T.J. LeCheminant to the Secretary, War Widows' Guild, 17 May 1948, War Widows' Guild archives, WA Branch, Perth.

58 ibid.

59 War Widows' Guild, Minutes, Council, 1 November 1948, WA Branch, Perth.

60 War Widows' Guild, Minutes, Executive Committee, 26 November 1948, WABranch, Perth.

61 War Widows' Guild, Minutes, Council, 1 November 1948, WA Branch, Perth.

62 War Widows' Guild, Minutes, Executive Committee, 20 May 1949, WA Branch, Perth.

63 War Widows' Guild, Report of Secretary, 4 May 1949, WA Branch, Perth.

64 War Widows' Guild, Minutes, Executive Committee, 7 February 1949, WA Branch, Perth.

65 War Widows' Guild, Minutes, Council, 4 August 1948, WA Branch, Perth.

66 'Register of Heritage Places – Permanent Entry: Esplanade Reserve', Heritage Council of Western Australia, Perth, 2003; Stan Gervas, *Sunday mornings in Perth*, Gervas Books, Maylands, 2003, p. 107.

67 'Register of Heritage Places – Permanent Entry: Esplanade Reserve', p. 8.

68 War Widows' Guild, Report of Secretary, AGM, 4 May 1949, WA Branch, Perth.

69 Interview with Margaret Hateley and Beryl Haneman, 22 October 2010.

70 War Widows' Guild Circular, December 1949, WA Branch, p. 1.

71 *Guild News,* June 1980, p. 4.

72 ibid.

73 Interview with Alan Forsyth, 18 December 2008.

74 War Widows' Guild, Report of Secretary, December 1949 – April 1950, WA Branch, Perth.

75 War Widows' Guild, Minutes, Executive Committee, 3 October 1949, WA Branch, Perth.

76 War Widows' Guild, Minutes, Executive Committee, 3 October 1949, WA Branch, Perth.

77 Interview with Alan Forsyth, 12 December 2008.

78 War Widows' Guild, Minutes, AGM, 3 May 1950, WA Branch, Perth.

79 War Widows' Guild, Report of Secretary, December 1949 – April 1950, WA Branch, Perth.

80 ibid.

81 ibid.

82 War Widows' Guild, Minutes, Executive Committee, 6 September 1949, WA Branch, Perth.

83 War Widows' Guild, Report of Secretary, AGM, 4 May 1949, WA Branch, Perth.

84 War Widows' Guild, Circular, August 1950, WA Branch, Perth.

85 The Brewery donated ice cream, Golden Mile Cordial Factory gave soft drinks, fruit was donated by the Kalgoorlie Fruit Supply and Jacksons gave ham, butter and tea. Coles donated one pound and Selfridges ten shillings towards tree decorations.

86 War Widows' Guild, Report of Secretary, December 1949 – April 1950, WA Branch, Perth.

87 ibid.

88 'Anzac Day Observance: Legacy of Wounds and Suffering', *West Australian*, 26 April 1950, p. 3, retrieved from http://nla.gov.au/nla. news-article47843868

89 'These People', *Western Mail*, 13 July 1950, p. 33, retrieved from http://nla. gov.au/nla.news-page3968352

90 Interview with Alan Forsyth, 12 December 2008.

91 War Widows' Guild, Circular, August 1950, WA Branch, Perth; Isis, 'War Widows' Guild Succeeds with Kiosk', *West Australian*, 22 September 1950, p. 16.

92 War Widows' Guild, Secretary's Report, 1951–1952, WA Branch, Perth.

93 H.F.E., 'The Cheekiest Customer', *West Australian*, 5 April 1952, p. 19, retrieved from http://nla.gov.au/nla. news-article49025034

Chapter 4: Housing plans and a Royal Visit?

1 Quoted in 'Broadcast by King: Message to Empire', *Sydney Morning Herald*, 26 December 1941, p. 5, retrieved from http://nla.gov.au/nla. news-article17780537. The quote also appears on the cover of each edition of *Guild News*.

2 Clark, *No Mean Destiny*, p. 111.

3 ibid., p. 112.

4 Re-establishment Pamphlet no. 6: War widows' entitlements, Repatriation Commission, Adelaide, 1946.

5 'Repat Stop Pensions to Widows', *Argus*, 6 June 1949, p. 3, retrieved from http://nla.gov.au/nla.news-article22733263

6 Kay Keavney, '1965: Same Motto – and £2m. in Housing', *Australian Women's Weekly*, 8 September 1965, p. 7, retrieved from http://nla.gov.au/nla.news-article46239761

7 Lisa Allan, 'Going your way', *Argus*, 27 September 1952, p. 3, retrieved from http://nla.gov.au/nla.news-article23204090

8 Quoted in Clark, *No Mean Destiny*, p. 114.

9 'War Widows' Guild President Replies to Mr Barnard', *Canberra Times*, 17 June 1949, p. 1, retrieved from http://nla.gov.au/nla.news-article2809436; 'Editorial: For 10,000 dead men', *Australian Woman's Weekly*, vol. 17, 2 July 1949, p. 18, retrieved from http://nla.gov.au/nla. news-article47223573

10 'Charges Minister with "Heartless Cruelty"', *Mecury*, 17 June 1949, p. 5, retrieved from http://nla.gov.au/nla. news-article26631093

11 'War Widow Remark: "Private Joke"', *Sydney Morning Herald*, 17 June 1949, p. 10, retrieved from http://nla. gov.au/nla.news-article18119433

12 'Editorial: For 10,000 Dead Men', p. 18.

13 'War Widow Leader: Mr Barnard is Critical', *Sydney Morning Herald*, 16 June 1949, p. 4, retrieved from http://nla.gov.au/nla.news-article18119433

14 'Editorial: For 10,000 Dead Men', p. 18.

15 Clark, *No Mean Destiny*, p. 116.

16 'RSL wants £12,000 for War Memorial', *West Australian*, 22 July 1950, p. 5, retrieved from http://nla.gov.au/nla.news-article47876345

17 'Inquiry into Allegations: Morals of War Widows', *Mecury*, 3 March 1950, p. 1, retrieved from http://nla.gov.au/nla.news-article26683361

18 Jessie Vasey, 'If I were Minister for Repatriation', *Argus*, 3 March 1950, p. 2.

19 'War Widows' Morals: No Inquiry', *Sydney Morning Herald*, 4 March 1950, p. 4, retrieved from http://nla.gov.au/nla.news-article18150753

20 'War Widows' Morals', *West Australian,* 4 March 1950, p. 7, retrieved from http://nla.gov.au/nla.news-article47832850

21 '"Gloomy Day Not Wanted," Says Mrs Vasey', *Argus*, 29 April 1949, p. 3, retrieved from http://nla.gov.au/nla.news-article22725317

22 Jessie Vasey, 'Today is a Day of Memories', *Argus Woman's Magazine,* 25 April 1950, p. 2, retrieved from http://nla.gov.au/nla.news-article22824607

23 War Widows' Guild, Circular No 15, March 1950, Melbourne Branch.

24 'Korean War 1950–1953', Australian War Memorial, Canberra, retrieved from www.awm.gov.au/atwar/korea.asp; 'British Commonwealth Occupation Force (BCOF)', Australia's involvement in the Korean War, retrieved 29 June 2012 from http://korean-war.commemoration.gov.au/armed-forces-in-korea/british-commonwealth-occupation-force.php

25 *Out in the Cold: Australia's Involvement in the Korean War 1950–1953*, Department of Veterans' Affairs, Canberra, 2010, p. 12; 'The Cold War and the Crisis in Korea – How Was Australia Involved?', retrieved 25 June 2012 from http://korean-war.commemoration.gov.au/cold-war-crisis-in-korea/australias-involvement-in-korean-war.php

26 P.J. Scully, 'Spence, Louis Thomas (1917–1950)', *Australian Dictionary of Biography*, National Centre of Biography, Australian National University, retrieved from http://adb.anu.edu.au/biography/spence-louis-thomas-11741/text20993; 'High tribute to Spence', *Courier Mail*, 4 October, p. 1, retrieved from http://nla.gov.au/nla.news-article50030539

27 Olwyn Green, *The Name's Still Charlie: A Remarkable Story of Courage and Love*, University of Queensland Press, St Lucia, 1993, pp. 241, 253.

28 'Collie Man Killed: Casualty in Korea War', *West Australian*, 5 October 1950, p. 1, retrieved from http://nla.gov.au/nla.news-article47890389

29 'Casualties from WA: Men killed in Korea', *West Australian*, 2 November 1950, p. 1, retrieved from http://nla.gov.au/nla.news-article47895312; 'Family notices: Deaths on Active Service', *West Australian*, 3 November 1950, p. 1, retrieved from http://nla.gov.au/nla.news-article47895505

30 'Letters to the Editor', *West Australian*, 18 December 1950, p. 11, retrieved from http://nla.gov.au/nla.news-article48142134

31 'Australian Death-roll of 38 in Korean War', *West Australian*, 11 January 1951, p. 1, retrieved from http://nla.gov.au/nla.news-article48145753

32 'Royal Visit to Begin on March 1, 1952', *Canberra Times*, 23 February 1951, p. 1, retrieved from http://nla.gov.au/nla.news-article2822321

33 War Widows' Guild, Minutes, Executive Committee, 5 February 1952, WA Branch, Perth.

34 'Perth's Farewell to Sir James', *Western Mail*, 5 July 1951, p. 8, retrieved from http://nla.gov.au/nla.news-article39111592

35 'Public Servant and Friend of People: Many Tributes to Late Sir James Mitchell', *West Australian*, 27 July 1951, p. 3, retrieved from http://nla.gov.au/nla.news-article48982445; 'Sir James Mitchell dies in sleep', *Argus*, 27 July 1951, p. 5, retrieved from http://nla.gov.au/nla.news-article23076377

36 Peter Boyce, 'Gairdner, Sir Charles Henry (1898–1983)', *Australian Dictionary of Biography*, National Centre of Biography, Australian National University, retrieved from http://adb.anu.edu.au/biography/gairdner-sir-charles-henry-12522/text22533

37 War Widows' Guild, Minutes, Executive Committee, 13 November 1951, WA Branch, Perth.

38 'King Disappointed by Cancellation of Proposed Tour', *Mercury*, 11 October 1951, p. 3, retrieved from http://nla.gov.au/nla.news-article27053881

39 War Widows' Guild, Minutes, Executive Committee, 5 February 1952, WA Branch, Perth.

40 ibid.

41 'Poignant Scene in House', *Canberra Times*, 7 February 1952, p. 1, retrieved from http://nla.gov.au/nla.news-article2848092

42 'King George VI Dies Peacefully in Sleep: Deep Mourning throughout British Commonwealth', *Canberra Times*, 7 February 1953, p. 1, retrieved from http://nla.gov.au/nla.news-article2848092

43 'Funeral Service in Chapel at Windsor for Late King George VI', *West Australian*, 18 February 1952, p. 1, retrieved from http://nla.gov.au/nla.news-article49015936

44 'Thousands Fill Perth Churches: Day of Mourning for Late King George VI', *West Australian*, 18 February 1952, p. 3, retrieved from http://nla.gov.au/nla.news-article49015954

45 'Violets for Mourning', *West Australian*, 15 February 1952, p. 7, retrieved from http://nla.gov.au/nla.news-article49015630

46 War Widows' Guild, Minutes, Executive Committee, 4 March 1952, WA Branch, Perth.

47 War Widows' Guild, Minutes, Executive Committee, 29 April 1952, WA Branch, Perth.

48 'Nation Pays Homage to the Fallen', *West Australian*, 26 April 1952, p. 1, retrieved from http://nla.gov.au/nla.news-article49028406

49 War Widows' Guild, Minutes, Executive Committee, 5 August 1952, WA Branch, Perth.

50 'Museum Data Exchange: National Flower Day photographic collection', History SA, retrieved 14 June 2012 from museumex.org/has/2824

51 Jean Chetkovich and Deborah Gare, *A Chain of Care: A History of the Silver Chain Nursing Association*, The University of Notre Dame Australia Press for The Silver Chain Nursing Association, Perth, 2005, p. 133.

52 'National Flower Day', *Western Mail*, 18 September 1952, pp. 6, 36, 62, retrieved from http://nla.gov.au/nla.news-article39353490; 'Perth's Third National Flower Day', *Western Mail*, 18 September 1952, p. 50, retrieved from http://nla.gov.au/nla.news-article39353532

53 War Widows' Guild, Minutes, Council, 28 April 1953, WA Branch, Perth.

54 Quoted in Clark, *No Mean Destiny*, p. 151.

55 ibid., p. 152.

56 '"Spying" on War Widows to Go', *Mercury*, 17 July 1953, p. 3, retrieved from http://nla.gov.au/nla.news-article27166423

57 War Widow's Guild, Circular, Number 23, Melbourne Branch, quoted in Clark, *No Mean Destiny*, p. 152.

58 'Off to Crowning', *Argus*, 9 April 1953, p. 9, retrieved from http://nla.gov.au/nla.news-article23241506; 'Australians will dress smartly at coronation', *West Australian*, 5 May 1953, p. 20, retrieved from http://nla.gov.au/nla.news-page3793429; 'They were guests of the queen', *Argus*, 29 May 1953, p. 16, retrieved from http://nla.gov.au/nla.news-article23247249

59 'Two Australians Appointed to Privy Council', *West Australian*, 1 June 1953, p. 1, retrieved from http://nla.gov.au/nla.news-article55807419

60 War Widows' Guild, Minutes, Executive Committee, 5 June 1953, WA Branch; interview with Margaret Hateley and Beryl Haneman, 22 October 2010.

61 'Boer War to Vietnam', NAA, retrieved 20 June 2012 from www.naa.gov.au/collection/explore/defence/conflicts.aspx; 'Korean War 1950–53', NAA, retrieved 5 March 2010 from www.awm.gov.au/atwar/korea.asp

62 See *Guild News* and executive minutes between June 1950 and July 1953.

63 '"They Fought for Liberty": Queen Honours 20,000 War Dead', *Argus*, 19 October 1953, p. 1, retrieved from http://nla.gov.au/nla.news-article23320353; 'Queen Unveils Memorial at Runnymede: Air Force Men Remembered', *Cairns Post*, 19 October 1953, p. 1, retrieved from http://nla.gov.au/nla.news-article42816966

64 Clark, *No mean destiny*, p. 158.

65 War Widows' Guild, Minutes, Executive Committee, 3 November 1953, WA Branch, Perth.

66 Interview with Patricia Milne, 26 March 2010.

67 Jenny Gregory, *City of Light: A History of Perth Since the 1950s*, City of Perth, Perth, 2003, p. 22.

68 Interview with Patricia Milne, 26 March 2010.

69 Gregory, *City of Light*, p. 24.

70 John Smith, *Fear, Frustration and the Will to Overcome: A Social History of Poliomyelitis in Western Australia*, PhD thesis, Edith Cowan University, Perth, p. 229.

71 Gregory, *City of Light*, p. 23.

72 War Widows' Guild, Minutes, AGM, 18 May 1954, WA Branch, Perth.

73 Interview with Margaret Hateley and Beryl Haneman, 22 October 2010; 'Ex-Service Parade', *Western Mail*, 18 March 1954, p. 9, Supplement: Western Mail Royal Tour Itinerary for WA, retrieved from http://nla.gov.au/nla.news-article39366602

74 Quoted in Damousi, *Living with the Aftermath: Trauma, Nostalgia and Grief in Post-war Australia*, p. 10.

75 'Widows' Guild Not to Attend Anzac Service', *Argus*, 22 April 1954, p. 8, retrieved from http://nla.gov.au/nla.news-article26604406

76 ibid.

77 'We Widows Will Be at the Shrine, She Says', *Argus*, 24 April 1954, p. 7, retrieved from http://nla.gov.au/nla.news-article26605044

78 Damousi, *Living with the Aftermath*, p. 13.

79 War Widows' Guild, Minutes, Executive Committee, 4 May 1954, WA Branch, Perth.

80 War Widows' Guild, Minutes, Executive Committee, 4 May 1954 and 3 May 1955, WA Branch, Perth.

81 ibid.

82 *Guild News*, December 1956, p. 1.

83 War Widow's Guild, Annual Report, May 1955 – May 1956, WA Branch, Perth.

84 *50 Years of Achievement*, documentary, Australia, 1995.

85 Clark, *No Mean Destiny*, pp. 146–7.

86 *50 Years of Achievement*.

87 Clark, *No Mean Destiny*, p. 147.

88 War Widows' Guild, Minutes, Executive Committee, 5 February 1952, WA Branch, Perth.

89 War Widows' Guild, Minutes, Executive Committee, 4 December 1951, WA Branch, Perth.

90 War Widow's Guild, Annual Report, May 1955–May 1956, WA Branch, Perth.

91 War Widows' Guild, Minutes, Executive Committee, 1 February 1955 and 3 May 1955, WA Branch, Perth.

92 War Widows' Guild, Minutes, Executive Meeting, 3 July 1956, WA Branch, Perth.

93 Interview with Gwen McDowell, 23 October 2009.

94 ibid.

95 War Widows' Guild, Minutes, Council, 21 November 1956, WA Branch, Perth; War Widows' Guild, Minutes, Executive Committee, 4 August 1958, WA Branch, Perth; War Widows' Guild, Minutes, AGM, 19 May 1959, WA Branch, Perth.

96 War Widows' Guild, Minutes, Executive Committee, 7 May 1957, WA Branch, Perth.

97 *Guild News*, December 1958, p. 2.

98 Interview with Alex MacDonald, 12 March 2010.

99 War Widows' Guild, Minutes, Executive Committee, 1 October 1957 and 5 November 1957, WA Branch, Perth.

100 War Widows' Guild, Minutes, Executive Committee, 6 February 1958, WA Branch, Perth.

101 'News and Notes', *West Australian*, 4 November 1954, p. 2, retrieved from http://nla.go.au/nla.news-article52962722

102 Michael Fine, *The Responsibility for Child and Aged Care: Shaping Policies for the Future*, SPRC Discussion Paper No. 105, Social Policy Research Centre, University of New South Wales, Sydney, 1999, retrieved from www.sprc.unsw.edu.au/media/File/dp105.pdf

103 War Widows' Guild, Minutes, Executive Committee, 3 February 1959, WA Branch, Perth; War Widows' Guild, Minutes, Council, 17 February 1959, WA Branch, Perth.

104 War Widows' Guild, Minutes, Executive Committee, 14 October 1958, 3 February 1959, WA Branch, Perth.

105 *Guild News*, July 1960, p. 4.

106 War Widows' Guild, Minutes, Executive Committee, 5 January 1960, WA Branch, Perth.

107 War Widows' Guild, Minutes, Council, 18 August 1959, WA Branch, Perth.

108 *Guild News,* October/November 1960, p. 2.

109 *Guild News*, October 1959, p. 2.

110 War Widows' Guild, Minutes, Council, 18 August 1959, WA Branch, Perth.

111 War Widows' Guild, Minutes, Council, 15 March 1960, WA Branch, Perth.

112 *Guild News*, July 1960, p. 2.

113 'War Veterans' Home', file, Anzac House archives, Perth.

114 War Widows' Guild, Minutes, AGM, 16 May 1961, WA Branch, Perth.

115 *Guild News*, August 1961, p. 2.

116 *Guild News*, May 1971, p. 2.

117 *Guild News,* August 1961, p. 2.

Chapter 5: End of an Era

1 *Guild News*, May 1961, p. 2.

2 *Guild News*, July 1960, p. 6.

3 *Guild News*, August 1961, p. 3.

4 Gregory, *City of Light*, p. 3.

5 Annual Report 1960–61, in *Guild News*, August 1961, p. 3.

6 *Guild News*, August 1962, p. 4.

7   Perth City Council (PCC): Council Property Esplanade Kiosk, File No. G7/7, Lease Document 323, Box 1442.

8   ibid.

9   Interview with Alan Forsyth, 12 December 2008.

10   PCC: Council Property Esplanade Kiosk, File No. G7/7, Lease Document 323, Box 1442.

11   ibid.

12   ibid.

13   War Widows' Guild, Minutes, Executive Committee, 14 May 1963, WA Branch, Perth.

14   War Widows' Guild, Minutes, Executive Committee, 5 October 1964, WA Branch, Perth.

15   War Widows' Guild, Minutes, Council, August 20, 1963, WA Branch, Perth.

16   *Guild News,* August, 1963, p. 2.

17   *Guild News,* June 1964, p. 5.

18   *Guild News,* June 1964, p. 2.

19   *Guild News,* November 1963, p. 2.

20   'Major-General Sir Douglas Kendrew 1963-1973', The Constitutional of Western Australia, retrieved 16 June 2012 from www.centre. wa.gov.au/ExhibitionsOnline/ GovernorsAndPremiers/Governors/ Pages/Kendrew.aspx

21   *Guild News,* November 1963, p. 2.

22   Interview with Gwen McDowell, 23 October 2009.

23   War Widows' Guild, Minutes, Executive Committee, 7 March 1966, WA Branch, Perth.

24   Interview with Beryl Haneman and Margaret Hateley, 20 October 2010.

25   *Guild News,* June 1964, p. 6.

26   'Victor Ketterer', *The AIF Project,* 2009, retrieved 4 September 2009 from http://www.aif.adfa.edu. au:8080/showPerson?pid=164190

27   *Guild News,* February 1967, p. 4.

28   Ken Inglis, 'Return to Gallipoli', in J. Lack (ed.), *ANZAC Remembered: Selected writings by K.S. Inglis,* University of Melbourne,

Department of History, Melbourne, 1998, pp. 29-39.

29   'Australia and the Vietnam War', retrieved 10 February 2011, http:// vietnam-war.commemoration.gov.au

30   Gregory, *City of Light,* pp. 124-30.

31   War Widows' Guild, Minutes, Executive Committee, 2 November 1964, WA Branch, Perth.

32   Dr Guy Henn, Condolence motion, Legislative Assembly, 28 April 1998, online version.

33   War Widows' Guild, Minutes, Council, 23 November 1964, WA Branch, Perth.

34   Deputation from War Widows' Guild, 7 December 1964, in Minutes, Council, 19 January 1965, WA Branch, Perth.

35   ibid.

36   ibid.

37   War Widows' Guild, Minutes, Executive Committee, 4 October 1965, WA Branch, Perth.

38   *Guild News,* July 1966, p. 2.

39   War Widows' Guild, Minutes, Council, 20 October 1964, WA Branch, Perth.

40   *Guild News,* June 1964, p. 5; War Widows' Guild, Minutes, Executive Committee, 5 October 1964, WA Branch, Perth.

41   *Guild News,* June 1964, p. 4.

42   *Guild News,* November 1963, p. 3.

43   Clark, *No Mean Destiny,* pp. 199-200.

44   Extracts from Minutes of a Meeting of the Board of Directors of Vasey Housing Auxiliary (War Widows' Guild) Ltd., 15 March 1966, Vasey Family Papers, MS 3782, box 15 folder 92, NLA; additional details located in Clark, *No Mean Destiny,* pp. 172, 199, 204, 210, 211.

45   Cec Baldwin to Robert Vasey, 22 April 1966, Vasey Family Papers, MS 3782, box 15 folder 92, NLA.

46   Cec Baldwin to Robert Vasey, 29 June 1966, Vasey Family Papers, MS 3782, box 15, folder 92, NLA.

47 *Guild Digest,* December 1966, p. 11.
48 Clark, *No Mean Destiny,* p. 214.
49 *Guild Digest,* December 1966, p. 11.

Chapter 6: 'Carry on the Magnificent Work'
1   *Guild News,* December 1966, p. 2.
2   *Guild Digest,* December 1966, p. 3.
3   War Widows' Guild, Minutes, Executive Committee, 3 October 1966, WA Branch, Perth.
4   *Guild Digest,* December 1966, p. 4.
5   Interview with Alan Forsyth, 12 December 2008.
6   A. MacDonald, personal communication, 21 February 2011.
7   *Guild Digest,* December 1966, p. 4.
8   ibid., p. 11.
9   ibid., p. 3.
10 Until 1963, Jessie Vasey had been referred to as the federal president, but at the federal conference that year it was voted to use the terms national president and national conference. Thus when Janet Mayo was elected, she was given the title of national president.
11 Clark, *No Mean Destiny,* p. 70.
12 *Guild News,* December 1966, p. 2.
13 Quoted in *Guild News,* December 1966, p. 2.
14 *Guild News,* December 1966, p. 3.
15 *Guild News,* December 1966, pp. 2–4.
16 *Guild News,* October 1967, p. 3
17 *Guild News,* October 1967, pp. 6–7.
18 War Widows' Guild, Minutes, Executive Committee, 6 July 1954, WA Branch, Perth
19 Interview with Beryl Haneman and Margaret Hateley, 22 October 2010.
20 War Widows' Guild, Minutes, Executive Committee, 3 July 1963, WA Branch, Perth.
21 War Widows' Guild, Minutes, Executive Committee, 23 July 1963 and 4 February 1964, WA Branch, Perth.
22 *Guild News,* December 1967, p. 2.
23 War Widows' Guild, Minutes, National Conference, 16–20 October 1967, p. 6.

24 *Guild News,* May 1967, p. 4.
25 War Widows' Guild, Minutes, Council, 17 April 1967, WA Branch, Perth.
26 Stewart Bovell, Minister for Lands, to Gwen Forsyth, 14 November 1967. War Widows' Guild – stage 1, PP572/1, WA70, NAA, Perth.
27 The area of land that is now Forsyth Gardens is officially part of the suburb of Menora, which came into existence in 1954, but all documentation for this time period, including official forms from the Minister of Lands, states it as part of Mount Lawley.
28 *Guild News,* June 1969, p. 2.
29 *Guild News,* June 1968, p. 2.
30 ibid., p. 4.
31 ibid., p. 6
32 *Guild News,* September 1968, p. 2.
33 *Guild News,* June 1969, p. 3.
34 'Nightingale Medal for WA Woman', *West Australian,* 22 May 1969, p. 33.
35 Wendy Birman and Victoria Hobbs, 'Ferguson, Jean Elsie (1909–1979)', *Australian Dictionary of Biography,* National Centre of Biography, Australian National University, retrieved 1 December 2011 from http://adb.anu.edu.au/biography/ferguson-jean-elsie-10166
36 *Guild News,* August 1962, p. 4.
37 *Guild News,* June 1970, pp. 2–3; Peck Estate file, War Widows' Guild archives, WA Branch, Perth.
38 'Peck, John Henry (1886–1928)', *Australian Dictionary of Biography,* National Centre of Biography, Australian National University, retrieved from http://adbonline.anu.edu.au/biography/peck-henry-8007
39 F.S. Flynn, Senior Trust Officer, WA Trustees, to Mrs MacDonald, 18 September 1984, War Widows' Guild archives, WA Branch, Perth.
40 'Probate on bequest necessary, *West Australian,* n.d., n.p., Peck Estate file, War Widows' Guild archives, WA Branch, Perth.

41 Wallace and Gunning Barristers & Solicitors to War Widows' Guild, 26 March 1970, Peck Estate file, War Widows' Guild archives, WA Branch, Perth.

42 *Guild News,* November 1969, p. 2

43 *Guild News,* June 1968, p. 2.

44 War Widows' Guild, Minutes, National Conference, 14–17 October 1969, p. 2.

45 ibid., p. 9.

46 ibid., pp. 7–8.

47 Interview with Alex MacDonald, 12 March 2010.

48 A. Forsyth, personal communication, 21 February 2011.

49 ibid.

50 ibid.

51 *Guild News,* February 1971, p. 3.

52 *Guild News,* May 1971, p. 3.

53 Janet Mayo to all state Guilds, 15 December 1970, War Widows' Guild archives, WA Branch, Perth.

54 *Guild News,* December 1971, p. 2.

55 *Guild News,* August 1972, p. 2.

56 ibid. At the time of the announcement, the war widows' basic weekly pension rate was $20 with an additional $8.50 domestic allowance.

57 *Guild News,* August 1972, p. 2.

58 ibid.

59 *Guild News,* June 1973, p. 4.

60 *Guild News,* August 1972, p. 4.

61 *Guild News,* June 1974, p. 2.

Chapter 7: Still Fighting

1 Alison Alexander, *A Wealth of Women: Australian Women's Lives from 1788 to the Present,* Duffy and Snellgrove, Sydney, 2001, p. 264.

2 Mary Turner, *The Women's Century: A Celebration of Changing Roles, 1900–2000,* National Archives, Surrey, 2003, p. 124.

3 Alexander, *A Wealth of Women,* pp. 261, 301.

4 David Horner, *Australia's Military History for Dummies,* Wiley Publishing, Milton, 2010, p. 356.

5 Paul Toose, *Independent Enquiry into the Repatriation System,* Australian Government Publishing Service, 1975, p. 5.

6 Toose, pp. 743, 762.

7 Toose, p. 660.

8 Toose, p. 661.

9 Toose, p. 40.

10 ibid.

11 Quoted in Toose, p. 21.

12 Toose, p. 625.

13 Toose, p. 41.

14 War Widows' Guild, Minutes, Executive Committee, 5 April 1976, WA Branch, Perth.

15 Clem Lloyd and Jacqui Rees, *The Last Shilling: A History of Repatriation in Australia,* Melbourne University Press, Carlton, 1994, p. 330.

16 War Widows' Guild, Minutes, National Conference, October 1973, War Widows' Guild of Australia archives, Canberra, p. 11.

17 War Widows' Guild of Australia, Minutes, Special Meeting of War Widows' Guild Australia, 7 April 1973, Canberra.

18 ibid.

19 War Widows' Guild, Minutes, Executive Committee, 6 August 1973, WA Branch, Perth.

20 War Widows' Guild, Minutes, National Conference, October 1973, War Widows' Guild of Australia archives, Canberra, p. 22.

21 War Widows' Guild, Minutes, National Conference, October 1973, War Widows' Guild of Australia archives, Canberra, p. 4.

22 War Widows' Guild, Minutes, Executive Committee, 1 April 1974 and 3 June 1974, WA Branch, Perth.

23 War Widows' Guild, Minutes, Executive Committee, 1 July 1974, WA Branch, Perth.

24 Letter from E. Mills to Mrs Forsyth, 27 May 1974, War Widows' Guild

archives, WA Branch, Perth.

25 War Widows' Guild, Minutes, Executive Committee, 1 July 1974, WA Branch, Perth; letter from Gwen Forsyth to Mrs E. Mills, 25 May 1974, War Widows' Guild archives, WA Branch, Perth; letter from E. Mills to Mrs Forsyth, 27 May 1974, War Widows' Guild archives, WA Branch, Perth.

26 *Guild News*, December 1973, p. 3.

27 The Department of Repatriation and Compensation was known as the Repatriation Department from 1917 to 1974. It became known as the Department of Repatriation and Compensation for a brief time during 1974 and 1975 before returning to the title of Repatriation Department, again briefly, before a further name change saw it become the Department of Veterans' Affairs (DVA) in 1976. See 'Veterans' Case Files – Fact Sheet 54', NAA, retrieved from www.naa.gov.au/collection/fact-sheets/fs54.aspx

28 Gwen Forsyth to W.G. Hayden, 15 July 1974, War Widows' Guild archives, WA Branch, Perth.

29 Bill Hayden to Gwen Forsyth, 16 August 1974, War Widows' Guild archives, WA Branch, Perth.

30 War Widows' Guild, Minutes, Executive Committee, 2 September 1974, WA Branch, Perth.

31 *Guild News*, February 1975, p. 3.

32 War Widows' Guild, Minutes, Executive Committee, 7 July 1975, WA Branch, Perth; War Widows' Guild, Minutes, Executive Committee, 5 July 1976, WA Branch, Perth; *Guild News,* October 1976, p. 2.

33 *Guild News*, February 1975, p. 3; *Guild News*, October 1976, p. 2.

34 Interview with Marj Hassett and Iris Rowtcliff, 22 June 2009.

35 ibid.

36 ibid.

37 War Widows' Guild, Minutes, Executive Committee, 7 July 1975, WA Branch, Perth.

38 *Guild News*, June 1975, p. 2.

39 *Guild News*, December 1975, p. 6.

40 Interview with Marj Hassett and Iris Rowtcliff, 22 June 2009.

41 War Widows' Guild, Minutes, Executive Committee, 16 January 1967, WA Branch, Perth.

42 Quoted in Norma King, *The Voice of the Goldfields: 100 Years of the Kalgoorlie Miner*, Hocking and Co., Kalgoorlie, 1995, p. 166.

43 *Guild News*, June 1973, p. 3.

44 M. Domeyer, personal communication, 15 August 2012.

45 War Widows' Guild, Minutes, Executive Committee, 5 January 1976, WA Branch, Perth.

46 M. Domeyer, personal communication, 15 August 2012.

47 L. Anderson, personal communication, 16 October 2012.

48 Gregory, *City of Light*, p. 208.

49 Gregory, *City of Light*, p. 203.

50 Anzac House and Club Board of Management, Minutes, n.d., Anzac House archives, Perth.

51 'A Short History of Anzac House', in pamphlet for official opening of the new Anzac House, 14 November 1981, Anzac House archives, Perth.

52 Anzac House and Club Board of Management, Minutes, 26 May 1976, Anzac House archives, Perth; 'A Short History of Anzac House'.

53 War Widows' Guild, Minutes, Executive Committee, 5 July1976, WA Branch, Perth.

54 *Guild News,* August 1976, pp. 5–6.

55 War Widows' Guild, Minutes, Executive Committee, 7 February 1977, WA Branch, Perth.

56 'Lawson Apartments', Heritage Perth, retrieved from heritageperth.com.au/properties/Lawson-apartments

57 'Register of heritage places – permanent entry: Esplanade Reserve', Heritage Council of Western Australia, Perth, 2003, p. 2.

58 *Guild News*, May 1977, p. 2.

59 ibid.

60 ibid.

61 ibid.

62 ibid.

63 Interview with Marj Hassett and Iris Rowtcliff, 22 June 2009.

64 *Guild News*, May 1977, p. 2.

65 *Guild News*, July 1977, p. 2.

66 ibid., pp. 2, 4.

67 *Guild News*, November 1977, p. 3.

68 ibid.

69 *Guild News*, June 1979, p. 4.

70 *Guild News*, June 1978, p. 3.

71 ibid.

72 *Guild News*, June 1977.

73 War Widows' Guild, Minutes, Executive Committee, 7 November 1977, WA Branch, Perth.

74 *Guild News*, June 1978, p.2.

75 *Guild News*, June 1974, p. 8.

76 ibid.

77 *Guild News*, June 1978, p. 2.

78 *Guild News*, June 1979, p. 2.

79 Gwen Forsyth to Elva Elliot, 30 January 1979, War Widows' Guild archives, WA Branch, Perth.

80 Gregory, *City of Light*, p. 220; Geoffrey Bolton, 'Way 1979: Whose Celebration?' in Lenore Layman and Tom Stannage (eds), *Celebrations in Western Australian History*, Studies in Western Australian History X, April 1989, Centre for Western Australian History, Nedlands, pp. 15–20.

81 Gregory, *City of Light*, p. 223.

82 'Register of heritage places – permanent entry: Esplanade Reserve', p. 2.

83 Gregory, *City of Light*, p. 223.

84 *Guild News*, June 1980, p. 4.

85 *Guild News*, June 1979, p. 3.

86 *Guild News*, May 1971, p. 4.

87 *Guild News*, June 1979, p. 5.

88 War Widows' Guild of Australia, Minutes, National Conference 14–17 October 1969, Canberra, p. 19.

89 War Widows' Guild, Minutes, National Conference, October 1973, War Widows' Guild of Australia archives, Canberra, p. 10.

90 War Widows' Guild, Minutes, National Conference, October 1975, pp. 18–19; War Widows' Guild of Australia archives, Canberra, p. 18; *Guild News*, March 1980, p. 5; *The Guild News*, February 1981, p. 4.

91 *Guild News*, June 1980, p. 4.

92 *Guild News*, February 1981, p. 4.

93 *Guild News*, June 1980, p. 4.

94 *Guild News*, June 1981, p. 2.

95 *Guild News*, August 1980, p. 2; *Guild News*, June 1981, p. 2.

96 War Widows' Guild, Minutes, Executive Committee, 3 March 1980, WA Branch, Perth.

97 *Guild News*, August 1980, p. 2.

98 Interview with Sue Wilson, 29 October 2013.

99 L. Beaman, personal communication, 19 November 2012.

100 Interview with Iris Rowtcliff, Marj Hassett and Pearl Thomson, 28 July 2008.

101 S. Wilson, personal communication, 15 March 2013; interview with Robin Bowden and Doreen Basley, 2 November 2009.

102 Interview with Betty Walker, 17 November 2008.

103 According to Joy Smith, personal communication, 2 February 2015, a parlour car was 'a type of coach, which ran continuously from Fremantle to Perth and back. There was no timetable, you just waited until one came along. If they saw you, they'd stop for you whether you were actually waiting for them or not. They were designed to fit about ten passengers (two rows of four and

a row of two), but in war the parlour cars were often overloaded.'

104 ibid.

105 ibid., 17 November 2008.

106 *Guild News*, June 1981, p. 2.

107 ibid.

108 War Widows' Guild, Minutes, Executive Committee, 1 June 1981, WA Branch, Perth.

109 War Widows' Guild, Minutes, National Biennial Conference, September 1981, p. 2.

110 Some of this correspondence is held in Guild Archives, WA Branch, Perth.

111 *Guild News,* November 1979, p. 4; correspondence between Marjorie Le Souef and Gwen Forsyth, War Widows' Guild archives, WA Branch, Perth.

112 War Widows' Guild, Minutes, National Biennial Conference, September 1981, p. 17.

113 Clark, *No Mean Destiny*, pp. 254–5.

114 Clark, *No Mean Destiny*, p. 262.

115 Clark, *No Mean Destiny*, p. 267.

116 *Guild News*, February 1982, p. 5.

117 ibid.

118 Interview with Marj Hassett, Pearl Thomson and Iris Rowtcliff, 28 July 2008.

119 Interview with Marj Hassett, Pearl Thomson and Iris Rowtcliff, 28 July 2008.

120 *Guild News,* February 1981, p. 5; February 1986, p. 3; War Widows' Guild, Minutes, Executive Committee, 3 November 1989 and 7 December 1981, WA Branch, Perth.

121 War Widows' Guild, Minutes, AGM, 17 May 1982, WA Branch, Perth.

122 *Guild News*, June 1982, p. 5; War Widows' Guild, Minutes, Executive Committee, 7 June 1982, WA Branch, Perth.

123 *Guild News*, June 1981, p. 5.

124 *Guild News*, June 1983, p. 9.

125 ibid.

126 War Widows' Guild, Minutes, AGM, 16 May 1983, WA Branch, Perth.

127 'A tribute to Mrs A.L. Forsyth, OBE', *Tapis*, November 1983, p. 5.

128 ibid.

129 Interview with Alan Forsyth, 12 December 2008.

130 *Guild News*, June 1980, pp. 3–4.

Chapter 8: Changing of the Guard

1   War Widows' Guild, Minutes, Council, 23 May 1983, WA Branch, Perth.

2   War Widows' Guild, Minutes, AGM, 21 May 1984, WA Branch, Perth.

3   Interview with Alex MacDonald, 12 March 2010.

4   ibid.

5   ibid.

6   *Guild News*, August 1978, p. 5.

7   ibid.

8   *Guild News*, February 1979; see also 'Ferguson, Jean Elsie (1909–1979)', in *Australian Dictionary of Biography – Online Edition*, retrieved 3 September 2009.

9   Interview with Marjorie Hassett, Pearl Thomson and Iris Rowtcliff, 28 July 2008.

10 ibid.

11 Interview with Doreen Taylor, 21 January 2009.

12 ibid.

13 War Widows' Guild, Minutes, AGM, 20 May 1985, WA Branch, Perth.

14 War Widows' Guild, Minutes, Executive Committee, 5 September 1989, WA Branch, Perth.

15 *Guild News*, September 1986, p. 2.

16 According to the website TuTiempo.net, Brisbane's weather had maximums ranging from 24 to 28°C during the conference and with no rain other than a downpour of almost 12 mm on 25 September 1986.

17 Letter from Gloria MacDonald to Mrs E. Elliot, 25 June 1984, War Widows' Guild archives, WA Branch, Perth.

18 *Guild News*, September 1986, p. 2.
19 War Widows' Guild, Minutes, Executive Committee, 9 March 1987, WA Branch, Perth; J. Knight, personal communication, 2 March 2012.
20 Roslyn Burge, *No Peacetime Cinderellas: War Widows' Guild of Australia NSW Ltd*, War Widows' Guild of Australia, NSW Ltd., Sydney, 2008, p. 211.
21 War Widows' Guild, Minutes, Executive Committee, 3 October 1977, WA Branch, Perth.
22 Toose, p. 621.
23 ibid.
24 War Widows' Guild, Minutes, Council, 16 February 1977, NSW Branch, Sydney, quoted in Burge, *No Peacetime Cinderellas*, p. 211.
25 War Widows' Guild, Minutes, Executive Committee, 1 November 1976, WA Branch, Perth.
26 Burge, *No Peacetime Cinderellas*, p. 211.
27 ibid.
28 War Widows' Guild, Minutes, Executive Committee, 4 May 1987, WA Branch, Perth.
29 War Widows' Guild, Minutes, Executive Committee, 6 April 1987, WA Branch, Perth.
30 War Widows' Guild, Minutes, Executive Committee, 26 May 1987, WA Branch, Perth.
31 War Widows' Guild, Minutes, Executive Committee, 24 February 1986, WA Branch, Perth.
32 Jessie Vasey to war widows, October 1945, War Widows' Guild archives, WA Branch, Perth.
33 John Clarke, *Report of the Review of Veterans' Entitlements*, Commonwealth of Australia, Canberra, pp. 223–4.
34 War Widows' Guild, Minutes, Executive Committee, 3 August 1987, WA Branch, Perth.
35 War Widows' Guild, Minutes, Executive Committee, 9 March 1987, WA Branch, Perth.
36 Interview with Iris Rowtcliff, Marj Hassett and Pearl Thomson, 28 July 2008.
37 War Widows' Guild, Minutes, Executive Committee, 4 November 1985, WA Branch, Perth; *Guild News*, June 1989, p. 1.
38 War Widows' Guild, Minutes, Executive Committee, 5 February 1952, WA Branch, Perth.
39 Interview with Iris Rowtcliff, Pearl Thomson and Marj Hassett, 28 June 2008.
40 ibid.
41 ibid.
42 War Widows' Guild, Minutes, Executive Committee, 6 April 1987, WA Branch, Perth; *Guild News*, June 1987, p. 4.
43 Interview with Iris Rowtcliff, Pearl Thomson and Marj Hassett, 28 June 2008.
44 ibid.
45 ibid.
46 Interview with Marj Hassett and Iris Rowtcliff, 22 June 2009.
47 *Guild News*, December 1988, p. 3.
48 War Widows' Guild, Minutes, Executive Committee, 3 July 1989, WA Branch, Perth.
49 Interview with Margaret Southwood, 25 November 2009.
50 ibid.
51 ibid.
52 ibid.
53 War Widows' Guild, Minutes, Executive Committee, 2 May 1988 and 4 July 1988, WA Branch, Perth.
54 Interview with Iris Rowtcliff, Pearl Thomson and Marj Hassett, 28 June 2008.
55 ibid.
56 Interview with Iris Rowtcliff and Marj Hassett, 22 June 2009.

57 *Guild News*, June 1989, p. 3; December 1989, p. 2.
58 Interview with Iris Rowtcliff, Pearl Thomson and Marj Hassett, 28 June 2008.
59 ibid
60 ibid.
61 ibid.
62 ibid.; Iris Rowtcliff, personal communication, 24 June 2013.
63 War Widows' Guild, Minutes, Executive Committee, 4 September 1989, WA Branch, Perth; Clem Lloyd & Jacqui Rees, *The Last Shilling: A History of Repatriation in Australia*, Melbourne University Press, Carlton, 1994, p. 383.
64 *Guild News*, June 1990, p. 2; Lloyd & Rees, *The Last Shilling*, p. 383.
65 Premier Peter Dowding to Prime Minister Bob Hawke, 24 November 1988 and Barry McKinnon, Leader of the Opposition, to Mr J.P. Hall, State President, RSL, 29 November 1988, Minutes, Unit and Kindred Association, Hospital Integration Committee, Anzac House archives, Perth.
66 War Widows' Guild, Minutes, Executive Meeting, 1 May 1989, WA Branch, Perth.
67 'Speech for the Prime Minister Opening of New Theatre Block, RGH Concord', 7 March 1990, retrieved from http://pmtranscripts. dpmc.gov.au/transcripts/00007943. pdf
68 War Widows' Guild, Minutes, Executive Meeting, 9 March 1990, WA Branch, Perth.
69 *Guild News*, June 1990, p. 2.
70 War Widows' Guild of Australia, Western Australia to Chairman, Unit and Kindred Association, n.d., Anzac House archives, Perth.
71 War Widows' Guild, Minutes, Executive Meeting, 2 July 1990, WA Branch, Perth.

72 Unit and Kindred Association, Hospital Integration Committee, Minutes, 19 December 1990, Anzac House archives, Perth.
73 Unit and Kindred Association, Hospital Integration Committee, Minutes, 27 March 1991, Anzac House archives, Perth.
74 'Repatriation Hospital Plan Wins Support', *West Australian*, 26 November 1991, p. 34.
75 ibid.
76 Ben Humphreys to The Editor, *Subiaco Post*, 15 October 1992, n.p.
77 Unit and Kindred Association, Hospital Integration Committee, Minutes, 27 March 1991, Anzac House archives, Perth.
78 Unit and Kindred Association, Hospital Integration Committee, Minutes, 16 July 1991, Anzac House archives, Perth.
79 Unit and Kindred Association, Hospital Integration Committee, Minutes, 24 August 1993, 8 September 1993, 16 September 1993 and 1 October 1993, Anzac House archives, Perth.
80 Rosyln Davies, *Everyone's a Hero: Stories from the First Seventy Years at an Amazing Hospital*, Ramsay Health Care Australia Pty Ltd, Fremantle, 2010, pp. 61–2.
81 *Guild News*, February 1994, p. 3.
82 Davies, *Everyone's a Hero*, p. 64.
83 *Guild News*, June 1994, p. 2.

Chapter 9: Leaving a Legacy
1 War Widows' Guild, Minutes, Executive Committee, 24 May 1993, WA Branch, Perth.
2 ibid.
3 War Widows' Guild, Minutes, Executive Meeting, 1 May 1995, WA Branch, Perth.
4 *Guild News*, June 1995, p. 2.
5 Interview with Iris Rowtcliff, Pearl Thomson and Marj Hassett, 28 June 2008.

6   *Guild News*, December 1995, p. 2.
7   ibid.
8   Australia Remembers commemorative stamps, 1995, copy held in War Widows' Guild archives, WA Branch, Perth.
9   *Guild News*, February 1997, p. 2.
10 Interview with Anne Lopez, 18 March 2009.
11 *Guild News*, June 1997, p. 4
12 Interview with Fran Aggiss, 24 September 2009.
13 Interview with Doreen Taylor, 21 January 2009.
14 Interview with Ruth Moir and Jean Bloomfield, 29 September 2009.
15 ibid.
16 ibid.
17 ibid.
18 Interview with Fran Aggiss, 24 September 2009.
19 ibid.
20 'President's report, 1990 AGM' in *Guild News*, June 1990; War Widows' Guild, Minutes, Executive Meeting, 2 April 1990, 4 February 1991 and 6 May 1991, WA Branch, Perth.
21 Interview with Fran Aggiss, 24 September 2009.
22 Gregory, *City of Light*, p. 298.
23 Interview with Margaret Southwood, 25 November 2009.
24 Interview with Fran Aggiss, 24 September 2009.
25 Interview with Doreen Taylor, 21 January 2009.
26 *Guild News*, September 1999, p. 15.
27 Interview with Margaret Southwood, 25 November 2009.
28 Interview with Iris Rowtcliff and Marj Hassett, 22 June 2009.
29 *Guild News*, June 2000, p. 3.
30 *Guild News*, June 2000, p. 3.
31 *Guild News*, November 2000, p. 7.
32 *Guild News*, November 2000, p. 7.
33 War Widows' Guild, Minutes, Executive Committee, 5 May 1997, WA Branch, Perth.
34 War Widows' Guild, Minutes, Executive Committee, 4 June 1979, WA Branch, Perth.
35 War Widows' Guild, Minutes, AGM, 21 May 1984, WA Branch, Perth.
36 War Widows' Guild, Minutes, Executive Committee, 2 August 1993, WA Branch, Perth.
37 *Guild News*, June 1994, p. 2.
38 Mrs Shaw's view is supported by an international research paper on aging, which argues that in 1986, 4.4% of the Australian population over 65 years of age were living in nursing homes, while only 2.4% were living in hostel type accommodation, which provided 'congregate living and personal and social care but not continuous nursing care.' It became a 'major policy concern ... to change the balance between nursing home and hostel care.' (See Joan Van Nostrand, Anna Howe, Betty Havens, David Bray, Wim van der Heuvel, Tor Romoren & Robert Clark, *Overview of Long-Term Care in Five Nations: Australia, Canada, the Netherlands, Norway and the United States*, US Department of Health and Human Services, September 1995, retrieved from aspe.hhs.gov.daltcp/reports/1995/5overvie.htm)
39 War Widows' Guild, Minutes, Executive Committee, 7 June 1994, WA Branch, Perth.
40 War Widows' Guild, Minutes, Executive Committee, 6 November 1995, WA Branch, Perth.
41 War Widows' Guild, Minutes, Executive Committee, 5 May 1997, WA Branch, Perth.
42 *Guild News*, June 1996, p. 3.
43 *Guild News*, June 1997, p. 2.
44 J. Knight, personal communication, 13 August 2012.
45 *Guild News*, May 2001, p. 5.
46 'War Widows' Gift to UWA', *Uniview Magazine*, February 2001, p. 3.

47 *Guild News*, August 2002, inside cover.
48 *Guild News,* September 2001, p. 6.
49 Interview with Robin Bowden and Doreen Basley, 2 November 2009.
50 ibid.
51 ibid.
52 ibid.
53 *Guild News*, July 2003, p. 13.
54 ibid.
55 ibid.
56 Burge, *Everyone's a Hero*, p. 128.
57 War Widows' Guild, Minutes, Executive Committee, 6 May 1996 and 4 March 1997, WA Branch, Perth.
58 Marjorie Le Souef to residents of Forsyth Gardens, 15 October 2001, Forsyth Gardens file, War Widows' Guild archives, WA Branch, Perth.
59 *Guild News*, December 2001, p. 2.
60 J. Knight, personal communication, 12 August 2012.
61 'WA War Widows Told to Pack Up and Leave', *West Australian*, 11 January 2002, n.p.
62 *Guild News*, April 2002, p. 2.
63 ibid.
64 'WA war widows told to pack up and leave', *West Australian*, 11 January 2002, n.p.
65 *Guild News*, April 2002, p. 2.
66 Marjorie Le Souef, quoted in 'Guild Replies to War Widows', *West Australian*, 16 January 2002, n.p.
67 Marjorie Le Souef, 'Statement from the War Widows' Guild of Australia (WA) Inc', 15 January 2002, War Widows' Guild archives, WA Branch, Perth.
68 Marjorie Le Souef to residents of Forsyth Gardens, 7 January 2002, Forsyth Gardens file, War Widows' Guild archives, WA Branch, Perth.
69 *Guild News*, April 2002, p. 2.
70 *Guild News*, August 2002, p. 2.
71 Interview with Hazel Donald, 27 August 2012.
72 *Guild News*, July 2003, p. 4

73 War Widows' Guild, Minutes, Executive Committee, 17 February 2003, WA Branch, Perth.
74 'Opening the War Widows' Guild Community and Administration Centre as part of the WA War Widows' Guild Annual General Meeting', Speeches/Transcripts, Former Minister for Veterans' Affairs, copy in War Widows' Guild archives, WA Branch, Perth.
75 ibid.
76 J. Knight, personal communication, 12 August 2012; interview with Hazel Donald, 27 August 2012.

Chapter 10: Remembrance and Recognition
1 Quoted in Burge, *No Peacetime Cinderellas*, p. 65.
2 Clark, *No Mean Destiny*, p. 158.
3 Alistair Thomson, *Anzac Memories: Living with the Legend*, Oxford University Press, Melbourne, 1994, p. 189.
4 Mark McKenna, 'Anzac Day: How Did It Become Australia's National Day?' in Marilyn Lake (ed.), *What's Wrong with Anzac: The Militarisation of Australian History*, UNSW Press, Sydney, 2010, p. 111.
5 ibid., pp. 110–34.
6 See Marina Larsson, *Shattered Anzacs: Living with the Scars of War*, 2009, UNSW Press, Sydney, 2009.
7 Robert Manne, 'A Turkish Tale: Gallipoli and the Armenian Genocide', *The Monthly*, February 2007, retrieved from www.themonthly.com.au/issue/2007/february/1327543545/robert-manne/turkish-tale-gallipoli-and-armenian-genocide
8 Interview with Florence Gordon, 10 August 2010.
9 Interview with Anne Lopez, 18 March 2009.
10 Shirley Hands, 'Shirley Hands' visit to Singapore and Malaysia', *Guild News*, April 2002, insert.

11 'Bali Bombing', This Day in History, History Channel, retrieved from www.historychannel.com.au/classroom/day-in-history/detail.aspx?dayId=379

12 'Afghanistan, 2001–present', Australian War Memorial, retrieved from www.awm.gov.au/atwar/afghanistan

13 'The Second Gulf War', Australian War Memorial, retrieved from www.awm.gov.au/atwar/gulf

14 John Clarke, Doug Riding & David Rosalky, *Report of the Review of Veterans' Entitlements*, Commonwealth of Australia, Canberra, 2003, p. v.

15 ibid., p. xi.

16 *Guild News*, November 2003, p. 9.

17 'Government increases rent assistance for war widows', 2 March 2004, press release, retrieved from www.navalassoc.org.au/DVA%20VA%20016%202Mar04.htm

18 War Widows' Guild of Australia [background paper on continuation of pension on remarriage or upon forming a de facto relationship], M1425, NAA, Perth.

19 War Widows' Guild, Minutes, Executive Committee, 3 October 1977, WA Branch, Perth.

20 John Clarke, Doug Riding & David Rosalky, *Report of the Review of Veterans' Entitlements*, Commonwealth of Australia, Canberra, 2003, pp. 430–31, retrieved 18 October 2013 from www.dva.gov.au/pensions_and_compensation/pensions_and_rates/clarke_review/Documents/ch19_22.pdf

21 J. Knight, personal communication, 12 June 2013.

22 Peter Husling to Marjorie Le Souef, 4 March 2002, War Widows' Guild archives, WA Branch, Perth.

23 Marjorie Le Souef to the Hon. Bruce Billson MP, 7 August 2006, War Widows' Guild archives, WA Branch, Perth.

24 War Widows' Guild of Australia, National Conference, Minutes, 16–19 October 2006, p. 18.

25 J. Knight, personal communication, 12 June 2013.

26 'Claim for $25,000 Ex-gratia Payment by a Surviving Spouse', Australian Government Department of Veterans' Affairs, retrieved 18 October 2013 from www.dva.gov.au/dvaforms/Documents/D9077.pdf

27 J. Knight, personal communication, 20 August 2012.

28 J. Knight, personal communication, 20 August 2012; Guild pay ledger records, War Widows' Guild archives, WA Branch, Perth.

29 Norma Whitfield, 'National President's Message', *Guild News*, November 2005, p. 3.

30 'Veteran Fulfils a Poignant Dream to Return', *West Australian*, 13 September 2005, p. 13.

31 *Guild News*, November 2005, p. 2.

32 In 2001, Marjorie Le Souef had been approached by another war widower who wished to join the organisation. A pension for war widowers had been introduced in 1991, and as the national constitution allowed for such an inclusion, Marjorie contacted the man (see *Guild News*, September 2001, p. 16). Bert Donald became a member in June 2003.

33 'Australia's Military Involvement in Afghanistan since 2001: A Chronology', Parliament of Australia, retrieved 24 February 2014 from www.aph.gov.au/About_Parliament/Parliamentary_Departments/Parliamentary_Library/pubs/BN/1011/MilitaryInvolvementAfghanistan

34 *Guild News*, December 2006, p. 2.

35 ibid.

36   Dr John Shepherd, 'Address Given at the 60th Anniversary of the War Widows' Guild', 29 November 2006, War Widows' Guild archives, WA Branch, Perth.

37   Interview with Florence Gordon, 10 August 2010.

38   ibid.

39   ibid.

40   ibid.

41   Interview with Sue Wilson, 29 October 2013.

42   ibid.

43   ibid.

44   ibid.

45   War Widows' Guild of Australia, National Conference, Minutes, 16–19 October 2006, p. 12.

46   WA State Report, War Widows' Guild of Australia, National Conference, 16–19 October 2006.

47   Marie Cooke, 'Australian War Widows: A Case Study to Challenge Public Policy', *Australian Journal of Social Issues*, vol. 38, no. 4, 4 November 2003, pp. 465–75.

48   S. Wilson, personal communication, 25 March 2013.

49   Interview with Robin Bowden and Doreen Basley, 2 November 2009.

50   Interview with Hazel Donald, 27 August 2012.

51   WA State Report, War Widows' Guild of Australia, National Conference, 16–19 October 2006, WA Branch, Perth.

52   Kim Morgan-Short, 'A Younger Widow Tells Her Story', *Guild News*, December 2011, pp. 8–9.

53   Interview with De'Arne Prosser, 27 November 2013.

54   ibid.

55   ibid.

56   ibid.

57   ibid.

58   See Joy Damousi, 'War Widows Remember' in *Living with the Aftermath*, pp. 9–35.

59   See Marina Larsson, *Shattered Anzacs: Living with the Scars of War*, 2009, UNSW Press, Sydney, 2009; and Tanja Luckins, *The Gates of Memory: Australian People's Experiences and Memories of Loss and the Great War*, 2004, Curtin University Books, Fremantle, for further details about this.

60   Interview with Sue Wilson, 29 October 2013.

Epilogue

1   A. Blood, personal communication, May 2012.

2   Dr John Shepherd, 'Address Given at the 60th Anniversary of the War Widows' Guild', 29 November 2006, War Widows' Guild archives, WA Branch, Perth.

SELECT BIBLIOGRAPHY

GUILD ARCHIVES

Circular, Melbourne: War Widows' Guild, Victorian Branch, Melbourne, March 1950.

Ex-Servicemen's Organisations and Departments Concerned in the Re-establishment of Ex-service Personnel, Minutes, 11 March 1947, copy held in War Widows' Guild archives, WA Branch, Perth.

Ex-Servicemen's Organisations and Departments Concerned in the Re-establishment of Ex-service Personnel, (1947, July 26), Minutes, 26 July 1947, copy held in War Widows' Guild archives, WA Branch, Perth.

Guild Digest, War Widows' Guild, NSW Branch, Sydney, December 1966.

Guild News, War Widows' Guild, WA Branch, Perth, 1954–2015.

Le Souef, Marjorie, *Discharge from the Army*, unpublished autobiographical narrative, Perth, 2005.

Transcript of radio interview, Mr Clements and Mrs Gahan, Post War Bulletin, No. 53, n.d.

Transcript of radio interview, Mr Clements and Mrs Learmonth, Post War Bulletin, No. 61, 2 September 1947.

War Widows' Guild Council Minutes, 1947–1993.

War Widows' Guild Executive Minutes, 1946–2014.

War Widows' Guild of Australia, National Conference Minutes, 1947, 1967–1975, 1981, 1992–1996, 2008–2014.

Weaving School, various papers.

INTERVIEWS

Fran Aggiss, 24 September 2009

Doreen Basley and Robin Bowden, 2 November 2009

Hazel Donald, 27 August 2012

Alan Forsyth, 12 December 2008

Florence Gordon, 10 August 2010

Phyllis Grlusich and Robert Jones, 19 May 2011

Marjorie Hassett and Iris Rowtcliff, 22 June 2009

Marjorie Hassett, Iris Rowtcliff and Pearl Thomson, 28 July 2008

Margaret Hateley and Beryl Hanamen, 22 October 2010

David Heath, 11 May 2011

Anne Lopez, 18 March 2009

Alex MacDonald, 12 March 2010

Gwen McDowell, 23 October 2009

Patricia Milne, 26 March 2010

Ruth Moir and Jean Bloomfield, 29 September 2009

De'Arne Prosser, 27 November 2013

Eva Roach, 31 March 2009

Maureen Rose, 24 May 2011

Margaret Southwood, 25 November 2009

Doreen Taylor, 21 January 2009

Laurel Taylor, 7 May 2009

Helen Treloar, 4 June 2010

Betty Walker, 17 November 2008
Graham Walker and Peggy Litchfield,
12 May 2011
Sue Wilson, 29 October 2013

Australia, 1995.
60th Anniversary of War Widows' Guild,
radio interview, 720 ABC Perth,
28 November 2006.

PRIVATE PAPERS AND ARCHIVAL MATERIAL

2/28 Infantry Battalion August –
September 1943 (1943), AWM52
2nd Australian Imperial Force and
Commonwealth Military Forces unit
war diaries, 1939–45 War. Australian
War Memorial, Canberra.
Anzac House and Club Board of
Management, Minutes, Anzac House
archives, Perth.
'A Short History of Anzac House', in
pamphlet for official opening of the
new Anzac House, 14 November 1981,
Anzac House archives, Perth.
Papers of Mavis Thorpe Clark, MS
7847, National Library of Australia,
Canberra.
Personal Papers of Prime Minister
Chifley, Correspondence 'W', part 1,
1947–1948, retrieved from http://
recordsearch.naa.gov.au/scripts/
Imagine.asp
Perth City Council (PCC), *Council
Property Esplanade Kiosk*, File No.
G7/7, Lease Document 323, Box 1442.
Perth City Council archives, Perth.
Unit and Kindred Association, Hospital
Integration Committee, Minutes,
Anzac House archives, Perth.
Vasey Family Papers (VFP), MS 3782,
National Library of Australia,
Canberra.
'War Veterans' Home', file, Anzac House
archives, Perth.
War Widows' Guild of Australia
[background paper on continuation
of pension on remarriage or upon
forming a de facto relationship],
M1425, NAA, Perth.
War Widows' Guild – Stage 1, PP572/1,
WA70, NAA, Perth.

AUDIO VISUAL

50 Years of Achievement, documentary,

REPORTS

Clarke, John, Riding, Doug and Rosalky,
David, *Report of the Review of
Veterans' Entitlements*, Commonwealth
of Australia, Canberra, 2003.
Fine, Michael, *The Responsibility for Child
and Aged Care: Shaping Policies for the
Future*, SPRC Discussion Paper No.
105, Social Policy Research Centre,
University of New South Wales,
Sydney, 1999, retrieved from www.sprc.
unsw.edu.au/media/File/dp105.pdf
Register of heritage places – permanent
entry: Esplanade Reserve, Heritage
Council of Western Australia, Perth,
2003.
Toose, Paul, *Independent Enquiry into the
Repatriation System: Report*, Australian
Government Publishing Service, 1975.
Van Nostrand, Joan, Howe, Anna, Havens,
Betty, Bray, David, van der Heuvel,
Wim, Romoren, Tor and Robert
Clark, *Overview of Long-Term Care in
Five Nations: Australia, Canada, the
Netherlands, Norway and the United
States*, US Department of Health and
Human Services, September 1995,
accessed from aspe.hhs.gov.daltcp/
reports/1995/5overvie.htm

BOOKS AND ARTICLES

Aitken-Swan, Jean, *Widows in Australia:
A Survey*, Council of Social Service of
New South Wales, Sydney, 1962.
Alexander, Alison, *A Wealth of Women:
Australian Women's Lives from 1788
to the Present*, Duffy & Snellgrove,
Sydney, 2001.
Austen, Tom, *Western Images: Western
Australia in Pictures from the Colonial
Era to the Present*, St George Books,
Perth, 1996.
Bolton, Geoffrey, 'Way 1979: Whose
Celebration?' in L. Layman and T.

Stannage (eds), *Celebrations in Western Australian History*, Studies in Western Australian History X, April 1989, Centre for Western Australian History, Nedlands, pp. 15–20.

Burge, Roslyn, *No Peacetime Cinderellas: War Widows' Guild of Australia NSW Ltd*, War Widows' Guild of Australia, NSW Ltd., Sydney, 2008.

Chetkovich, Jean and Gare, Deborah, *A Chain of Care: A History of the Silver Chain Nursing Association*, University of Notre Dame Australia Press for Silver Chain Nursing Association, Perth, 2005.

Clark, Mavis Thorpe, *No Mean Destiny: The Story of the War Widows' Guild of Australia 1945–85*, Hyland House Publishing, South Yarra, 1986.

Cody, Les, *Ghosts in Khaki: The History of the 2/4th Machine Gun Battalion*, Hesperian Press, Victoria Park, 1997.

Cooke, Marie, 'Australian War Widows: A Case Study to Challenge Public Policy', *Australian Journal of Social Issues*, vol. 38, no. 4, 4 November 2003, pp. 465–75.

Court, Vicki, *War Widows' and Widowed Mothers' Association of Victoria: The First 82 Years*, War Widows' and Widowed Mothers' Association of Victoria, Melbourne, 2005.

Damousi, Joy, *The Labour of Loss: Mourning, Memory and Wartime Bereavement in Australia*, Cambridge University Press, Cambridge, 1999.

Damousi, Joy, *Living with the Aftermath: Trauma, Nostalgia and Grief in Post-War Australia*, Cambridge University Press, Cambridge, 2001.

Davies, Rosyln, *Everyone's a Hero: Stories from the First Seventy Years at an Amazing Hospital*, Ramsay Health Care Australia Pty Ltd, Fremantle, 2010.

Ewen, Murray, *Colour Patch: The Men of the 2/4th Australian Machine Gun Battalion 1940–1945*, Hesperian Press, Perth, 2003.

Garton, Stephen, *The Cost of War: Australians Return*, Oxford University Press Australia, Melbourne, 1996.

Gervas, Stan, *Sunday Mornings in Perth*, Gervas Books, Maylands, 2003, p. 107.

Green, Olywn, *The Name's Still Charlie: A Remarkable Story of Courage and Love*, University of Queensland Press, St Lucia, 1993.

Gregory, Jenny, *City of Light: A History of Perth Since the 1950s*, City of Perth, Perth, 2003.

——— (ed.), *On the Homefront: Western Australia and World War II*, University of Western Australia Press, Nedlands, 1996.

Grose, Peter, *An Awkward Truth*, Allen & Unwin, Crows Nest, 2009.

Ham, Paul, *Kokoda*, Harper Collins, Pymble, 2004.

Hoffman, Peter, *Honours Denied: The Documented Life of Herman August Kuring in Peace and War, 1895–1941*, Perth, 2005.

——— *Australia's Military History for Dummies*, Wiley Publishing, Milton, 2010.

——— *General Vasey's War*, Melbourne University Press, Carlton, 1992.

Hough, David, *Boans for Service: The Story of a Department Store 1895–1986*, Estate of F.T. Boan, Perth, 2009.

Inglis, Ken, 'Retun to Gallipoli', in J. Lack (ed.), *ANZAC Remembered: Selected Writings by K.S. Inglis*, University of Melbourne, History Department, Melbourne, 1998, pp. 29–39.

Jalland, Pat, *Changing Ways of Death in Twentieth-Century Australia: War, Medicine and the Funeral Business*, UNSW Press, Sydney, 2006.

Lake, Marilyn and Reynolds, Henry (eds.), *What's Wrong with Anzac: The Militarisation of Australian History*, UNSW Press, Sydney, 2010.

Larsson, Marina, *Shattered Anzacs: Living with the Scars of War*, UNSW Press, Sydney, 2009.

Le Souef, Leslie, *To War Without a Gun*, Artlook, Perth, 1980.

Lloyd, Clem and Rees, Jacqui, *The Last Shilling: A History of Repatriation in Australia*, Melbourne University Press, Carlton, 1994.

Luckins, Tanja, *The Gates of Memory: Australian People's Experiences and Memories of Loss and the Great War*, Curtin University Books, Fremantle, 2004.

Lyons, Mark, *Legacy: The First Fifty Years*, Legacy Co-ordinating Council in conjunction with Lothian Publishing Company, Melbourne, 1978.

Manne, Robert, 'A Turkish Tale: Gallipoli and the Armenian Genocide', *The Monthly*, February 2007, retrieved 18 October 2013 from www.themonthly.com.au/issue/2007/february/1327543545/robert-manne/turkish-tale-gallipoli-and-armenian-genocide

Masel, Philip, *The Second 28th: The Story of a Famous Battalion of the Ninth Australian Division*, John Burridge Military Antiques, Swanbourne, 2000.

McKernan, Michael, *The Strength of a Nation: Six Years of Australians Fighting for the Nation and Defending the Homefront in WWII*, Allen & Unwin, Crows Nest, 2008.

McKenna, Michael, and Ward, Stuart, '"It Was Really Moving, Mate": The Gallipoli Pilgrimage and Sentimental Nationalism in Australia', *Australian Historical Studies, 129*, 2007, pp. 141–51.

Out in the Cold: Australia's Involvement in the Korean War 1950–1953, Department of Veterans' Affairs, Canberra, 2010.

Page, Charles, *Wings of Destiny: Wing Commander Charles Learmonth, DFC and Bar and the Air War in New Guinea*, Rosenberg Publishing, Sydney, 2008.

Re-establishment Pamphlet no. 6: War Widows' Entitlements, Adelaide: Repatriation Commission, Adelaide, 1946.

Stewart, Noel, 'Lady Mitchell: A Governor's Wife' in *As I Remember Them*, Artlook Books, Perth, 1987, pp. 31–36.

Summers, Anne, *Damned Whores and God's Police*, 2nd edn, Penguin Books, Ringwood, 1994.

Thomson, Alistair, *Anzac Memories: Living with the Legend*, Oxford University Press, Melbourne, 1994.

Turner, Mary, *The Women's Century: A Celebration of Changing Roles, 1900–2000*, National Archives, Surrey, 2003.

War Widows: Notes on War Pensions and Repatriation Benefits, Repatriation Commission, Melbourne, 1953.

Wheeler, Lorraine, 'War, Women and Welfare', in R. Kennedy (ed.), *Australian Welfare: Historical Sociology*, Macmillan, South Melbourne, 1989.

Wood, Ernest, Hodgkin, Mary and Wood, Adrian, *If This Should be Farewell: A Family Separated by War: The Journal and Letters of Ernest and Mary Hodgkin 1942–45*, Fremantle Arts Centre Press, Fremantle, 2003.

WEB RESOURCES

Birman, Wendy and Hobbs, Victoria, 'Ferguson, Jean Elsie (1909–1979)', *Australian Dictionary of Biography*, National Centre of Biography, Australian National University, retrieved from http://adb.anu.edu.au/biography/ferguson-jean-elsie-10166

Black, David, 'Collett, Herbert Brayley (1877–1947)', *Australian Dictionary of Biography*, National Centre of Biography, Australian National University, retrieved from http://adb.online.anu.edu.au/biogs/A0800/3B

'Boer War to Vietnam', NAA, retrieved from www.naa.gov.au/collection/explore/defence/conflicts.aspx

Citation for Distinguished Flying Cross – REL/15999.001 – Distinguished Flying Cross and Bar: Wing Commander C.C. Learmonth, 14 and 22 Squadron,

RAAF, retrieved from http://cas.awm.
gov.au/item/REL/15999.001

Heywood, Anne and Robinson, Penny,
'Voluntary Aid Detachments
(VAD) (1914–)', *The Australian
Women's Register*, 2003/2009,
retrieved 21 March 2011 from
http://www.womenaustralia.info.
biogs/AWE0491b.htm

Korean War 1950–1953 (n.d.), Australian
War Memorial, Canberra, retrieved
from www.awm.gov.au/atwar/korea.
asp

Mcphee, John, 'Grieve, Rachel
(1885–1977)', *Australian Dictionary
of Biography*, National Centre of
Biography, Australian National
University, retrieved 13 October 2011
from http://adb.anu.edu.au/biography/
grieve-rachel-10368

Peck, John Henry (1886–1928),
Australian Dictionary of Biography,
National Centre of Biography,
Australian National University,
retrieved 21 May 2009 from
http://adbonline.anu.edu.au/biogs/
A110194b.htm

Scully, P., 'Spence, Louis Thomas
(1917–1950)', *Australian Dictionary
of Biography*, National Centre of
Biography, Australian National
University, retrieved from
http://adb.anu.edu.au/biography/
spence-louis-thomas-11741/text20993

'Victor Ketterer', *The AIF Project*, 2009,
retrieved 4 September 2009 from
http://www.aif.adfa.edu.au:8080/
showPerson?pid=164190

'Korean War 1950–53', NAA, retrieved
5 March 2010 from www.awm.gov.au/
atwar/korea.asp

'World War 2 Accident Kills 59 and
Injures over 100 – Port Moresby
Airfield – 7 September 1943', retrieved
24 May 2010 from www.australian-
pow-ww2.com/history_24.html

ACKNOWLEDGEMENTS

Writing is often seen as a solitary task, and indeed it must be, but through the research and writing of this book, I have come to appreciate that writing is necessarily a collaborative process. This book would not be what it is without every person who has been part of that collaboration.

My greatest thanks and admiration go to the members of the War Widows' Guild of the past and present; I am indebted to those who welcomed me into their midst and trusted me with their stories. And to the children of those founding war widows who dared to challenge the status quo to improve the quality of life for thousands of women in similar circumstances, thank you for sharing the memories of your mothers with me, and enriching the narrative in the process.

To the members of the executive committee, I have been encouraged by your faith in my ability to communicate the story of your organisation. To Jenny Knight, Sally Carver and Anita Atkin, thank you for your ongoing commitment to the wellbeing of all war widows in Western Australia, and for the friendship you have extended to me.

Editing has taken place in several stages over a number of years. Firstly, I am indebted to Dr Ffion Murphy for her honest and thorough supervision of my original manuscript, submitted as a Master of Arts thesis in 2012. Later, my grandfather John Prince was brave enough to point out several major structural issues that I needed to address for the narrative to work. Finally, thank you to Janet Blagg at Fremantle Press for your incredible gift of fine tuning the words on the page. It has been a privilege to have your editorial expertise. I am also very grateful to Jane Fraser, Claire Miller, Naama Amram and the rest of the team at Fremantle Press for believing in this book and smoothing the publication process for me. Thank you also to Carolyn Brown for her exquisite cover – the book would not be the same without her design.

I would like to acknowledge the assistance of archivists at the National Library of Australia, National Archives of Australia, the Australian War Memorial and the Battye Library. I am particularly indebted to those at the National Library of Australia who are responsible for Trove, the digital archive of Australian newspapers. The Perth City Council provided me with access to previously unopened files on the Esplanade Kiosk and Naomi Lam searched the Anzac House archives for information pertaining to the Guild. I am also grateful to the staff of the Edith Cowan University Library, in particular its document delivery service which enabled me to access texts and resources otherwise unavailable to me.

Joy Damousi's groundbreaking research into the emotional journey of war widows has been invaluable, as has Mavis Thorpe Clark's prior work on the War Widows' Guild as a national body. I wish to acknowledge Clark's family for allowing me to quote from her work. I am also grateful to the Vasey Family, who have permitted me to quote extensively from Jessie Vasey's words, reproduce documents she penned and include various photographs. Prime Minister John Curtin's condolence letter to Jessie Vasey is reprinted with permission from the Department of the Prime Minister and Cabinet. John Perry gave permission to reproduce Alma Figuerola's painting of Jessie Vasey. Charles Page gave generously of his time and knowledge of the Second World War, sharing information about Marjorie Le Souef and her marriage to Charles Learmonth. West Australian Newspapers kindly gave permission to reproduce the photo of Gloria MacDonald receiving her OAM.

Thank you to my dear friend Sonia Helbig; we have been encouraging each other to persevere with our writing for twenty years, and it was she who showed me the tiny advertisement requesting a writer to compile a history of the War Widows' Guild. I am also grateful to my 'Tuesday night girls' who sustain and encourage me in life and faith, and to the staff at Cranked for endless pots of tea and a distraction-free writing space. Finally I would like to thank my husband Matt for his ongoing support, and my children Charlie and Alessandra for their interest not only in the project but in the war widows who meet at the Marjorie Le Souef Administration and Community Centre each Monday.

INDEX